JA#

A Pilgrimage of Faith

BAPTISTS

HISTORY, LITERATURE, THEOLOGY, HYMNS

General Editor: Walter B. Shurden is the Callaway Professor of Christianity in the Roberts Department of Christianity and Executive Director of the Center for Baptist Studies, Mercer University, Macon, Georgia.

John Taylor, *Baptists on the American Frontier: A History of Ten Baptist Churches*
   Edited by Chester Young
Thomas Helwys, *A Short Declaration of the Mystery of Iniquity*
   Edited by Richard Groves
Roger Williams, *The Bloody Tenant of Persecution for Cause of Conscience*
   Edited by Richard Groves
   Edwin Gaustad, Historical Introduction
James A. Rogers†, *Richard Furman: Life and Legacy*
Lottie Moon, *Send the Light: Lottie Moon's Letters and Other Writings*
   Edited by Keith Harper
James Byrd, *The Challenges of Roger Williams: Religious Liberty, Violent Persecution, and the Bible*
Anne Dutton, *The Influential Spiritual Writings of Anne Dutton: Volume 1: Letters*
   Edited by JoAnn Ford Watson (Fall 2003)
David T. Morgan, *Southern Baptist Sisters: In Search of Status, 1845-2000* (Fall 2003)
William E. Ellis, *"A Man of Books and a Man of the People": E. Y. Mullins and the Crisis of Moderate Southern Baptist Leadership* (reissue in paperback Fall 2003; hardback 1985)
Jarrett Burch, *Adiel Sherwood: Baptist Antebellum Pioneer in Georgia* (Winter 2003)
Anthony Chute, *A Piety Above the Common Standard: Jesse Mercer and the Defense of Evangelistic Calvinism* (Spring 2004)
William H. Brackney, *A Genetic History of Baptist Thought* (Fall 2004)
Henlee Hulix Barnette, *A Pilgrimage of Faith: My Story* (Fall 2004)

A Pilgrimage of Faith

My Story

Henlee Hulix Barnette

Mercer University Press
Macon, Georgia
25th Anniversary

ISBN 0-86554-942-7
MUP H679

© 2004 Mercer University Press
1400 Coleman Avenue
Macon, Georgia 31207
All rights reserved

First Edition

The paper used in this publication meets the minimum
requirements of American National Standard for Information
Sciences—Permanence of Paper for Printed Library Materials,
ANSI Z39.48–1992.

Unless otherwise noted, Scripture quotations are from the King
James Version of the Bible.

Library of Congress Cataloging-in-Publication Data

Barnette, Henlee H.
A pilgrimage of faith : my story / Henlee Hulix Barnette.-- 1st ed.
    p. cm.
Includes bibliographical references and index.
ISBN 0-86554-942-7 (alk. paper)
1. Barnette, Henlee H. 2. Baptists—United States—Biography. I. Title.
BX6495.B37A3 2004
286'.092--dc22

                                                              2004014655

To my children
John Alexander
Wayne Ford
Martha Ann
James Randolph
All gifts from God

Contents

Acknowledgments

Many persons contribute to the making of a book. It is impossible for me to identify all of those who had a part in this one. Three friends must be thanked. I could not have completed "my story" without their help.

I am deeply grateful to Dr. Walter "Buddy" Shurden, distinguished Baptist historian and Chairman of the Roberts Department of Christianity at Mercer University, for his careful critique of the manuscript. He gave it greater precision and a larger perspective.

Dr. Paul Debusman, reference librarian of distinction, read the typed manuscript, and verified data and source materials. He also made positive recommendations toward consistency in the use of upper and lower cases and other stylistic matters.

Paul Simmons, Ph.D., made valuable contributions to this work by confirming dates, clarifying events and suggesting additions that made for a fuller story.

I am deeply grateful to Catherine McAuley who typed the handwritten chapters and helped bring order out of chaos, making constructive comments as to structure, sequence of chapters and clarity of expression. She demonstrated the patience of Job, the computer skills of a rocket scientist and the power to see things through. Her enthusiasm and optimism made it a pleasure project.

Preface

At the age of ninety I decided to write a story, my story, describing in simple terms my pilgrimage as a human being. It is a story written for my children and their children's children. Perchance it will inspire some of them to tell their stories to their children.

There is always the temptation when writing about oneself to omit the wrinkles and warts. To overcome this temptation an effort has been made to be as objective, accurate and comprehensive as possible based on memory and date books from 1931.

My story is made up of several mini-stories and is written in simple terms and narrative style. Contemporary writers have turned to the narrative style to get their messages across. Before recorded history, it was done by oral tradition. Perhaps the Bible is the best example of the use of the narrative method. Jesus and the prophets used it. Both told dramatic stories that are unforgettable. I have avoided big words and complex sentences. Chapters are brief and this makes it possible to read one or two in a few spare moments. I hope that others down the line will be inspired to do a more complete genealogical study of the Barnette family. By so doing they will know more about where they came from, who they are and where they are going or should go.

I take full responsibility for any errors in the finished product. If I have wounded any soul by unfair remarks, I ask forgiveness. My aim has been to meet God's standard for interpersonal relations summed up by the prophet Micah: "To practice justice, love mercy, and walk humbly with God."

In an age of disconnection, I hope that this writing will keep us Barnettes connected long after I have made the Great Transition. In the days ahead the tension between faith and reason is bound to become more intense. So, may you, dear ones, continue to grow in grace and knowledge of the Lord Jesus Christ.

—Henlee Hulix Barnette

Foreword

Walter B. Shurden

I can say it no other way: Henlee Hulix Barnette is one of a kind. How many others do you know with the name of Hen-Lee? Indeed, how many others do you know with the name of Henlee Hulix? As Frank Stagg once said of Penrose St. Amant, "When someone says, 'Penrose,' everybody knows who the subject is." For almost a half century now among theological professionals and thousands of seminarians among white Baptists of the South, when one says, "Henlee," a very distinct image appears.

You can *hear* the image. It speaks very, very slowly. In fact, it speaks so slowly that you may think that the deliberate and dedicated rural drawl is a kind of feigned brag about being from Sugarloaf Township, North Carolina. If you did not know better, you may think you were talking to a fellow who had just brought his watermelons into town, peddling them from the back of his pick-up truck at what is hopefully a profitable intersection. Henlee would delight in your thinking that! Because eventually, in a moment of intellectual tête-à-tête, he will quietly ask you a question or utter a line that causes you to awaken to the reality that you are talking with someone who certainly did *not* ride into town on the back of a watermelon truck.

Because of the pervasiveness of higher education in America today, many people falsely equate graduation with education. Henlee, a high school dropout in the seventh grade, went back to the ninth grade at age twenty-two and graduated from high school at age 25. From there he not only graduated from Wake Forest University, and the Southern Baptist Theological Seminary, he "got educated" along the way. Later as professor of Christian Ethics at Southern Seminary he would teach thousands of ministers to learn to think biblically and critically, while urging them to act compassionately and courageously.

When you hear "Henlee," you not only *hear* the image, you *see* the image. He walks like he speaks, with a slow gait. Often standing up straight and arching his back with hands on hips, he looks you in the eye when talking to you. Too busy with important concerns to pay much attention to sartorial matters, Henlee, so the legend goes, had a long-running competition with his best friend, Wayne Oates, to see who could purchase the best clothes at the cheapest price. One-upmanship had to do with less, not more. While some of the "less, not more" motif originated in a cultural background, much of it came from a commitment to the Christian way.

When you hear "Henlee," you can *hear* and *see* an image. But you can also *feel* the image. The feeling is unmistakable; it is that of Christian compassion. Rooted in the same cultural background as the theme of "less, not more," Henlee's background of hard work in cotton mills and poverty in childhood certainly contributed to the compassion that has characterized his life. Hard work and poverty, however, do not always result in a life of compassion. Indeed, they often produce bitterness, petulance, and smallness of soul. I am convinced, therefore, that one could never understand much at all about Henlee Hulix Barnette apart from his transformative teen-age Christian experience. It was a religious experience that issued in a life of authentic personal piety and genuine social concern. Henlee's recounting of his first encounter with the Holy in life is too good to make you wait a few pages to read it.

"A revival was in progress at this church in North Kannapolis and my mother, a devout Christian, was much in prayer for me and my father. My neighbor was a weaver with a fourth grade education. One evening after dinner he approached me while I was sitting in the swing on the front porch of the mill house on Maple Hill and invited me to church. I declined. He persisted and got my promise to go with him the next night.

"At a North Kannapolis shack, where a short time before the owner had shot my neighbor, I found one fellow, Red Joines, and told him we were going to church. At first he objected, but then reluctantly followed. We sat on the back bench made of slabs, in the wooden frame church. The minister, the Reverend Wade H. James, preached. His topic was 'The Great Physician' based on Jeremiah 8:22: "Is there no balm in Gilead, is there no physician here?" He gave the invitation to be healed by the Great Physician.

After two persons came to my side pleading that I accept Christ as my personal Saviour, I went to the mourner's bench. There among the mourners I said to the Lord, 'Here is my life, take it and use it for your glory.' There came over me a peace I had never known. I felt that I had been cleansed, forgiven of my sin, and healed. I felt like I had been washed clean and had become a new person. This was 18 September 1931. I was nineteen years old.

"In that same meeting my father, who did not attend church, made his profession of faith. Neither of us knew the other was there. My mother in the congregation shouted and clapped her hands praising God."

In that recollection of his conversion experience, Barnette tells the reader not only about himself and the source of much of his later Christian compassion, he describes much about the religious life of the South among poor white Baptists in the 1930s. It was a time of revivals when sincere Christians unapologetically "exhorted" the non-Christian, when the "mourners" bench welcomed sinners as well as saints, and when lives like Henlee's were "born again." Henlee remembered the specifics: The name of the preacher, the title and text of the sermon, where he sat that night in church, the promise he made to Christ, the feelings that swept over his nineteen year old soul, and the date, "18 September 1931." The specifics remind one of Blaise Pascal, the mathematician/philosopher, who pinned the date of his conversion on a sheet of paper to his inside coat pocket. On the paper, he wrote, "FIRE!"

While they were on the faculty at Southern Seminary together, Wayne Oates, Henlee's best friend, had already published dozens of books in the field of pastoral care, and his popularity was soaring. Henlee finally got a book published by Westminster Press, the Presbyterian publishing house no less! It was a small book, but it sold like hotcakes. One day, in the midst of the euphoria of his success and elated at all the good things happening to him, Henlee walked into his office, and he spotted in the middle of his desk a big, puffy, pouch of Bull Durham tobacco: a symbol of the tobacco road from which he came! Henlee has that same pouch of tobacco in his house to this very day. Beneath the pouch of Bull Durham was an unsigned note, obviously written by his closest friend in the world. The note beneath the pouch read, "Remember where you came from." Henlee never forgot.

"HENLEE." If you knew him personally, the sound of the name would conjure for you the unmistakable and distinctive sound of his voice. The sound of the name also would cause you to envision his rather lanky physique, and it would inevitably bring the image of compassion to your mind. My first year of teaching church history at Southern Baptist Theological Seminary in 1976 was Henlee's last year of teaching there. Henlee took me under wing, offered friendship and guidance, and over numerous lunches he told me bits of the story of his life, in which I delighted. I am, therefore, delighted anew that he has shared that story with a wider public and that he has shared it in the Mercer University Press's series on "Baptists." Henlee is one! And he is one of a kind.

Walter B. Shurden
Callaway Professor of Christianity
Executive Director,
The Center for Baptist Studies
Mercer University
June 9, 2004

From left to right: William Randolph Barnette and Nancy Webster Barnette. Henlee's paternal grandparents.

Seated, left to right: Romulus R. Kerley, my maternal grandfather and William "Billy" Kerley, my maternal great-grandfather. Standing, left to right: me, Henlee Barnette and Winnie Kerley Barnette, my mother. Four generations. The Kerleys lived near Taylorsville, North Carolina.

One room log cabin. Birthplace of Henlee Barnette, born 14 August 1911 in Sugarloaf Township, Alexander County, near Taylorsville, North Carolina. Photo ca. 1970.

My father, William Alexander Barnette—Registrar of Deeds, Alexander County, North Carolina. Married Winnie Kerley.

My mother, Winnie Kerley—married William Alexander Barnette, 4 April 1908. She was sixteen. They were married for fifty-four years. He died at seventy-seven in 1962. She died at eighty-one in 1972 in Kannapolis, North Carolina.

Left to right: A boy named Henlee, Will Barnette, Mazo and Mama. Photo ca. 1914.

CUTTING ROOM PERSONNEL, at Plant 1 are shown in this 1928 photo. The photo was provided by David Blackwelder, first shift spare hand in the cutting department. Mr. Blackwelder, who has 52 years of Cannon service, started in Plant 1's No. 1 weave and has been in the cutting department since 1928. Aiding him in providing identification of those in the photo was Charles Taylor, another company veteran. Mr. Taylor, with 50 years of service, started in No. 5 weave and has been in the cutting room since 1937. Those in the photo, left to right, are as follows: First

row — Jim Rowland, Bill Reading, Red Simpson, Smoot Kiser, unknown, Ralph Strickland, Pete Clawson, Mr. Shap, Roy Pothel, James Hudson, Whitey Wilson, Charlie Perkins, Henry Pitts, Clyde Fesperman, Leroy Perkins, Snub Link, Shorty Haseltine, Ray King. Second row — Mr. Bollard, Mr. Collins, V. P. Wilson, Mr. Critz, Glenn Childers, David W. Blackwelder (still working), unknown, unknown, Ed James, Raymond Clawson, Herman Miller, Jim Punch, Ed Swing, Curtis Hudson, unknown, Johnny Hughes, Melvin Talbot, Lewis Demarcus.

Charles Overcash, Lindsay Russell, Rufus McKinney, (recently received 50-year service emblem), unknown, Vernon Crisco, Jake Farley, Jophis Phillips. Third row — Manuel Yost, Mac McDonald, unknown, Chester Seaford, Bill Parrish, Lee Walls, Raymond Ashby, James Helms, unknown, Lee Moose, Ralph Marlowe, Pop Woodard, Harrah Suther, George Bastian, Shorty O'Kelly, Jake Casble, Douglas Roseman, Henry Deese, Charles Taylor, Adam Waller, Robert Reisler, Mr. Steele, Odell James, John Litaker. Fourth row — Russ Harrington, Boyd Honeycutt,

Frank Kennerly (works in washcloth department), Carl Pethel, Andy Propst, Kingsley Reid, Bill Pelbel, Ray Crisco, Ray Reese, Garvel Denny, Luther Crose, Henlee Barnett, Lynn Reever, John Rhine, Henry Deese, Sidney Blackwelder, Howard Wike, Conley James, Lewis Hartis, Russ Walts, Perry Woodard, Earl Demarcus, Florence Alexander, Fred Reese, Emanuel Edison, unknown, John Beagg, Bill Gibson, Brance Hubbard, Boyd Zimmerman, Lonnie Demarcus, Merle Demarcus, and Tom Deese.

Cannon News Vol 11, No 9 April 27, 1981 a Publication of employee of Cannon Mills, N.C.

Cutting Room Personnel at Cannon Mills at Plant One, 1928. Henlee standing in back row, second to left of open doorway. Henlee entered the mill in 1925 at age thirteen. Note the children employed at the mill and none of the workers is smiling.

Henlee Barnette's senior picture, Wake Forest University Yearbook, 1940.

Henlee Barnette at Wake Forest University with Thad Eure, Secretary of State.

Henlee, a member of Wake Forest's student legislature, 1940.

Union Gospel Mission building, Louisville, Kentucky. Henlee was
pastor and superintendent of this mission from 1941 through 1946.

Memorial Day Service at old Union Gospel Mission. Henlee and
children are shown between the windows. 1940's.

Clarence Leonard Jordan,
Ph.D., born 29 July 1912, died
29 October 1969. Founder
Koinonia Farm, Co-founder of
Habitat for Humanity. He had
few personal photos made. We
worked together at the Old
Haymarket Mission, Louisville,
Kentucky 1941-42.

Among my professors at Harvard
was Dr. Paul Tillich, University
Professor.

Henlee Barnette shaking hands with Nikita Khrushchev, Premier of
U.S.S.R., in his office in the Kremlin (1957) while American
Conference members await their turn.

At the conference table with Khrushchev in the Kremlin, 1957. Henlee Barnette
number four on the right.

Henlee Barnette, Professor of Christian Ethics, with new book *Introducing Christian Ethics*, published by Broadman Press, Nashville, Tennessee, 1961. Translated into Chinese and Korean.

Henlee Barnette and Martin Luther King, Jr. discussing the role of the Southern Baptist Seminary in the Civil Rights Movement (April 19, 1961).

Left to right: Henlee Barnette, Martin Luther King, Jr., Nolan Howington (Professor of Preaching) and Allen Graves (Dean of the School of Religious Education) in Barnette's office, The Southern Baptist Theological Seminary, April 1961.

Private John Barnette, rose to rank of Captain. Enlisted U.S. Air Force 1968. Served in Vietnam.

Wayne Barnette as a high school senior. Draft resister. Educated in Europe. Professional translator of Germanic and Slavic languages.

Our Didactic. Standing is Dr. Bill Bradnan. University of Louisville, School of Medicine, 1983. Henlee Barnette, the seminar leader, is not pictured.

Clinical Pastoral Education (CPE) University of Louisville, School of Medicine, Department of Psychiatry. Wayne Oates is third from left.

Henlee Barnette, Portrait, December, 2003, Black & White (no coat, with suspenders) with book *A Theology for the Social Gospel*, by Walter Rauschenbusch. (Barnette wrote his doctoral dissertation on Walter Rauschenbusch)

1

Heritage

It is not what you leave your offspring, but whom you leave them that really counts.

Life is a pilgrimage of faith. Pilgrimage is a term which I have always used to describe my faith journey. It came to me in the ninth grade in school when the teacher assigned me to read John Bunyan's *Pilgrim's Progress*, the first book I ever seriously read all the way through. *Nota bene* that I use faith instead of spiritual pilgrimage. Spirituality is a notoriously ambiguous and vaporous word. It can become too individualistic and lose its ethical dimension or veer off into New Age spirituality.

"Faith is turning your dreams into deeds; it is betting your life on the unseen realities" (Heb 11:1, *Cotton Patch Version of the New Testament*). Life is a faith pilgrimage in which we encounter all sorts of challenges and crossroads along the way to the Promised Land.

Faith-shaping Factors

We are all a part of what we have seen and heard. We are shaped by the things that impinge upon our minds, souls and spirits. The formation begins *in utero*. Actions and attitudes of our mothers even before we are born affect our health and attitude. When we are newborns, prayers, songs and loving words help to determine our health and happiness as we grow toward maturity. This is why it is imperative that parents obey the laws of nature and do nurturing love.

Some things over which I had no control have been formative in my life. Take my ancestors, for example. I am the product of some human beings who go all the way back to Adam and who, as time progressed, became identified as Barnett (e added later). Beyond the sixteenth century, I have no idea of my family. According to Anthony Jones and Peter Schaun, the Barnetts came from Northern Ireland. The progenitor of my line of Barnetts in the United States was John Barnett, born 20 May 1678 in Londonderry, Ireland (Northern Ireland). His descendant, William Barnett immigrated to America prior to 1730, settling his family in Hanover Township, now Dauphin County, Pennsylvania.[1]

The Barnetts migrated south, some settling in Virginia. My branch of the Barnetts settled in Granville County, North Carolina, just across the Virginia state line. Eventually some of them settled in the mountains of Wilkes County, North Carolina, including my great, great, great, great-grandfather Jesse, born in 1755 in Granville County. He named his son James (b. 1800), who eventually married Alice Holder. James became the father of ten children, three daughters and seven sons, one of whom was Robert Edmond who was my great-grandfather. All seven brothers were soldiers in the Civil War, or the War Between the States (1861–1865), all serving in companies C and D of the North Carolina troops during the war. All but one—Randolph S. Barnett—were casualties of the war. Some are buried in Virginia where they died. Robert Edmond died at age twenty-nine. He was survived by a son named Randolph, my grandfather. Young Randolph was adopted by John Smith; there were no legal procedures as prevail today so he did not change his name to Smith. Randolph settled near Taylorsville in Alexander County bordering on Wilkes County. None of the Barnetts on either side of the family owned slaves. They were too poor. But they were patriotic and were loyal to the South at a great sacrifice—their lives.

---

[1] See Douglas Clayton Barnette, *Barnett Family*, printed privately, Conover NC, 1981; Peter Schaun and Anthony Jones, *The Index to the Colonial and State Records of North Carolina, Genealogical Abstracts of Revolutionary Files*, (National Historical Publishing Co., Waynesboro TN, 1990, 59–60); Charles William Barnett, ed., *Battle of Point Pleasant: First Battle of the Revolution* (Parsons, WV, 1998 McClain Printing Co., 1998). Genealogical Abstracts of Revolutionary War Pension Files, Abstracted by Virgil D. White, National Historical Publishing Co., Waynesboro TN 1990, I:160. Index to the Colonial and State Records of North Carolina (Broadfoot Publishing Co., Wilmington NC, 1993), compiled by Stephen B. Weeks, 22:59.

Barnett Brothers Who Fought in the Civil War

James Barnett's seven sons participated in the Civil War on the Confederate side. They were:

James William Barnett enlisted on 1 October 1863 and served in Company C, 56th Regiment, North Carolina Troops. He died in combat 25 July 1864 at Richmond, Virginia and was buried there.

James T. Barnett, Jr. was born in 1827 and died in 1862 of pneumonia while in military service. He is buried in the Confederate Cemetery in Richmond, Virginia.

Robert Edmond Barnett, my great-grandfather, was born in 1834 and died August 1862, a member of the North Carolina Troops (1861–1865), a private in Company D, 18th Regiment. He died of wounds at home on leave in Wilkes County, North Carolina in 1862 at the age of twenty-nine.

Randolph S. Barnett—the only brother who survived the war—joined the North Carolina Troops, a private in Company D, 13th Regiment in September 1862. He died 4 September 1907.

Jesse M. Barnett joined the North Carolina Troops, a private in Company C, 4th Regiment. He enlisted June 1862 and at age twenty-four died on 28 February 1862 from wounds received in combat.

Noel J. Barnett belonged to the North Carolina Troops, a private in Company D, 33rd Regiment. He died in a military hospital on 15 September 1861.

Josiah M. Barnett belonged to the North Carolina Troops, a private in Company D and Company B, First Regiment. He entered military service in July 1861 and died 4 April 1862 at age twenty. (For more information, see Douglas Clayton Barnette, *Barnette Family*.)

On my mother's side of the family were Kerleys and Deals. The Kerleys were Scotch-Irish. They were workaholics, a close-knit clan and God-fearing. Grandfather and Grandmother Kerley were blessed with ten children, six girls and four boys. The Kerleys had annual reunions. Everyone knew everyone in the clan. There was only one common-law marriage in the whole tribe. To this day, the Kerleys gather annually at the old home place of great-grandfather Kerley, about four miles southeast of

Taylorsville, North Carolina. Kerleys and kin from all over the nation gather for renewal of spirit, good food and fellowship.

My grandfather, Romulus Rosfer Kerley, was justice of the peace in Sugar Loaf Township near Taylorsville, North Carolina. He held court on the front porch of his country store, came out of his house and performed marriages in the front yard for lovers in buggies drawn by a horse or a mule, and made the best corn liquor in the county. After Congress passed prohibition in 1919 he kept right on making it, so I was told, for the government. One of Grandfather Kerly's descendants has the log book recording all the ingredients and amounts produced. As a child I played with other children in Grandfather's still-house. When we broke some whiskey bottles, that broke up our playhouse gathering privileges.

The maternal side of my mother's family was of German lineage, the Diehls. During World War I, the name was changed from Diehl to Deal to avoid criticism and persecution. They came from Frankfort in the province of Brandenburg, Germany. On 9 September 1738, William Diehl arrived at Philadelphia, Pennsylvania, on the good ship Glasgow. From Pennsylvania, he moved to North Carolina near Newton. William married Susannah Icard, and from this union came six sons and five daughters. My grandmother, Amanda Magnolia Diehl was born 16 May 1871, the daughter of Miles and Lettie Webster Diehl. She married Romulus Rosfer Kerley. Issue from this union totaled ten children, including my mother Winnie Helen Kerley, who was born 12 October 1890.[2]

Grandfather Randolph Barnett was a large and physically strong man. He married Nancy Webster who was small but a strong and patient person. She worked hard and never complained about their rigorous life together. They had practically nothing to start with. Their first home was a cabin with a plank in the wall for a table. Both drank hot water in cups because coffee cost too much. I well remember seeing them sip hot water from cups just as if it were real coffee. They knew how to live on cornbread for breakfast.

Randolph and Nancy (we called her Mammy) made their own lye soap from ashes. After washing your face with it, you felt that it was going to crack and fall off. I remember seeing Mammy card wool and cotton by hand

---

[2] See Rom C. Deal, *Deal-Stafford Genealogical History*, Taylorsville NC: *Taylorsville Times,* 1939.

and spin it on an old spinning wheel and later knit it into socks. Randolph worked the fields in his bare feet in the summer.

Randolph was a lay preacher of the Baptist faith. I heard him preach at his home to groups that would gather there on Sunday afternoons. I still recall how hushed the group would be when he read the Bible and spoke. Tears often would run down his face as he earnestly explained about the good news of salvation.

Randolph was a man of discipline. The children were encouraged to study hard and to read the Bible. When the children were small and did wrong he thumped them on the head with his huge fingers. Like father, like son. My own father, William, punished me the same way. The thump was like a hammer blow on my young head. As the children grew older, Randolph used a leather whip on the boys. Nancy would beg him not to whip them so hard.

Birth and birthplace influence one's faith journey. My place of birth was in North Carolina about five miles northeast of Taylorsville, the county seat of Alexander County in Sugarloaf Township. At that time there was not a paved road or street in the county, including Taylorsville. I became familiar with all those dirt roads in the county, for at the age of eleven I served as a water boy on a road gang that maintained those roads. Salary: twenty-five cents a day. I loved to fish in the clear streams during lunchtime while the workers ate.

Taylorsville had no water or sewage system, no parks, no hospital in the town, not even in the county. It boasted of two physicians and two dentists, one garage, one livery stable, one calaboose (jail), one small hotel and the Joe Watts restaurant. The train track from the outside world ended in Taylorsville. Also, there was a small cotton mill with typical mill houses for the employees. There also was a so-called "nigger town," to which Negroes were relegated.

Alexander County was predominantly Anglo-Saxon and Scotch-Irish Protestant when I arrived on the scene. The topography was well suited to this population's geographic roots: half mountain and half piedmont. Most were farmers and poor.

Place and time of birth impact one's faith. The year of my birth was 1911 and the world has never been the same since the events of this date – at least not for me. William Howard Taft was president. The federal government cracked down on monopolies and filed suits against US Steel and the American Tobacco trusts. The first US cross-country airplane flight was completed in eighty-two hours by pilot C. P. Rogers.

A loaf of bread was five cents, a gallon of milk thirty-five cents, a new Ford seven hundred fifty dollars and a gallon of gas only ten cents.

Abroad, Italy declared war on Turkey. Sun Yat-Sen was elected provisional president of China after a revolution that resulted in the displacement of the Manchu dynasty which had survived two thousand five hundred years.

Nineteen hundred and eleven was the year that was. There were no televisions, no microwaves, videos, tape recorders, ballpoint pens, computers, air conditioners, credit cards, or many of the comforts and conveniences we enjoy today.

We lived an extremely simple life. Most current "necessities of life" would have seemed to us luxuries. At Christmas the children often received only an orange (we saved the peelings to eat when they dried), some raisins and a stick of candy. In short, we lived in prudent poverty. When I was a little chap, we would go to both grandparents' houses in a buggy or a wagon. Later we traveled in a Model T Ford with a bright copper radiator. When it rained, we would put up the black oil isinglass curtains. When we ran into a mud hole and got stuck—a common event—all of us had to get out and push. Since the fenders on the Model T hung straight out over the untreaded tires, the spinning wheels would throw mud all over us.

Among the joys of going to Grandfather Barnett's was the abundance of apples, grapes, molly pops, dried fruit, cantaloupes and watermelons upon which we gorged. There was no candy or ice cream. Too, we would play in the woods, and run up and down the road on stick horses.

A picture on the wall in Grandfather Barnett's house made a lasting impression on me. It portrayed Jesus with little children around him – red, yellow, black and white. Two lessons were learned from this small painting: Christ loves children, all the children of the world.

Grandfather Randolph died in 1935. A wagon drawn by a mule carried his body in a homemade pine coffin to Mt. Hebron Baptist Church for the funeral. He was buried in the church cemetery at the foot of Sugar Loaf Mountain.

As I have indicated, Nancy was a quiet, patient and humble person. I recall visiting her after she and Randolph had moved from the Sugar Loaf area to Rocky Face Mountain. Due to the fact that neighbors were difficult, Grandfather Randolph felt it best to move away rather than to go on feuding. Grandfather had died 8 September 1935, and Nancy was to be cared for by Romulus, her youngest son. When I arrived, she was sitting quietly in an old chair outside an old boarded shack because the old home had burned with all of its furnishings. I noticed that her arm was badly swollen just above her wrist. I was amazed to discover that it was broken and that she had been left alone for some time. I was angered that she had been so neglected, not even having been seen by a doctor despite her obvious injury. I packed her things, put her in my car and took her to my home in Kannapolis, North Carolina, about fifty miles away. Here she spent the balance of her days under the good care of my own mother. Grandmother Barnett died 8 August 1938 at the age of eighty.

On Nancy's side, I could only trace the family to her father, Francis Marimane Webster, born about 1827 and died in 1879. Her mother was Sara Kerley Webster, born about 1830 and died in 1905. Nancy had two brothers and one sister. Perhaps there were more, but I have found no further data to this effect. The name of the sister is not known, but one brother, Charles Webster, was killed when the mules ran away with him while hauling a load of wood. The other brother, Alexander, "Alex" for short, was a bachelor and carried the mail by horse and buggy from Taylorsville, the county seat of Alexander County, to the Wilkes County line at Pores Knob. He blew a bugle (about three feet long) to let the people know that he was coming with the mail. The sound resounded through the hills and the folks came to the road to get their mail or to mail letters. I saw the old bugle many times and tried to blow it – with little success because it took a lot of skill and wind. Like his sister, Nancy, Uncle Alex came to our home to be cared for by my mother in his final years. He was born 10 March 1851 and died 23 December 1923.

Uncle Alex was something of a philosopher with a twinkle in his eyes when he made a witty observation. He was of slender build, had a handlebar mustache and dressed very simply, except for a cowboy hat with some decorations on the band. He rigged up an ingenious fly-fan which, operated by a foot pedal, oscillated above the table. Since his house was not sealed up, he set up high boards around his bed to block the cold drafts. He was a Democrat. There was nothing unusual about that except that practically all of his relatives were Republicans. And in Alexander County in those days, it was a disgrace to be a Democrat; there was almost as much contempt for Democrats as there was for revenue officers.

Before Uncle Alex came to our home to live, my brother and I had to carry his meals to him to his place back in some woods about a quarter of a mile. I was about eleven and my brother about nine years old. Our parents were strong Republicans and we boys were galled by the fact that we had to carry food to "a damn Democrat."

Unless he was ill, Uncle Alex never missed a court session at the court house in Taylorsville. He was fascinated by the lawyers' arguments during the trials.

Francis Marimane Webster, Alex's father and my maternal great-grandfather, fought in the Civil War for the South. During his time in the army, he wrote a number of letters to his wife, which reveal something of his character. The following letter was written 22 August 1863:

> State of Virginia camp near army CH
> Dear Wife and Children
> By the kind and tender Mercies of all mighty God I am once more permitted to drop you a few more lines to let you all know that I am not well yet but I am a heep better than I have bin. I am tolerable harty not forgitting to hope that these few may reach you safely and find you all enjoying good health. I have no news, important news to write to you only I want to see you all very bad so bad I cannot tell by pen and ink how I do want to see you all tho I hope that the time will come that we will all meet once more. I will state to you that I have some money and some books and two finger rings and a piece for the girls and also some buttons for the little boys. I have sent you seventy dollars and I want you to pay Benjamin Watts five dollars and the rest you may spend for anything that you need for it. It is no much account any way and anything that you need and can get for it get it. I also send you the book by R. C. Barnes.
> I will inform you that we have very good preaching here every night and day. I want you to write me and let me know all the best news that you can find out in the good old state of N.C. Tell me whether there is any prospect of peace there or not. So I don't know as I have anything more to write that is worth your attention so I'll close by saying that I hope that you will excuse

bad writing and spelling and everything there in that you might find a midst in my hurried letter. So I remain your affectionate husband until death.

    M. Webster to Sarah Webster

    Written by the hand of J. Walker a member of my company.

Perhaps Francis was ill or wounded and could not write the letter himself.

A second letter is as follows:

30 December 1863 Virginia

Camps near Liberty Mills

My loving wife I avail myself with opportunity of writing to you a few lines to let you know that I am well and hearty thanks be to God for his mercies hoping these few will come safe and soon to hand and find you and the children all well and hearty and doing well. I can say to you that I received your letter that gives me great pleasure to hear from you and to hear you was all well and doing well. I think you have made a very good trade in swapping your cow for a milk cow if she is a good young and you have done well to make the swap. I want you to write me about your hogs if they will make you meat enough to do you or not. Write to me and let me know how much corn you made. If you think you will need more you had better look out in time. Sarah, I want you to take good care of my little apple trees till I come home, if I ever do.

I want you to write about my bees if they are all alive and how many you have now. You wrote to me to get a furlow and come home, but there is no chance to get a furlow now, but I hope the time is not far distance until my furlow will roll around. They are furlowing men one man from a company at a time. It will come to my turn before long. Times is all calm and still here now. I don't hardly think there will be fighting this winter here. Sarah no one can tell how bad I want to see you and my God blessed little children. I hope by the goodness and mercies of almighty God to meet you again in this world you and all the children, but if I never see you no more in this world I hope to meet you all in heaven on the right hand of God's throne. There the soft hand of God will wipe all tears from our eyes. Write to me soon. Your kind husband until death. Francis M. Webster to Sarah Webster and family.

    Marimane Webster to Sarah Webster

After the war, Francis returned to his mountain home and family. The story goes that one day while he was chopping down a tree, it fell on him and killed him.

The marriage of Randolph and Nancy was blessed with four children—two girls and two boys. I knew them all. Ervie ("Chick"), from whom I received some data about her father Randolph, was still living in August 1968 near Sugar Loaf Mountain. She married Will Wyke and there were three children: two girls, Hexie and Alvie, and one son, Alvin. Mary, Randolph's and Nancy's second daughter, married Carl Mitchell. There were several children born to them. William and Romulus were Randolph's and Nancy's two sons. Romulus was the youngest of the four children. His first wife died and he later married Vada Brown. There were several children from this marriage. Uncle Rom, as we called him, was drafted in World War I. I recall when he boarded the train at Taylorsville, North Carolina, to leave for camp along with a number of other young men. There were tearful farewells amidst the waving of small US flags by those who saw them off. A few weeks later Uncle Rom went AWOL, came home and hid in the corn crib on his father's farm. His elder brother William who was too old for the draft, persuaded the runaway to return to the army's jurisdiction. Uncle Rom spent some time in the brig—a military prison—and was eventually released. Probably to his great relief, he did not have to go overseas to fight.

While in the army Uncle Rom picked up some sort of disease that plagued him the rest of his life. He was routinely in and out of veterans hospitals, seeking relief from recurring symptoms. He died in the Oteen Military Hospital near Asheville, North Carolina, in 1967.

After the death of his second wife, Vada, Uncle Rom moved into a small hollow (now known as Barnett's Hollow) in the mountains of Sugar Loaf township. Here his children, when they married, built their small houses and began to raise their families. Uncle Rom lived in a cave and raised goats. In 1965 I visited this hollow. I saw Uncle Rom with one of his goats on the hillside (his beard was as long as the goat's!). I walked up to him and spoke. When I asked him if he knew me, he said, "No." When I identified myself, all he said was "How are you?" It had been about twenty-five years since I had seen him! I asked him about his children. He informed me that they lived in the hollow with the exception of one daughter, Shirley, who had gone to Washington DC, to be a secretary in the White House! He couldn't remember whom she had married.

William Alexander Barnette, eldest son of Nancy and Randolph, was my father. Will, as he was popularly addressed, was a tall and rather handsome man. He and Winnie, a petite woman of strong character, first met and courted while she lived at Grandma Lettie Deal's home. Winnie lived in the Deal home for two years because she enjoyed doing so and because her grandmother needed the younger woman's assistance. Winnie and two female cousins would meet young men on Sunday afternoons at Grandma Deal's. One girl could play the organ, so they sang, laughed and talked. Will did not have the courage to ask for Winnie's hand. After all, she was only sixteen years old and he was twenty-two. So he got Dugan Bumgartner, a friend of Winnie's father, to ask permission on Will's behalf for the couple to marry. I can understand why Will was reluctant to speak for himself. Grandfather Kerley was a good-sized man whose reddish face and prominent handlebar mustache only added to the aura of his already imposing presence. Permission eventually being given, they were married in Alexander County by J. W. Pharr, Justice of the Peace,[3] on 4 April 1908 after a courtship of one and a half years.

At first the newlyweds lived with Will's parents; next, nearby in a two-room house on the Old Crouch place, until Randolph built a cabin for the couple on Sugar Loaf Mountain. The old cabin still stood when last I visited the area in August 1999. Here Will and Winnie brought into the world their first child, a daughter named Mazo. I was their first son, born later in a one-room log cabin several miles away. Will and Winnie had gone to her father's place to plant a crop in the spring and summer of 1911. I was born 14 August 1911, in the log cabin built to rent to a person who wanted to farm the land. The time came for me to be delivered. Dad borrowed a mule and a buggy and drove to find a midwife named Mrs. Bady. She was not at home. Dad drove back to the cabin as fast as he could and then went for another "granny."

In the meantime, I was born. My Grandmother Kerley witnessed my birth. Another woman who had never had any children was also present. She was Aunt Becky Boles, who just sat by the fireplace. Mama had said, "He is gunna be born and I ain't gunna wait." So I was "just born" and they

---

[3] My father also became a Justice of the Peace and performed marriages. The first couple he married lived on a mountaintop, and he went up there with his young wife, Winnie, to perform the wedding.

covered me up without my umbilical cord being cut. After an hour or so Dad came in with a midwife named Mrs. Bumgartner who took one look at the situation and exclaimed: "Godalmighty! What did you sent fur me fur? Why didn't you take him up and fix him up? Wuddin' no use in me a comin." Whereupon she took a pair of scissors, cut the umbilical cord and I was fully born! My birth certificate reads "attendant at birth Mrs. Bumgartner (midwife.)" Mom stayed in bed nine days because her own mother insisted upon it.

Winnie went through pregnancies and gave birth to her first three children without seeing a doctor. Loomis, the third child, a boy, was born on Sugar Loaf Mountain. A fourth child, a son named Baines, was born in Taylorsville. He was delivered by Doc Edwards, one of the town's three doctors. Usually Doc Edwards, who customarily wore a brown derby hat, would ride a horse to make his calls. When it was time for Baines to be born, however, he had only to walk a short distance to our house.

After I was born, we moved back to the cabin on Sugar Loaf Mountain. My memory of living on Sugar Loaf Mountain is punctuated by several incidents. When I was only three years old, I recall going to the old spring-house where we kept milk and butter cooled and got buckets of water from the spring which flowed directly into the little structure. Another thing I recall is that I threw a rock into the creek that ran behind the house—and, tumbling, followed the rock into the creek! My father, working nearby, grabbed me before I went completely under the water. I remember that a lad named Fred Bently lived on nearby Pine Mountain. He would come to our house, take my sister Mazo's dolls away and then taunt her. She never forgot "mean old Fred Bently."

Out on the mountain we had no phone or access to a hospital. (In those days, you went to the hospital to die.) Town doctors rode horses to see patients. Pharmacies were considered well stocked if they had castor oil, sulfur and molasses to clean out the parasites that not uncommonly infested our bodies. Molasses made the foul-tasting medicine go down easier. Other readily sought-after medicinals were potato poultices for boils and Cardui, a patented medicine for "women's problems." Corn liquor was used for a variety of bodily pains. When suffering from a cold we took a "dram," a spoonful or a glass of whiskey depending on size, age and need of the patient. These were folk-medicines. We had to believe in faith healing for we had no access to modern medicine. If your side hurt you turned a rock over, spat under it and went back to work confident the ritual would soon provide relief for the discomfort.

Will's friends urged him to run for the office of Registrar of Deeds in Alexander County. He ran on the Republican ticket, was elected to the office in 1914 and served two terms.

After my father became the Registrar of Deeds in November 1914, we moved from Sugar Loaf Mountain to Taylorsville, so Dad could be close to his place of work. Our first home was across the street from the courthouse, near the jail or "calaboose" as it was called. Next, we moved to a frame house built on high pillars (no underpinning) in the Highland section of Taylorsville along the old Wilkesboro Road. What I especially recall about living there was the story circulating that gypsies were in town and that they kidnapped children. I was afraid to go out of the house alone. We also visited a man in the neighborhood who had a wind-up mechanical toy that caused me awe. The toy was the likeness of a Negro that danced on a tin box. It was called the "Dancing Coon." One day a man came along on a motorcycle and let Dad ride it. He fell off. Mama forbade him to ever get on another one and her obedient husband complied.

Soon we moved to another house in the Highlands, closer to the county courthouse. It was here that Baines, another brother, was born. To keep me out of the way, Dad gave me a hammer and some nails. I drove nails in wood while Doc Edwards delivered the baby. On one occasion Mama put me in the basement of the house for misbehaving. I broke the window, climbed out and ran to the courthouse. Dad brought me back home and gave me a good switching. I had a habit of following Dad to the courthouse and this usually resulted in a spanking.

I loved to go to the courthouse with Dad. I regularly made a scene mornings when he started in that direction, and it became apparent that I was not intended to go with him. I was fascinated with his office, especially the "stenographers" (secretaries), the typewriters and the large books in which the deeds were recorded. Also, I liked to climb the pyramid stairs on the façade of the courthouse. Then, too, I met a lot of people and listened to cases as they were tried in the courthouse. Sometimes I got to "pick the jury" by reaching into a glass jar and picking out twelve pieces of paper on which were written the names of those called upon to serve. Perhaps the best thing about this operation was that when the job was done the observing officials would toss me pennies, nickels and dimes. Thus enriched, I was able to buy candy and chewing gum. A favorite was a stick of OK Gum, mine for merely a penny.

From the Highlands, we moved to the Baines Norris house on Taylorsville's main street. "Aunt" Lula Watts lived across the street. She was the one who finally stopped me from running to the courthouse after Dad. One day she shamed me for this and told me I was too big to be behaving in such a manner.

The Carl Rogers family lived on the other side of the property from us. Mazo, Loomis, Baines and I played with their children, Cecil, Turner and a set of twins. One day when Turner and I were playing in our barn, I set it on fire. Dad kept a beautiful racehorse and a cow in the barn. I struck a match, lighted some chaff and the smoke boiled up. We could not put out the flames and we ran to our houses in a panic. Dad and several neighbors put out the fire "bucket brigade" style by taking water from the only supply that was handy, a well in our back yard. I thought I was in for a real serious whipping, but Dad just scolded me—and that was enough. I had learned my lesson about playing with matches.

Turner Rogers's goal in life was to fly a plane. I wanted to drive a racing car. Turner ultimately became a major general in the United States Air Force and later served as Secretary of the Air Force. In 1967 I gave a series of lectures at Chevy Chase Baptist Church in Washington D.C. Turner attended the lecture on war and peace, and I introduced him as the lad who more than fifty years previously helped me set my father's barn on fire. A letter from Turner in 1987 noted that I was his oldest friend, having enjoyed that relationship for some seventy years.

Another event during our stay at the Baines Norris house was my entrance into the first grade at school. Mom had to switch me to the school. Once I got there, I enjoyed it because we colored a lot of things like apples and turkeys. I was a timid soul, however, and would not ask to be "excused" for personal needs, suffering until I got home and availed myself of the privacy of our own facilities.

The second grade was boring. We had a tough, grouchy teacher, Miss Laura Hedrick. Once she beat me on the head with two pencils because I jumped out of my seat after being stuck in the bottom with a safety pin by

Oneal Moose, a mean student who sat behind me. I do not recall being in the third grade, but I spent two happy years in the fourth grade! In the fifth grade I learned two things: the 100th Psalm (the teacher made me stay in until I "learned it by heart") and a statement from the Sir Roger de Coverley Papers in *The Spectator*. The old gentleman made the observation that there is "much to be said on both sides" of every question. Through the years I have tried to look at both sides of every issue. This, I believe, has kept me from maintaining a one-track mind.

It would be so much easier just to see one side of a problem, but I feel compelled to examine both sides of an issue. This approach has greatly affected my teaching in college and seminary. It became my foundational pedagogical or teaching principle. I made it a practice to encourage my students to examine all aspects of an issue, to look at both the "pros and cons" of every problem or situation. People who represented different sides of a controversial issue were routinely visiting lecturers in my classes. For example, I have had Martin Luther King, Jr. and the head of the White Citizens' Council of Louisville lecture my students. One day I might have a labor leader speak in class and the next a representative of management, or perhaps an anti-war and a pro-war speaker. Students were free to make their own decisions about the issues. I also freely gave my own opinion on each matter discussed.

I remember the sixth grade very well. The teacher was in love with our principal, Clyde Campbell. She insisted I wear a necktie and part my hair in the middle just like the principal did. She even gave me some ties, expecting that I wear them. I refused. She kept me after class and told me I might as well leave school since I was not taking it seriously. She was certain I would never amount to anything anyway. After a few weeks in the seventh grade, the teacher asked me who wrote Edgar Allen Poe's *The Raven*. I told him I did not know. The class laughed. I walked out that day and never returned.

In 1918 we moved into the Jim Watts house, about four houses up the street toward town. It was a large frame building with a long front porch that included a swing. Evelyn, my parents' second daughter, was born here. That year the "flu" epidemic—influenza—descended upon us. We were told to wear asafetida, a brown gum resin with a pungent odor, in a small bag around our necks to ward off the disease. It was a worthless effort. Our whole family came down with the flu. Dad took it first, I followed and then the whole family became ill. It was so cold that winter that we all slept in the front room where there was a fireplace. Uncle Rom brought us wood and our next door neighbor, Mrs. Eckerd, baked up skillets of cornbread and left them on the front porch.

I recall struggling just to walk down the long hall to the back porch where I had to draw water from the well. I had to lean against the walls to get there and back to the front room. Since I was one of the first to come down with the flu, I was on my feet sooner than the others and had to wait on them.

Mama was very ill. Doc Edwards came and instructed us to fill fruit jars with hot water and pack them around her. She survived somehow! Once I was sent to the store for some things the family needed. I went to Campbell's Grocery, stood at the door, told the clerk what I wanted and he proceeded to get it. No one was allowed to enter stores for fear of spreading the flu. It seemed to me at that time like a five-mile hike to the store, but actually it was only about a quarter of a mile.

A vivid memory from those days was the black hearse drawn by two black horses that regularly passed by our house, bearing the bodies of those who had died of influenza. I could see the caskets through the black-tasseled glass windows of the hearse, and I wondered if one of us would be next to make the final journey to the grave yard in that somber carriage. More than twenty million people died worldwide during that epidemic, more people than had died during the hostilities of World War I. Our family, however, survived.

In the days when our family lived in the Jim Watts house, I stepped on a broken Coke bottle at the old hand pump on the school grounds. That resulted in a severe gash to my left foot. Someone had broken the bottle and its sharp fragments lay beneath the water accumulating around the pump. Big John Edwards, son of Doc Edwards and dubbed the "meanest boy in town," carried me on his shoulder all the way home. John ran to the courthouse for Dad. Doc Edwards arrived on his roan horse, carrying his instruments and medicine in the saddle bags. While three people held me on the bed, the doctor put seven stitches in my foot. No painkillers of any kind were administered. No wonder they had to hold me down! I had to crawl around for the next two weeks to keep the weight off of the foot, and then Dad fixed up an old crutch for me to use.

In the Spring of 1919 we moved to Round Top Mountain, about ten miles from Taylorsville. Here we did some gardening and kept cows and gathered apples. Dad and I would go down to the creek, watch the bees drink and then follow them to their holes in the trees and get the honey. One day a swarm of bees settled outside the house and Mama promptly hived them.

On Round Top Mountain I learned a valuable lesson that served me well in my professional life. One of my chores was to drive the cows from the beautiful green meadow across the creek to the barn at the close of day. With milk bags and bellies full, they slowly wound their way home. I quickly learned to walk, not behind the animals, but to the side. This is a good principle to follow to avoid stepping in ecclesiastical and political piles of various sorts.

In the fall of 1919 we moved back to Taylorsville, into the Wilson house near the railroad track in the east section of town. Here my father planted eight small water oak trees in the front yard. I was proud of those trees. Fifty years later, I drove by that house. A man sat under the shade of one enormous tree—a water oak. Despite the passing of so many years, at least one of the trees planted by Will Barnette had survived and thrived.

I stopped and asked if I could take a picture of the tree. "Sure, it doesn't belong to me," he said. I informed him that my father had planted the tree. He said he enjoyed sitting under it in the heat of the day. My father never had that pleasure. The tree was a commentary on much of my father's life. He did many good things that did not seem to bring him any immediate benefit. Will Barnette planted a number of "good trees" under the shade of which he never sat.

I first learned to ride a bicycle while we lived at the Wilson place. I had gotten a job as a water boy on a road gang. The pay was twenty-five cents a day. My job was to carry water for Dad and Mr. Montgomery, who operated the road scraper. I drew my pay envelope just like others did and saved enough money to buy a bike. John Edwards placed me on the handlebar and rode me down Main Street. In the process my foot was caught in the large sprocket and chain, gashing my heel. It would be weeks later before I finally learned to ride that bike, and that with the help of the girl next door!

I had to walk all the way across town to the school, from city limit to city limit. Once on the way home, I encountered my first cigar. Really, it was a cigar butt that I found on the roadside near the town cemetery. After two puffs, I began to turn green and then white, and fell over on the bank. I had previously smoked rabbit tobacco behind our barn, but had never tackled anything so potent as a genuine cigar. It was a pale and shaky Henlee who staggered home that day.

It was at the Wilson house where Uncle Alex came to die. He left his own place, a house and several acres in a wooded area about a quarter of a mile from where we lived. After Uncle Alex died, we moved into his former home. An uncle moved us with his truck. The Barnette children enjoyed playing in the woods near the house. At this time Dad operated a grocery store just across from the courthouse. He sold a lot of goods on credit, and it was a hardship when some of his customers did not pay up. He later built a filling station and a garage near the First Baptist Church of Taylorsville.

One day I was playing on the courthouse grounds and found a twenty-dollar bill. In those days that represented a small fortune. My father would not let me spend it until full inquiry was made as to who might have lost it. He even ran an ad in the local paper stating that money had been found and could be claimed by the owner. No one ever came forward to claim it. At the insistence of Rob Moose, the local optician and a member of the town's brass band, I used the money to buy a trumpet with a view to playing in the band. I blew it so much that my lips became swollen. It was not long before I gave up on the whole idea of becoming a musician and sold the trumpet.

Two games were popular among boys in those days: pitching tobacco tags at a drawn line and shooting marbles for keeps. I became an expert at marble shooting and always had a bag full of them.

Dad traded cars in connection with the garage business and gave me an old Model-T Ford when I was twelve years old. The local constable ordered me to stop driving it because I was too young. Indeed, when I slid down from the seat to reach the foot pedals, I could not see over the windshield!

Dad never stuck very long with one job. After four years as Registrar of Deeds, he engaged a variety of enterprises. First, he drove a truck that pulled a road scraper to maintain the county roads. This was about 1919 and there was not a single paved road in the whole county. As Registrar of Deeds, Dad signed the bonds ($50,000) to pave the streets of Taylorsville and to put in the water and sewage system.

After Dad quit the road job, he worked in Rufus Reid's garage as a mechanic. Later he opened the grocery store, then built the filling station along with a garage of his own. The garage is still standing and doing business. Before this, however, he opened a barber shop with a pool hall in the back. This is where I learned to shoot pool. Dad was a good barber but left that career behind to pursue the grocery business. At one time he also ran a taxi service and for a while was a horse trader. Dad eventually sold the garage and filling station and bought an apple orchard on one of the mountains about ten miles from Taylorsville. I had to help him fix up the old road that led up to the orchard, out of which I also had to dig up many an old stump.

At one point, someone helped himself to the apples in the orchard and the rails of the fence that surround it. The thief used the apples to make mash for whiskey and burned the rails to distill it. By the time Dad and I found the place where the still had been located, it was gone.

When we lived out in the mountains, we made a little money by taking peach seeds, dried fruit and "sassafras" bark to town and selling them. I guess some patent medicine company bought these items from the stores to which we sold them. As we returned home, we would pick up "a sack of pokes." These were sacks into which Bull Durham tobacco was put after we had clipped, turned, strung, tied and tacked the sacks together in bundles of twenty-five. We were paid the grand sum of five cents per one hundred! Nevertheless it was a family affair and all of the children had a part in the work.

2

The Magnetic Mills

The golf links lie so near the mill that almost every day the
laboring children can look out and see the men at play.
—Sarah N. Cleghorn, *Quatrain*

Cotton mills seemed to possess magnetic power over people in the South, especially during the Great Depression. They drew people from the hinterlands: sharecroppers, the jobless and the poor. Since Alexander County was one of the poorest counties in the state of North Carolina, hundreds migrated from there to the mill town of Kannapolis looking for work.

In 1925 the Barnette family, all eight of us, moved from Taylorsville to Kannapolis. It was the middle of the Roaring Twenties, the age of the "flapper." Clara Bow, silent movies star whose strongest suit was her sex appeal, personified for many the spirit of the era. The first Miss America pageant was held in 1921. The Ku Klux Klan paraded freely in the streets of Southern and Mid-western cities. In 1919, prohibition became law in the United States. Babe Ruth was the most popular baseball player, and Al Capone ruled the Chicago underworld. In 1927 Charles Lindbergh made the world's first solo transatlantic flight. Women bobbed their hair and the hemlines of their dresses became daringly short. I recall that my own sister, at the age of about fourteen, had her hair bobbed and began to use makeup. In our small town she and her likeminded peers were considered "loose girls" by the more constrained. Stalin rose to power in 1928. Dr. Fleming accidentally discovered penicillin in that same year.

The Barnettes made the trip from Taylorsville to Kannapolis, about fifty miles, in an ancient model-T Ford. Along the way there were flat tires and a rainstorm. A family we did not know invited us into their home until the inclement weather passed.

Kannapolis was founded in 1906 by J. W. Cannon. Its unusual name comes from two Greek words that mean "loom" and "city," together resulting in "the city of looms." Main Street in Kannapolis boasted a large sign electrically illuminated with 1,800 incandescent bulbs declaring Cannon Mills Company the "World's Largest Manufacturer of Towels." A large cannon with a stack of cannon balls rested on top of the sign. In 1925 this was a real wonder for a lad like me who had never before seen an electrically lighted sign. Only Main Street, boasting about one dozen stores and businesses, was paved and had sidewalks. A small lake lay between Main Street and the illuminated Cannon Mills sign. One could walk or drive around the lake.

Cannon and Cabarrus, producing towels, sheets and pillowcases, were the two giant mills that dominated the town. Workers were paid in cash every two weeks, their money handed to them in envelopes. When the mills ran full-time with night or "grave yard" and day shifts, the workers labored ten hours a day, five and one-half days a week.

The mills provided basic housing for the workers. These "mill houses" were simple frame structures supported on brick stilts—no underpinning, no inside water, no inside toilet facilities. There were electric lights; a single cord with a light bulb dropped from the ceiling in each room. Heat for the whole house came from one fireplace, meaning that only that room was actually heated. There was typically only one water spigot on the house's back porch, the one source for household water. We were fortunate enough to have a front porch where we hung a swing. Of course, the superintendents and other "bosses" lived in nicer homes, but nothing luxurious.

Mill workers were religiously and politically conservative, especially the "mountain folk." The companies were wise to employ tenant farmers, sharecroppers and mountain people, for they were suspicious of labor unions. From 1918 to the 1990s repeated attempts were made to unionize the mill workers. They passionately fought against union organization, thanking God each time another unionizing effort failed.

Mr. Charles Cannon owned the mill that had his name and controlled the town. Kannapolis in 1925 was unincorporated and had no city officials. Mr. Cannon established his own police force, controlled the weekly newspaper and determined who from the town would run for political office. My friend Bedford Black, a lawyer, called Cannon a "benevolent dictator." Black knew this from experience. He decided to run for US Congress. Mr. Cannon informed Black that it was not yet his turn. Although Mr. Cannon had helped pay Black's way through college, the lawyer disobeyed his benefactor's wishes and ran for office anyway. Mr. Cannon ordered the local paper never to mention Black's name. *Time* magazine carried the story under the caption "Black Out."

Charles Cannon was in many ways benevolent. He built and supported the J. W. Cannon High School, named for his father, which I attended. He established the town's YMCA (Young Men's Christian Association), which was the social and recreational center of the community. Cost of membership? Just two dollars a year. There you could take a free shower, and you have the use of a towel costing only two cents. You could shoot pool, bowl and get a haircut for twenty-five cents. There was also a religious dimension to the program, which took on an evangelistic tone. During my school days I served as president of the High-Y and chairperson of the Personal Workers Club, an evangelistic group.

Kannapolis also had a theater, where for a dime you could see movies like "The Green Archer" or the great cowboy films starring the likes of Bob Steele, Hoot Gibson, Ken Maynard and others. The Keystone Cops, Buster Keaton and other movie comedians provided laughs.

Charles Cannon was a committed Christian, deeply involved in the community's religious life. On occasion he brought notable evangelists to the city, including Billy Sunday, who spoke at the YMCA. Cannon also subsidized the town's various churches with gifts of money and provided much appreciated public approval of their ministries. While his intent to be helpful was surely authentic, Cannon's active presence within the town's congregations—often to their benefit—may have muffled the prophetic voices of the preachers. Generally though, he enriched the religious experience and educational tone of the community.

Religion permeated much of the town's day-to-day affairs. Once some of Cannon's employees stole towels by stuffing them down their working overalls trouser legs. The pastor of the "holiness church" preached against stealing. Some of his parishioners brought stolen towels to Mr. Cannon and asked forgiveness. As a result, Mr. Cannon helped the congregation build a brand new brick building on a hill.

The town was predominantly white Anglo-Saxon. A few blacks lived in isolation at the edge of the town. I never saw a black person in town at night. A small mill town about three miles north of Kannapolis was segregated. I once saw a sign at that city's limits that read, "Nigger, don't let the sun go down on you in this town." Close by was a black community, which had the only black doctor in town. I was told that white folks went to him when they caught venereal diseases.

By the time I was thirteen years old I desperately wanted to work in the mills. My father took me in one of the mills and tried to persuade the boss man (called the second-hand) to give me a job. The second-hand said that he did not need any more "hands." Workers in cotton mills in those days were called "hands." But this did not stop me. I went back several times to the mills and I think I irritated and frustrated the boss-man until he finally gave me a job. I had to work ten hours a day, five and one-half days a week for eighteen cents an hour. I was so tired when I got home Saturday at noon that I did not feel like being a juvenile delinquent. I just fell across the bed with my overalls on.

The entire family went to work in the mill except the small ones and my mother. Mama managed the household and we brought our cash pay to her. She in turn gave us an allowance.

In those days, there were little or no retirement programs available to mill workers. One woman worked in the cotton mills for sixty years, beginning at the age of ten. As a child, she had to stand on a box to do her work. When she finally retired, her retirement pension was not enough to pay the rent. Her son, Dr. Wayne E. Oates, the distinguished psychologist and author who coined the term "workaholic," helped his mother make financial ends meet until she died.

I do not recall that any medical benefits existed for workers in those days. Once we were vaccinated for typhoid fever. This occurred, I suspect, because management feared that too many "hands" would become ill. When Franklin Delano Roosevelt was elected president in 1933 a minimum wage was soon instituted, as well as a legal limit for working hours per week. Especially during the winter months, we knew what it was to enter into the mills in the dark and come out in the dark, rarely enjoying sunshine during the week. But when the maximum was set for working hours, we got out at three-thirty in the afternoon. I will never forget that experience. I walked briskly and excitedly out of the mill past the gatekeepers; the sun was shining, I felt that the Kingdom of God had come. I suddenly felt guilty because I was not working.

There was only one black employee in the mill where I worked. He cleaned spittoons. Many of the men—there were no women—in the department where I worked chewed tobacco—Brown's Mule, Apple and other brands. Some dipped snuff—Rooster, TubeRose—by putting it under their lower lip. Someone had to clean out the cuspidors and no white person would do that especially unpleasant job.

I recall only one Chinese family—the Jungs—who ran a laundry in the town. To those of us who had never seen Asian people before, they seemed strange. But that family was beloved. I never heard a racial slur spoken against them. Eventually all the Jung children achieved the American dream with unusual success in business, in the military, science and education.

A few months after being hired in the mill, I was promoted from spreading towels to cutting towels, which paid more. We were on piecework and, if we chose, we could work ourselves to death. Sometimes a worker was put on the "stretch-out system." This meant that one worker would be fired and another would assume that job's duties plus his own without any additional pay. In other words, the "stretched-out" worker did the work of two for the pay of just one. Cutting certain towels caused injury to my fingers. I taped them to prevent blood from staining the towels. If this occurred, my pay would be docked.

By the time I was eighteen, I had a second-hand Model-T Ford Roadster, quite an achievement for a mill worker of my age. I was part of the Maple Hill Gang. On Sundays we would gather in my home and play Black Jack for cigarettes or pennies. In spite of prohibition, sometimes we managed to secure a pint of corn whiskey. That had the effect of livening up the group and the game.

After four years in the mill, my buddy and I went to Charlotte, North Carolina, about thirty miles away. There we sought to enlist in the United States Marine Corps. As the applicants stepped up to the sergeant recruiter, he would look each one over and then point to the next place to which they were to go for further examination. I heard the sergeant tell the skinny men to go around the corner, eat all the bananas they could and then come back. When I stepped up, he took one look at me and said, "You go around the corner, eat an anvil and come back." That ended my efforts to enter the military. I was super-skinny and often embarrassed about my appearance.

During the Great Depression, which began in 1929, we had little to live on. Our diet consisted of pinto beans, fatback meat, cornbread and sometimes milk. Our dessert was molasses and fatback gravy. When we could work a day or two in the mill, all our small income went to feed and clothe the family. I remember my Mama would go out in the country and pick blackberries and other fruit for canning so we would have something to eat in the winter. She bought a cow and kept her in a shed she put up in our tiny back yard. We had milk. What a blessing!

While employment in the mill was a source of survival and I am grateful for it, there were damaging results for me. After enduring the physical stresses of the kind of standing that particular job required all those years, the varicose veins in both of my legs protruded like ropes. They eventually required surgical removal, the expense of which the mill industry bore no share. Psychologically, the impact of the repetitive work was devastating. Standing in one place cutting towels, I wore a hole through an oak floor. Five years of rocking back and forth pulling towels through a two-bladed cutter left me feeling like a machine. In my memory, I often see that footprint I left on the floor of the mill.

We were expected to meet production. To this day, I feel compelled to produce something visible—a letter, an article, a chapter. Doing so drives away any intrusion of depression and satisfies my compulsion to show something concrete for my efforts.

To this day I still have nightmares of attempting to escape from the mills. In my dream, I get lost inside the mill and have to ask the way to the gates though I went in and out of them, to and from work, a thousand times. I never escape to freedom in my dreams, and I am always stopped by the guards at the gate.

I became a "hand" along with thousands of children who never had the opportunity to develop to their full potential. We were "hands," and nothing more. The mill machine was often given more importance than the person working at it. Some people never discovered that "hands" were connected—to heads, hearts, spirits and families.

Though the cutting room gang was tough there were few fights. I was fired once for fighting. The other guy apologized to me, and we worked together on a job outside the mill. He eventually went back to work in the same department in the mill. I was given a pink slip explaining why I had been fired. By ironic contrast, years later in the "enlightened" post-World War II era, a seminary colleague was dismissed without even the minimal courtesy of an explanation.

Social life in the cotton mill town consisted largely of dating a girl on Saturday night. A couple or a foursome might take a motor ride in the country or to a nearby town. A popular place in my day was Propts' Spring, where there were facilities for picnics. Sometimes we gathered on a street corner near the First Baptist Church and, accompanied by an instrument, sang. Even in those days, the guitar was a popular music maker.

As a teenager, I was shy around the girls. One who lived across the street from me would sit in her porch swing and sing to me, "Sweet Henlee, from sunny Tennessee. You'll love him when you see sweet Henlee." My embarrassment was unbounded.

My mother provided valuable counsel with reference to my relationship to the opposite sex. She never picked a girlfriend for me, but diverted me from those who pursued me. Now I thank my God for her, for the protection and the wise counsel she gave. She had married at age sixteen, but only after dating my father for over a year. They celebrated fifty-four wedding anniversaries and were blessed with eight children.

3

Conversion and Call

*All Christians are called to ministry regardless of how they
earn their daily bread.*

To escape boredom and in a search for excitement I began to hang out at the
"shacks"—little communities that had grown up around the one-man
controlled city of Kannapolis. There were Union Town, Pethel Town,
Centerview and North Kannapolis. These small communities usually had a
grocery store, a small restaurant and maybe a pool hall. Fights would break
out frequently. Sometimes someone would get shot or cut badly. Each
community had its own local tough guy, both feared and admired. In North
Kannapolis, my neighbor Charlie aspired to that role. Someone shot him and
my last sight of him was in his front yard on the mill hill with a bullet in his
side, cursing and crying, and vowing to kill his enemy.

Efforts were made to get me "saved" and into regular church
attendance by well-intentioned church members. My father and I did not
engage in church life. Aggressive "soul-winners" informed me that I was
going to hell if I did not get right with God. My response was, "I will have
plenty of company from your church membership." Other concerned folk
took a gentler approach. A colleague in the mill put his arm around my
shoulder and told me that he loved me and wanted me to be a Christian. I
could find no rude response to offer! That experience resulted in my
beginning to think seriously about becoming a Christian.

Most moving to me was the love and prayers of my mother. She was
my image of an authentic follower of the "Jesus Way." She took the Bible
seriously, went into the one "closet" of our mill home and prayed for me
(see Matt 6:6). She prayed over me for years, like the persistent widow in
the Bible (see Luke 18:1–5), until her prayers were answered.

Mama was a devoted member of the First Baptist Church. She was a Baptist by conviction, having formerly been a Lutheran. In the worst of times during the Great Depression she would save a few coins, tie them in the corner of her handkerchief and be off to church. She put those few precious coins in the offering plates as they were passed.

When her church established a mission Sunday School in North Kannapolis, Mama joined in the work and helped to build it into a church. She remained a faithful member there for more than thirty years.

As it happened, a revival was in progress at the fledgling church in North Kannapolis. My mother, inspired by the services, redoubled her prayers for me and my father. My neighbor was a weaver at the mills with a fourth grade education. One evening after dinner he approached me while I was sitting in the swing on the front porch of the mill house on Maple Hill and invited me to church. I declined. He persisted and got my promise to go with him the next night.

I was sitting on the same swing the next night and had forgotten about the promise. There was my neighbor before I realized it saying, "Let's go." I had not planned to be home, but he caught me. "O.K., I'll go. I am not a liar, but we must go by the shacks first." As I mentioned earlier, "the shacks" were the unsanctioned stores, restaurants and pool halls that had sprung up around the edges of Kannapolis. These were the places where the "toughies" hung around.

At a North Kannapolis shack, where a short time before the owner had shot one of my neighbors, I found one fellow, Red Joines, and told him we were going to church. At first he objected, but then reluctantly followed. We sat on the back slab bench in the wooden frame church. The minister, the Reverend Wade H. James, preached. His topic was "The Great Physician," based on Jeremiah 8:22: "Is there no balm in Gilead; is there no physician there?" He gave the invitation to be healed by the Great Physician. After two persons came to my side pleading that I accept Christ as my personal Savior, I went forward to the "mourner's bench." There among the other mourners—those under the sense of conviction who were seeking the forgiveness of their sins from God—I said to the Lord: "Here is my life, take it and use it for your glory." There came over me a peace I had never known. I felt that I had been forgiven of my sins, cleansed and healed. I felt like I had become a new person. This was 18 September 1931. I was nineteen years old.

In that same meeting my father, who like me had not been a churchgoer, made his profession of faith. Neither of us knew the other was there. In the congregation, upon witnessing the full answer to her prayers, Mama shouted and clapped her hands praising God.

Next day I went to work in the mill knowing that some of the workers would make unkind remarks and put temptations in my way. By the grace of God I was able to remain faithful to my commitment to Christ. I kept a New Testament and a small dictionary on my cutting table. At every opportunity I would read a few verses. When I quit the mill, I left those two books. Later I was told that my successor read that New Testament, became a Christian and a devoted churchman.

What happened to Red Joines, the tough guy, whom I persuaded to accompany me to the revival meeting? When the invitation was given to accept Christ as Savior, he went out the back door. I never saw him again. Some time later I was informed that he had killed a man and was under arrest. That evening at the revival turned out to be a radical turning point in both of our lives. In the words of an unknown poet:

> To every man there openeth a high way and a low, and
> Each must decide which way his or her soul will go.

The good news is that in 1998 Red's brother informed me the courts ultimately found Red not guilty of murder, but that he had acted in self-defense. In 1996 Red had become a Christian. After more than half-a-century, he too made his way, not out the church's back door, but to the mourner's bench—and there found new life.

I was baptized Sunday afternoon 4 October 1931 in Graber's Pond by the Reverend Napoleon Huneycutt, pastor of the Trading Ford Baptist Church near Salisbury, North Carolina. More than eighty others were baptized in that out-of-doors baptismal service. Following my baptism, I became a member of the North Kannapolis Baptist Church.

After joining the church, like some other church members following regular worship services, I stood outside and talked with those who did not return to the building for the young people's meetings. It so happened that

Mr. Clay Wilson—a man who stood about six feet, five inches tall—was appointed by the BYPU (Baptist Young People's Union) to recruit members. He exited the church, caught me by the nap of my neck, stretched me up and declared, "Young man, you ought to be in BYPU!" Of course, I could not argue with him and I proceeded to the meeting.

I had never before seen anything like that meeting. Four or five members of the group were given a part on the program. A youth group leader gave me a topic to talk about the next Sunday. It was wise that my part was brief because I had never made a speech before in my life, in or out of the church. During the week before I was to speak, I worked on memorizing every word, every comma and every period of my piece. When the day came for me to make my presentation I was scared, but I showed up at the BYPU meeting anyway. When the meeting's leader finally called on me to give my part, I stood up and suddenly felt like I was in outer-space. To this day I still do not know what I said, but I remember feeling good when I sat down. That day, it turned out, was the beginning of my speaking career.

Within a short while I was teaching a Sunday School class at North Kannapolis Baptist Church. From there I went with a fellow church member into the slum section of our city and engaged in prayer meetings. The place was called "Frog Holler," and there was a lot of bootlegging, gambling and other mischief going on. Sometimes, in the house where I was holding prayer meeting and trying to be in the Spirit, someone in the back room would be bottling up different sorts of spirits—corn liquor. The odor of it would drift right into where we were having our prayer meeting. But out of those prayer meetings there came a church anyway. We built a little frame church house on a lot that was donated by Charles Cannon and the Home Mission Board of the SBC. The church grew and finally built a beautiful church house; one of the finest in the city of Kannapolis. In 1998, of one hundred Baptist churches in North Carolina, this one ranked fifth in giving to the Lottie Moon Missions Offering (named after the female missionary saint of Southern Baptist life): $52,000! You have to remember the origins of this now vibrant congregation was from among the poor mill workers.

One evening after church my pastor at North Kannapolis Baptist Church came to me in the churchyard. I was standing out there alone and he asked, "Is God calling you to preach?" His question was like a thunderbolt hitting me because I had been wrestling with the matter. I did not know that he or anyone else knew about it and I had to admit that I did feel a calling. He then said a very wise thing: "The same God who calls to preach calls to prepare."

Though my pastor, the Reverend Wade James, had only an eighth grade education, he was one of he wisest men I ever knew. He later finished high school and went to college and seminary. Before leaving to complete his formal education, however, six churches came from the one he served. The congregation at North Kannapolis Baptist Church also saw about eight persons leave their ranks for the called ministry.

I had not finished high school. Brother James, as he was popularly called, took me and my trunk with few belongings and deposited me at Campbell College in Buies Creek, North Carolina. I stayed one-half day and caught a ride back to Kannapolis that afternoon. To say the least my pastor was surprised and a bit hurt. Since I had no money, I decided to return and take my chances at completing a high school education in the local public school. I met the principal, Mr. Bill Bullock, in the hallway of Cannon High School. I requested to be enrolled. He asked for my education record. I had none. He asked, "Well, what grade do you want to enter?" My response: "I'll try the ninth." He said "O.K." It was 1933 and, having spent the previous six years working in the mill, I was twenty-two years old.

My formal education finally got underway again that fall at Cannon High School. My classmates had already studied the first half of our algebra book when I first enrolled. That first month I made a zero. I went back to the first half of the book, discovered some basic principles and finished the course with a passing grade. I studied by lamplight, for we had moved from town to the woods. There was neither electricity nor indoor plumbing in our latest family dwelling, but those were luxuries I did not miss since they had not been a part of my life before anyway.

In spite of the long hours of study for school, I participated in YMCA activities, served as pastor of the new church in Frog Holler (properly called West Point), served another church in a nearby city, became president of the high school student body and became president of the Cabarrus County Red

Cross[1]. Graduation came 12 May 1936. I was twenty-five years old and would be twenty-six upon entering college.

About one year after my conversion, I preached my first sermon at the North Kannapolis Baptist Church. It was 14 August 1932, my birthday. The sermon subject: "What Shall I Do With Jesus?" (Matt 27:22) Its simple outline was as follows:

Introduction

There are many great questions today. No man ever asked a more important question than Pilate: "What shall I do with Jesus?"
1. It is a very personal question
    a. No one else can decide this for you.
    b. You will accept or reject faith for yourself.
    c. It is your choice whether you will go to heaven or to hell. (2 Cor 5:10)
2. Furthermore, the question
    a. Is not what shall I do with the church, or some creed or even baptism?
    b. It is "What shall I do with Jesus?"
3. Again, the question is "What shall I do with Jesus?"
    a. God tells us to listen.
    b. Jesus calls us with many invitations. (Matt 11:28; Rev 22:17)
        1b. Who invites us to faith?
        2b. Who is invited?
        3b. Result if accepted.
        4b. Result if rejected.

When I offered an invitation for listeners to respond, four teenagers made a profession of faith in Christ. They were my neighbors and went on to live their entire lives as committed believers in Christ: Claude Russell, David Robinette, Clara Lauder and Marshall Cloniker.

---

[1] See "High School Senior Busy," *Charlotte Observer* (6 October 1935).

On 14 September 1932 North Kannapolis Baptist Church, my home church, licensed me to preach the gospel and to exercise my gifts in the work of the ministry, with the exception of administering the ordinances of baptism and the Lord's Supper. That was a responsibility reserved for the ordained clergy. My church subsequently sponsored an ordination council, composed of twelve people from five Baptist churches, who examined my suitability for the ministry. I was ordained on 10 July 1935 in the North Kannapolis church. My ordination was required so that I could function without restriction as pastor of the West Point Baptist Church, which I had helped to found in 1935.

Today (July 2004) the church's membership exceeds 500. That congregation has ordained four ministers and an additional two missionaries. The church is active in its ministry to the community and beyond through outreach efforts by its youth and adult organizations to help people who have suffered any number of calamities, such as floods, hurricanes or fires.

While still in high school, I simultaneously served West Point Baptist Church as a "supply" pastor and First Baptist Church of Landis as its regular pastor. My first sermon at Landis netted me two dollars and twenty cents. That sum increased with each sermon. I resigned both churches in July 1936 and left for Wake Forest College.

4

Wake Forest College

A little learning is a dangerous thing;
Drink deep, or taste not the Pierian spring.
—Alexander Pope

In the fall of 1936 I left the mill town of Kannapolis in a 1928 Model-A Ford Coach with $50 in my pocket. I had finished high school earlier in the spring and was on my way to Wake Forest College. I had some apprehension about what lay ahead of me, but I also went in high hopes and excited about meeting my first college professors.

The first person I met at an old wooden dormitory on the campus of Wake Forest was a young student, Garland Hendricks. He greeted me and inquired as to who I was and where I was coming from. When he discovered that I was a ministerial student, he told me that he had been interim pastor at a nearby Baptist church and that he was trying to complete his Master of Arts degree at the college. He wondered if I would be interested in preaching in the church. He said they were looking for a minister to "hold a revival meeting." Of course, I was interested. He took me to the administration building to see Dr. W. R. Cullom, Chairman of the Department of Religion. He questioned me a bit about my pastoral experience. I told him that I had been pastor of two small churches in North Carolina. That was good enough! On the following Sunday, Dr. Cullom sent me to Corinth Baptist Church near Louisburg, North Carolina. The church soon called me as pastor and I remained there all through my college career. The young man who recommended me to Dr. Cullom was Garland Hendricks, who later became a professor at Southeastern Baptist Theological Seminary at Wake Forest after the college itself had moved to Winston-Salem, North Carolina.

Wake Forest College was founded by Baptists in 1834. It was located on Number One Highway about sixteen miles north of Raleigh, the North Carolina state capital. The college motto was *Pro Christo, Pro Humanitate*. Though the *Pro Christo* is absent from the emblem, Christ is there represented by the presence of the first two letters of his name in Greek. The college colors were old gold and black; *Dear Old Wake Forest*, the school song.

In 1936 the college was not coed (at least I never saw any females in my classes) and consisted of about five hundred students. Baseball was popular and attracted excellent players to the school. Tommy Burns, who later pitched for the New York Giants, and Ray Scorboro, who played for the Washington Senators were among my classmates. Many of the football players came from northern coal mining areas and had names that struck us Southern boys as strange, names such as Gugenski and Palansky. Basketball, tennis and golf also had some outstanding athletes representing the school. Our football coach, Peahead Walker, later became a coach at Yale University and there was joined by other coaching associates from Wake Forest.

The Euzelian and Philamathesian Literary societies, founded in 1835, were popular and sponsored distinguished speakers including Governor Joseph Melville Broughton, who himself had been a member of the Euzelian Society as a student. On 28 September 1937 the Euzelian Society heard Thomas Dixon, author of *The Clansmen*, a book that was made into the D. W. Griffith movie, *The Birth of a Nation*. A portrait of Dixon hung on the wall of the Euzelian Society. He earned more than one million dollars writing books—an enormous amount of money in his day. But he lost it all in the Great Depression. "Did I give up, sit around and moan? No! I said I would write better books and more books," declared Dixon. He continued: "I've lived the first chapter of life. When I go out of this life, I will just begin a new chapter." In my second year at college, I was the Euzelian Society's chaplain and became its president in my senior year.

In those years, upper classmen exercised a sort of informal but real authority over under classmen. As a freshman I was often threatened in notes sent by upper classmen. Among other things, they declared that I would get a free haircut some night—a traditional hazing prank played on freshmen at Wake Forest College. I was from a mill town, had worked in the slums of that town and had hung around plenty of tough places. I resented the threats and was in no mood to give satisfaction to any prankster. One evening a note was slipped under my door ordering me to dress in my Sunday best and to stand at a certain spot just outside Hunter Hall. I was bound to obey to some degree. Someone tipped me off that a bucket of water would hit me from the third floor. Down it came and I dashed aside, avoiding a drenching. My anger surged. I entered the building and quickly reaching the third floor, knife in hand, I dared the perpetrator to step out of his room. A student finally appeared and asked to see the note. He grabbed it, ran to the toilet and flushed it. I put my knife back in my pocket. That was the way we fought on the mill hill. But the message was sent. I never received another note, and my red hair remained its normal length.

While at Wake Forest I joined various organizations: the Golden Bough, the Ministerial Conference, the Euzelian Society, the Student Legislature, Omicron Delta Kappa, Delta Kappa Alpha and Chi Eta Tau. These relationships helped to form meaningful fellowship and some lasting friendships. I also was head of an unofficial group called the "Pappy Circle," because we were significantly older—in my case, about six years—than the other students. All the members of the circle did well in their chosen vocations. Among them were Wayne E. Oates, Nolan Patrick Howington, David Schrum and Claude Roebuck, three who became professors and one a physician. There were about a dozen in the circle.

Courses in the curriculum that challenged me were Latin under Dr. Hubert Poteat; English literature under Drs. Folk and Jones; anatomy under Dr. William (Billy) Lewis Poteat, who unfortunately did not complete his class that term due to health problems; Greek under Dr. George Paschal; religion under Drs. W. R. Cullom, O. T. Binkley and James Lynch; philosophy and psychology under Dr. A. C. Reid. These and other teachers provided me with a well-founded classical education. Their integrity, intellectual honesty, competency in their disciplines and spiritual vision left a lasting imprint upon me.

Student politics were an important part of my life at Wake Forest College. Harald Schaly, a Brazilian who had been in a couple of revolutions in that country, led us in a crusade to put non-fraternity students in key campus leadership positions in an upcoming election. The opposing parties met on the football field to fight it out. Tomatoes, eggs and garbage were thrown by the frat boys, while a brass band played on the back of a flat-bed truck. In the midst of the melee, I saw Schaly stab his finger at the face of a student named Castelberry and declare, "You ain't a gentleman!" Another ministerial student who had been a professional boxer before conversion, mounted the truck, put up his dukes and cried, "Come on! I'll take all of you on one at a time!"

We sort of made up when calmer voices prevailed and we were made aware of how stupid we were being. Our side, nonfrat, lost the battle. Schaly and I felt so guilty for how we had conducted ourselves that we went to Dr. Billy Poteat's grave in the cemetery across the railroad tracks and prayed. We asked God to give us the patience and brotherly love our great teacher possessed and expressed in his life. After the prayer we got back into my old purple Plymouth and drove to Sky Hill, so-called because most of the dwellings were occupied by ministerial students. A group was assembled on a porch. We drove up and yelled, "We lost the election!" No one said anything. Lo! It was a prayer meeting. The speaker was in the midst of the ten plagues in the Bible when we so rudely interrupted with our worldly news.

Some Remarkable Professors at Wake Forest

Dr. William (Billy) L. Poteat. One of the greatest professors I met while attending Wake Forest College (1936–40) was Dr. Billy Poteat. He had been president of the college for many years. During my student years, however, Dr. Billy—as he was affectionately known—had returned to the classroom to teach biology—with attention to the controversial subject of evolution. There had been an effort in the Southern Baptist Convention to have him fired while he was president. He was a great teacher. I had a course with him in anatomy and his method of teaching was unique. Behind the podium where he lectured there was a row of closets which contained all the parts of the human body, some in formaldehyde. He brought a human skeleton before the class in his first lecture. He pointed to the skeleton and his first words echoed a verse from the Old Testament: "We are fearfully and wonderfully made" (see Ps 139:14). His good natured humor was also immediately apparent as he next pointed to the coccyx, the four small segments of bone at the end of the spinal column, and said, "Young gentlemen, thereby hangs a tale; your tail."

One day on campus I saw Dr. Billy looking intently through a small microscope at something in his hand. I asked him what he was looking at. He said, "Take a look." I did and saw there were some very small and lovely flowers. Amazed at their beauty and size, I asked him where he found them. Dr. Billy answered, "This whole campus is covered with these flowers and we walk over them every day." It astounded me that Dr. Billy knew the name and type of every tree on the campus. According to him, there were sixty-five species of trees at Wake Forest College.

Dr. Billy was a committed Christian and always went to prayer meeting when he was in town. Often they called on him to pray. He would stand facing the congregation with eyes wide open, and looking up toward heaven would say, "Well, Lord, here we are again." He wrote a wonderful book entitled *Can a Man Be a Christian Today?* published by the University of North Carolina Press. At Dr. Billy's funeral, the pastor called attention to the book and asked, "Can a man be a Christian today?" The pastor then observed that Dr. Poteat proved the answer in the affirmative by how he had lived.

Dr. W. R. Cullom. During the 1930s, Dr. Cullom was Chairman of the Department of Religion at Wake Forest College. His lectures were often dry but always informative. I spent one summer as a guest in his home. At one point during that time, I was called away to another city to preach a revival meeting. Upon arrival there, I discovered that I had left my sermons back at Dr. Cullom's home. Making an urgent telephone call back to Wake Forest, I requested that Dr. Collum mail the sermons to me as quickly as possible. Eventually they arrived with a note from my summer host and professor. He wrote that he had a very difficult time getting the post office to handle the sermons because they were so dry they were flammable and dangerous. He had a rare sense of humor.

At the age of ninety-five, he and a fellow minister, who was himself ninety years old, would read together significant books on race and race relations. They had been brought up all of their lives in the South and were influenced by the customs and mores of the South in relation to race. Now in 1962, at ripe old ages, they were struggling to overcome their racial prejudice. They felt cramped by prejudiced customs and worked to break free of racism's subtle hold. The two elderly men also worked to open their neighbors' hearts and minds regarding the issue.[1]

Dr. Hubert Poteat. My Latin professor was Dr. Hubert Poteat. He would send us to the board to conjugate verbs and translate sentences from Latin into English. I recall that when one student put his work on the board, Dr. Hubert commended him and told him he had done the impossible. The student thought he was being given a great compliment. He had, however, conjugated a Latin noun—which is of course impossible! When students made stupid mistakes like this, Dr. Poteat would characteristically growl, "Go out on the campus and graze!" This was a euphemistic way of likening the target of his ire to a particularly dull beast of burden, a jackass.

Dr. Hubert was an accomplished musician, a distinguished organist and like his father, Dr. Billy Poteat, a progressive Southerner. He was a devoted member of the Masonic Lodge and succeeded comedian Harold Loyd as that organization's national leader.

Dr. N. Y. Gulley. In the 1930s, freshman students at Wake Forest were required to attend chapel during their first semester. The chapel services were usually conducted by a professor and occasionally led by a visiting minister. Dr. N. Y. Gulley, founder and one-time dean of the School of Law at Wake Forest, was an elderly gentleman when I heard him conduct the chapel service. Using Hebrews 12:1, "Let us lay aside every weight and the sin which does so easily beset us," he announced his subject as "Sins of College Students." In those days, Wake Forest University was an all male school and the professors often talked very frankly to us. There were three sins that he stressed in his talk: laziness, lying and lascivious lingering around the lewd ladies.

Professor A. C. Reid. One professor we students respected and feared at the college in the late 1930s was Dr. A. C. Reid, Professor of Philosophy and Psychology. He was nicknamed "Alternating Current Reid" and he *could* shock you. When the bell rang for classes to begin, he would lock the door and latecomers found themselves barred from the class.

Professor Reid believed there was a sacredness about his classroom. One could be dismissed from the class for carrying on a conversation while

---

[1] S. L. Morgan, Sr., "I Confess to Race Prejudice," *Western Recorder* (15 March 1962): p.7.

he was lecturing—or even for yawning loudly. On one occasion a ministerial student, who was a church pastor in nearby Raleigh, had his feet propped up on a seat when Dr. Reid entered the classroom. Dr. Reid whistled softly, as was his habit before saying something particularly serious. He then asked how the student would feel if, on the following Sunday, one of his church's deacons propped his feet up on a pew during services. The student responded that he would not like it. Dr. Reid said, so that the whole class could hear: "Then take your feet off of that seat. It is just as sacred as that pew in your church."

Edgar Estes Folk, Jr. A professor in the field of the modern literature, Edgar Estes Folk, Jr., was the son of Dr. E. E. Folk, Sr., distinguished editor of *Baptist and Reflector*, the Baptist state paper of Tennessee, as well as the author of several books. One was titled *Baptist Principles* and consisted of letters to his son and namesake, whose picture appeared in the volume.

Professor Folk assigned me the task of reading and reporting on Thomas Mann's great novel, *Joseph in Egypt*. My report's subject: "Ten Reasons Why Joseph Did Not Succumb To The Seductions of Mut-em-enet." ("Lily-armed Mut-em-enet," who tried to seduce Joseph, was Potipher's wife. See Gen 39.)

A quarter of a century later I took one of my sons to Wake Forest College, which by then had moved to Winston-Salem under the leadership of President Harold Tribble. (He had been one of my major professors at Southern Baptist Theological Seminary.) While on campus I introduced John to some of my former professors who were still teaching at Wake Forest. In the English Department we talked with Professor Aycock, a beloved and revered man. Huddled at a desk to my right I saw Professor Folk, who did not so much as look up from the material he was reading although he was in earshot of everything we were saying. I decided that we would not disturb Professor Folk and turned to leave. At that moment he exclaimed, "Give me ten reasons why Joseph did not succumb to the seductions of Mut-em-enet!"

Dr. George Paschal. My professor in classical Greek on the old campus of Wake Forest College was Dr. George Paschal. Sometimes we students came to class ill-prepared for our lessons. Perhaps we had not properly translated a portion from Homer's *Iliad*, or Xenophon's *Anabasis* or some other great work. Dr. Paschal would become angry and chastise us verbally for not doing the assignments as well as they deserved. He would declare he did not care whether we learned Greek or not, would walk to a window and stand there looking out for a while. A deathly silence in the classroom normally accompanied these moments, for we were loaded down with guilt for disappointing our teacher. Then Dr. Paschal would turn with tears in his eyes and say, "I do very much want you to learn Greek." For at least the next few days we would invariably come to class more fully prepared.

All the professors I had at Wake Forest College during my four years were men of competence in their disciplines and compassionate in their relationship with students. They took us seriously as persons, treated each student with respect. In return, our teachers earned our deep respect and high regard. It was this predominant spirit that gave Wake Forest College an atmosphere of academic excellence and made it a community of learning, faith and action.

Serving within the Churches

Corinth and New Sandy Creek Baptist Churches, small enough to be "half-time" congregations, called me as pastor while a student at Wake Forest College. At Corinth Baptist Church, the offering on the first Sunday I preached was two dollars and ninety-six cents. The deacons and I came to an agreement that each Sunday's offering was to serve as my salary. After a few Sundays, however, the deacons changed their minds. The offerings had grown to nearly fifty dollars, a lot of money for a small rural church in the midst of the Great Depression years of the 1930s.

A bit later, nearby New Sandy Creek Baptist Church—also a congregation meeting on a part-time basis—invited me to preach in view of a call. After the trial sermon, I was invited to return for the next worship service. During the second sermon, while sitting on the front pew, the chairman of the pulpit committee and some members of the board of deacons went to sleep. I just knew that I had blown it and would not be called as pastor. To my surprise the pulpit committee met and recommended me to the church. They called me to serve as their pastor. I later told the chairman of my fear that I would not be called because he had fallen asleep during that second sermon. His reply: "I heard you the first time and knew I could trust you. So I just took a nap." He turned out to be my most devoted supporter in that small congregation.

During a revival meeting at New Sandy Creek Church one summer I preached a message on "What to do when an earthquake comes." The sermon was based on Acts 16:25–26, the account in which the Apostle Paul was imprisoned for "exceedingly troubling" the city of Philippi. According to the Bible, an earthquake shook the city and threw open the doors of the prison. The Philippian jailor, seeing that Paul refused to escape and being deeply moved by his prisoner's faith, cried out "What must I do to be saved?" New Sandy Creek Church was filled to overflowing for the services. Since it rested on large stones without a foundation, it began gently to settle down. There was no panic, only a sigh of relief when the structure finally came to rest. Results of that meeting were rewarding. I soon thereafter baptized thirty new Christians in nearby Weldon's Pond.

In those days, racism was rampant in both rural and urban North Carolina. In 1936, one year before I became pastor of Corinth Baptist Church, a black man from the community around the church was charged with killing a white person. A mob tied him behind an auto and dragged him through the streets of Louisburg, the seat of Franklin County. They lynched him, cutting off his fingers and toes as gruesome souvenirs. Some time later, I was shocked to find a photo in a newspaper that captured a faithful member of my church standing near the lynched victim. The churchgoer may or may not have participated in the lynching, but he was there.

Reading the reports and talking to others about the events that led to this tragedy, I was inspired to preach on the Christian principles of love, justice, brotherhood and the value of every individual made in the image of God.

From 1936–1940, while a student at Wake Forest College, I drove to and from the two churches to fulfill my pastoral duties. I would often stop and pick up individuals "thumbing" for rides. During the Great Depression many people traveled by standing along highways, hoping to catch a free ride. Once I picked up a hitchhiker, a tough-looking customer, who soon asked, "Ain't you afraid to pick up strangers?" He leaned over toward me and asked threateningly, "Ain't you afraid somebody will stick a knife in your ribs?" I replied, "No." At the same time I pushed the accelerator to the floor board of my old purple Plymouth and the car quickly reached the speed of eighty miles an hour. I asked him, "See those telephone poles whizzing by?" He replied, "Yes." Then I declared, "When someone sticks a knife in my ribs, we take a telephone pole." My guest rider straightened up, sat back and began talking about religion.

On another occasion, I picked up two men. Both had been drinking and were headed for Raleigh, the capital of North Carolina. As we rode along I asked one of them to reach in the compartment of the car, get my Bible and read the sixth chapter of Romans, especially verse twenty-three: "For the wages of sin is death, but the gift of God is eternal life in Jesus Christ our Lord." Since I was not going to Raleigh, I let them out when our destinations caused our traveling directions to part. Even so, both men said they were turning around at that point and going back home.

My social life as a student was full of activities, including parties related to membership in a half-dozen campus organizations. Dates were frequent with Carolina's finest women from nearby college campuses, Meredith College in Raleigh and the University of North Carolina at Chapel Hill.

Other extracurricular activities included speeches made to the Masons and at school graduations, performing marriages, conducting funerals and occasionally speaking on-air at the radio station in Raleigh. Conducting revival meetings was my favorite form of ministry. At Peach Tree Baptist Church near Wake Forest, Wayne Oates—pastor, friend and fellow college student—and I joined in a revival meeting. Forty-two were baptized by Pastor Oates, a large number for a small rural church. Later I received a letter from Oates declaring that immersing forty-two people in baptism had left him exhausted. An expression of his warm sense of humor, he wrote that he planned to become a Methodist and just sprinkle new Christians.

Upon review of the schedules and date books kept from college days, I am surprised that I graduated *cum laude*!

5

The Beeches

Suppose we quietly agree that the seminary may die,
but we will die first.
—Professor John A. Broadus

Graduation day came at Wake Forest College on 27 May 1940. Graduates sat in the bleachers of the football field. As the governor of North Carolina spoke a storm displaying thunder and lightning was approaching in the distance. It reminded us of the blitzkrieg of Poland by Hitler's military forces in 1939, and the formation of the Axis Alliance of Germany, Italy and Japan in 1940. In June of that same year, France fell to the Axis powers.

With the approaching bad weather, the governor cut his speech short and we stood in the long line to receive our diplomas. Some graduates enlisted in the military. Others went on to teach, to practice law, to preach, to pursue business careers, or to study medicine. Nolan Howington, my roommate, and I remained on campus at Wake Forest until about the middle of September 1940 and then together left for the Southern Baptist Theological Seminary in Louisville, Kentucky. On the way, we stopped at his parents' home near Shelby, North Carolina. His parents were tenant farmers. Nolan had eleven brothers and one sister. When we ate dinner, it was at a banquet-sized table. Nolan had left the farm for Wake Forest College, where he had graduated *summa cum laude*. The following day we continued on to Louisville in my old purple Plymouth.

The president of Crozer Theological Seminary (Chester, PA), Dr. James H. Franklin, had offered me an assistant teaching position. But I had heard there were great teachers at Southern Seminary and was determined to continue my education there. So on 14 September 1940 we arrived at the seminary campus called "The Beeches," after the giant beech trees in front of what was its principal building, Norton Hall. Looking over the campus, we saw four buildings: Norton, Mullins, Rice and Judson Halls. There was also a small gymnasium on the campus. We were assigned to our rooms on the third floor of Mullins Hall.

Students were mostly from the Southern states, Baptist colleges and Baptist churches. A majority of them were single for we were still on the edge of an economic depression and younger people generally could not afford to marry. Too, there was a prevailing attitude that seminary ministerial students should not marry until they graduated. There was dating between seminary students and the Woman's Missionary Union Training School located at House Beautiful on Broadway Street in downtown Louisville.

Students worked in a variety of jobs to support themselves. Some were fortunate enough to serve as pastors of small churches in the city or out in the country. Others did everything from shining shoes to teaching Latin to Ph.D. students. One chap gained income through the expertise of distinguishing hens from roosters among newborn chicks.

During my first year at seminary my religious work was done at Waverly Tuberculosis Hospital, and at the Ormsby Village, a center for delinquent boys. I also served as a supply preacher for various country churches. A chapel speaker at the seminary, Dr. Clarence Jordan, challenged me to serve as pastor and superintendent of the Union Gospel Mission in the infamous Haymarket district of Louisville. I accepted. More about this later.

Faculty Members

Dr. John R. Sampey. There were a dozen faculty members in the 1940s and about five hundred students at the Southern Baptist Theological Seminary. Among the elders were Dr. John Richard Sampey, seminary president and professor of Old Testament. Isaiah was his favorite book of the Bible. Dr. Sampey was a student of the school's Founding Fathers. His theme song might well have been titled "Wine, Women and War." He was opposed to the liquor industry, an advocate for women and a proponent of a "just war" philosophy. I recall that Dr. Sampey presided in chapel and during World War II and challenged students to go into the military chaplaincy. He often corrected speakers after their chapel talks.

We dubbed Dr. Sampey "Tiglath-pileser" after the tough Assyrian king in the Old Testament. Of course, we would not dare call him that name to his face. He was a strict disciplinarian. If a student was caught cheating, Sampey would inform the student's family, his church, and announce in chapel that the student was on the way out of town.

The man was not without a keen sense of humor. In a legendary dialogue with a student named Pinnix, Dr. Sampey is reported to have asked the if God could lie, to which the student said "No."

Sampey: "Can we lie?"

Pinnix: "Yes, sir."

Sampey: "Could Robert E. Lee lie?"

Pinnix: "Yes, sir."

Sampey: "No sir, no sir! It's not on the record. I'm surprised to find a man who would say that he could lie. You must be a Yankee, Brother Pinnix."[1]

Some seminary students courted their girlfriends in Cherokee Park near the school. City law required that the dome light of a car be on when the vehicle was parked with occupants inside. One student and his girlfriend were caught parking one night without the benefit of that little light. The patrolling police officer ordered the couple to turn the dome light on. The student resisted the order. The officer arrested him but let the girl go free. When released from jail, the unwise student got the full Sampey treatment. At that time many students ate together in the Mullins dining room. When Dr. Sampey came to visit during mealtimes following the parking incident, we would often join in softly singing, "Keep the dome light burning while our hearts are yearning." We raised our voices to the tune of a popular World War I song—and almost closely following the original song's words. We substituted the original lyrics "home light" with our own more meaningful phrase: "dome light."

In the "Big Map Room" where Dr. Sampey taught his Isaiah class, a student asked if we would know each other in heaven. The professor's reply: "Do you think we will be bigger fools up there?"

Dr. Sampey was a distinguished scholar, statesman and prophet. As Hitler was coming to power, some Baptist attendants at the 1934 Baptist

---

[1] Inman Johnson, *Of Parsons and Professors* (Nashville: Broadman Press, 1959) 8–9.

World Alliance in Berlin were of the opinion that Hitler brought a "new Puritanism" to Germany because he opposed cigarette smoking and women wearing lipstick. Because of these stances, some Baptists were willing to overlook some of Hitler's unjust actions. Dr. Sampey, however, was a realist and believed that much was just not right in all the new German leader represented. He wrote, "Our Baptist brethren in Germany face a very grave crisis. They will find it difficult to be loyal both to Hitler and the Lord Jesus."[2]

Dr. Sampey was quick-witted, able to meet and best any verbal challenge. At one World Council of Churches meeting, a priest in a long robe and sporting an arrogant attitude looked at Dr. Sampey and condescendingly asked, "To what sect do you belong?" The reply, after a lingering look up and down his inquisitioner's robe: "I belong to the male sex; and what sex are you?"

As a great patriot and an advocate of a "just war" philosophy, Dr. Sampey strongly supported the United States' involvement in World War II. Fifty years after his passing in 1943, word was going around that Sampey had made a deathbed declaration that war was wrong, always wrong. Dr. Theron Price, formerly professor of church history at Southern Seminary and Sampey's close friend, asserts that he "had never heard him retract anything he had said" about war.[3]

Dr. William Owen Carver. Physically small but mentally a giant, William Owen Carver was professor of Missions from 1896 to 1943 at Southern Seminary. He laid the theological foundations for the most effective Southern Baptist Christian missions programs of the twentieth century. He attracted the best and the brightest students, who themselves would later establish colleges, seminaries and churches throughout Asia, South America, Europe and Africa. His courses were tough and called for serious study. He regularly asked questions we had not anticipated nor to which we found easy answers.

Dr. Carver shared with us a vision of world missions that was both clear and challenging. After all these years, I still remember his lectures on

---

[2] See *Western Recorder* (13 September 1934): 3.

[3] Barnette letter to T. D. Price, 7 January 1943. Dr. Price's response was penned on this letter and returned (not dated); letter in author's file.

missions in the "plan of the ages" to which he provided biblical and philosophical foundations.

Once when I was a graduate fellow (a professor's assistant: grading papers and teaching in the professor's absence) in Christian ethics, another graduate fellow in New Testament and a new student were in my office. The fellow was reading from the Greek New Testament for the benefit of the new student. I could hear the footsteps of Dr. Carver falling in the hallway. He passed by my office and suddenly stopped, turned and stood in the doorway.

Dr. Carver: "Did I hear someone reading from the Greek New Testament?"

Fellow: "Yes, Dr. Carver. I was reading for a new student from the book of Acts."

Dr. Carver: "In the last sentence you read, you missed a *de*."

He then turned, walked away and left all three of us astounded. This man *knew* his Greek New Testament. His teaching and writing certainly demonstrated the richest of biblical foundations.

Dr. William Hersey Davis. Known by his students as "the Big Doc," Dr. William Hersey Davis was my teacher in English New Testament and Senior Greek (1942–43). We belonged to Deer Park Baptist Church on Bardstown Road in Louisville. He was called the Big Doc because he was about six feet, four inches tall. He also supervised the library at Southern Seminary and directed the school's graduate program. He gave all the language exams for graduate students. In those days, three years of Koine Greek (New Testament) were required at the undergraduate level. Students had to be able to read the entire New Testament in Greek. At the graduate level (Ph.D. and Th.D.), a reading knowledge of Greek, Hebrew, German and another language other than English—usually Latin or French—was required. We had to read passages from Tischendorf's Latin commentary on the Greek New Testament along with twenty-three papyri letters (edited by Dr. Davis) that were written about AD 1 by farmers, soldiers and merchants. The spelling in these letters was bad. A large number of students routinely failed the tests.

Dr. Davis was very popular with the students. When he walked in the halls of the school, students would join him to hear what he thought about certain New Testament passages or issues of the day. He downplayed Christmas and Easter as pagan holidays.

I planned to do my graduate work with him as my supervisor until I discovered that he was already serving as supervisor for dozens of students. I switched to "Christian Sociology" under Dr. J. B. Weatherspoon and Dr. O. T. Binkley, who took over that discipline at the request of Weatherspoon. Dr. Davis never let me forget that I deserted him for "that little sociology stuff."

Davis and O. G. Poarch, who years later became my father-in-law, were roommates at Richmond University in Virginia. Here Davis played football and graduated with one of the highest grade-point averages ever attained at that institution. Since Poarch was a freshman, he had to serve the upper classman Davis. This included shining Davis's shoes, running errands, *et cetera*. They were contemporaries at Southern Seminary. Poarch participated in Davis's ordination at the Walnut Street Baptist Church and made better grades in Greek than Davis.

Admiring students imitated Dr. Davis by growing a small mustache and unconsciously imitating his mannerisms, one of which was to drop the voice into a sort of mumble. Once a student told Dr. Davis that he could not understand what the professor was saying in his classroom prayers. Big Doc's reply: "I was not talking to you."

Once at Deer Park Baptist Church, Dr. Davis and I were both participants in a deacon's ordination service. Mrs. Davis had cautioned her husband to "leave some time for Henlee to speak." Davis chose to address the word deacon and must have dealt with every instance in which it appears in the New Testament. It was an accomplished but long presentation. When it was finally my turn to speak, I exhorted the deacons to pray for, praise and pay the pastor. That took all of three minutes.

Dr. Jesse Burton Weatherspoon. Before assuming his teaching post at Southern Seminary, Dr. Jesse Burton Weatherspoon was the pastor of Highland Baptist Church in Louisville. My first encounter with him was in Mullins Hall after he had delivered a speech to a gathered group. I was impressed with what I heard and told him so. His response shocked me: "What are you going to do about it?"

Weatherspoon was professor of homiletics as well as Christian sociology. In his preaching class we had to perform. We sat two by two on wooden benches. I wrote my sermon topic on the board before my seatmate arrived. When he saw the topic, "The Pastor and Home Visitation," he exclaimed: "What a boring topic!" After a couple of others had preached it was my turn. My main point was that a home-going pastor results in a church-going people. Professor Weatherspoon remarked, "We have, heretofore, heard the general, but now we have heard the kernel." After class, Dr. Weatherspoon invited me to be his undergraduate teaching fellow.

I recall an instance when a student preached a sermon in class whose subject, content and conclusion bore absolutely no relationship to one another. He rambled and became bombastic. Dr. Weatherspoon was sharply critical of the sermon. The student exploded with anger at the criticism, declaring that God had given him the sermon and he had preached it at a recent Baptist associational meeting to great praise. Dr. Weatherspoon responded: "Young man, there are two ways to go through a door. You may turn the knob or knock it down. You knocked the door down."

Professor Weatherspoon was revising Dr. John A. Broadus's famous book on preaching titled *On the Preparation and Delivery of Sermons*. He also managed the Social Service Commission (forerunner to the Christian Life Commission of the Southern Baptist Convention), keeping the data for that organization in his office desk drawer. He widened the scope of the commission to include race relations, war and peace, marriage and the family. He helped secure the first full-time director, Dr. Hugh Brimm.

Weatherspoon had great influence within the Southern Baptist Convention. In his report to the Convention at St. Louis in 1954, he commended the Supreme Court of the United States for desegregating the public schools. Only Dr. Weatherspoon could have persuaded the Convention to pass such a progressive resolution on race relations during the socially turbulent 1950s.

When his wife, "Lady" as she was affectionately called, died, I went to his home on Pleasantview Avenue to offer a word of comfort. The first thing he said to me was, "Henlee, Lady is gone." After Dr. Weatherspoon's death, I gave his eulogy at a faculty retreat.

Dr. Olin T. Binkley. This Baptist saint and scholar joined the faculty at Southern Baptist Theological Seminary in 1944. He had previously taught at Wake Forest College 1938–1944), where I had taken his courses in Christian ethics. He was educated at Wake Forest College, Southern Baptist

Theological Seminary and Yale Divinity School, receiving a Ph.D. from Yale University. "Equipped with the finest of training, he made Christian ethics alive and relevant to the total scheme of Christian concerns."[4]

I became Professor Binkley's first teaching fellow in 1944 when he assumed responsibility for the ethics courses within the seminary's department of homiletics. I switched from being a fellow in homiletics to ethics with Weatherspoon's blessing. Dr. Binkley later persuaded President Ellis Fuller, Sr., to approve the establishment of a department of Christian ethics, of which Dr. Binkley became chairman.

In 1951, I joined Dr. Binkley as an associate professor. In 1952 Dr. Sydnor Stealey, president of Southeastern Baptist Theological Seminary, persuaded Professor Binkley to join that faculty. Hence, I assumed the chairmanship of the Christian ethics department at Southern in Louisville.

Our brief relationship as colleagues at Southern was a fruitful and enriching one. Dr. Binkley succeeded Dr. Stealey as president of the seminary at Wake Forest and served in that post from 1963–1974. He died 27 August 1999 of heart failure, at age ninety-one.

Dr. Binkley supervised my graduate work and dissertation titled "The Ethical Thought of Walter Rauschenbusch: A Critical Interpretation." In the late 1930s at Wake Forest College, Dr. Binkley introduced me to the writings of Rauschenbusch and I have maintained an interest in his thought ever since. I did not attempt to publish my dissertation because I wanted to continue to work with Southern Baptists. Rauschenbusch is widely recognized as the father of "the social gospel." Southern Baptists had a phobia about the term and the religious movement associated with it. With the full support of the seminary administration and the theological faculty, however, I did offer a seminar in Social Christianity that focused on a comparison of the themes of the Kingdom of God in Rauschenbusch's and Reinhold Niebuhr's works.

Dr. Binkley was a person with a Christ-like demeanor. Some referred to him as "the Walking Jesus." A man of integrity, he displayed the rare virtue of humility. As a scholar he was a man of intellectual honesty and possessed

---

[4] William Mueller, *A History of Southern Baptist Theological Seminary* (Nashville, TN, Broadman Press, 1959) 222.

a rare sensitivity towards others, especially the poor, the sick and the grieving.

Dr. Binkley's father, Joseph M. Binkley, was a farmer and pastor of one church for fifty-one years. When Olin was a student at Wake Forest College, he lived in prudent poverty. Money was scarce for his parents. In those days, they would send him five dollars whenever they could. During his sophomore year, he decided to stay home, work and earn money for school the next two years. When school let out for the Christmas break, he caught a ride to Harmony, North Carolina. He noticed his mother's hands were yellowed and blistered. He asked why, but she would not tell him. On Christmas morning at the breakfast table, he learned the truth when he turned his plate over. There he found seventy-five dollars, which his mother had made cracking black walnuts to sell. Tears came to his eyes and, in response to her selfless love, he completely surrendered his life to the Kingdom of God.

Dr. Binkley and I corresponded across half a century. When he could no longer write, his beloved wife Pauline wrote to me for him. In a letter to him in 1993, I acknowledged that he provided for me a model of Christian ministry, a passion for justice, an exemplar of intellectual honesty, a paragon as a teacher and a prophet who proclaimed "the whole counsel of God."

After Dr. Binkley's death in 1999, I wrote the following to his beloved wife and the inspiration of his life, Pauline:

> Know that I share with you the celebration of his life. I shall always remember him as a saint and a scholar. He possessed that happy combination of religious devotion and critical intelligence. He had a tender heart and a tough mind. How fortunate I was to have him as a teacher who saw things from the perspective of eternity.

All of my professors at Southern Baptist Seminary were men of God, men of integrity and caring followers of Jesus the Christ. I have described some of my professors in more detail. Others were Dr. Edward McDowell (Greek and New Testament), Henry C. Goerner (Church Missions), Inman Johnson (Speech and Music), J. M. Adams (Archaeology), Harold Tribble

(Theology), Gaines Dobbins (Religious Education), Sydnor Stealey (Church History). By 2001 they had all made the great transition to "the land from whence no traveler returns."

6

The Haymarket

I said, "Let me walk in the fields."
He said, "No, walk in town."
I said, "There are no flowers there."
He said, "No flowers but a crown."
—Anonymous

I first heard about the Haymarket in downtown Louisville when Clarence Jordan was the chapel speaker in Norton Hall at Southern Baptist Seminary in 1940 during my first year as a student. Clarence was the Long Run Baptist Association's newly appointed Director of City Missions. He declared that if there was a young preacher in the audience not looking for the safe harbor of a First Baptist Church of Podunk Hollow, there were 10,000 unchurched people in the Haymarket area. He challenged us to see for ourselves.

I accepted that challenge and began visiting one block in the community, hoping to persuade people to attend the Union Gospel Mission at First and Jefferson Streets with its neon sign that proclaimed "God is Love." Built as a residence in 1836, in 1881 the building was turned into a mission house by a reformed gambler named Steve Holcombe.

The Haymarket area is one of the oldest sections of Louisville. Before the turn of the twentieth century it was the marketplace to which farmers brought hay, fruit, vegetables and other goods to sell. When I arrived on the scene in 1941, the Haymarket was a slum. In the radius of three blocks from the mission at First and Jefferson Streets there were whiskey stores, honky-tonks, gambling dens, flop houses and places of prostitution. My ministry responsibilities covered the area from Jackson Street on the east to Third

Street on the west, Market Street on the north and Walnut Street (now Muhammad Ali Avenue) on the south.

A fellow student accompanied me on my first home visit to the Adams family, who lived on the top floor of an old tenement house. Mr. Adams informed me that the family had lived there for twenty years, and we were the first ministers to visit them. Across the next four years I discovered hundreds of unchurched people living throughout the area.

On Saturday, 6 September 1941, I had a conference with Dr. Clarence Jordan, Superintendent of City Missions for the Long Run Baptist Association, about becoming pastor of the Union Gospel Mission. With the permission of the Protestant Board, who controlled the mission property, Jordan and the Baptist mission board of trustees had begun to develop a ministry in the old building. Prior to the conference with Jordan, I had been conducting prayer meetings in the mission chapel on Wednesday nights.

On Monday, 17 September 1941, I was called by the Baptist mission board to be the pastor of the Union Gospel Mission. We worked out an agreement with Broadway Baptist Church whereby those who made commitments to Christ could become members of the church on Broadway and worship at the mission facility. Broadway Baptist Church had prominent citizens in Southern Baptist life among its members in those days. In the congregation were Mrs. George Washington Norton, Miss Mattie Norton, Mr. and Mrs. Charles Gheens, Dr. and Mrs. John R. Sampey and others.

On 13 September 1943 I was elected Superintendent of the Mission. This administrative work was in addition to my tasks as pastor, teaching fellow and graduate studies at the seminary.

Miss Asenath Brewster—a direct descendant of William Brewster, who made the passage from England to the New World on the Mayflower— served as the mission's director of religious education. Together we recruited as voluntary workers eleven men: ten students from the seminary and one from the University of Louisville School of Medicine, all of whom later became well-known in their own ministries. Among these were Kermit Schmidt, who became a missionary to Brazil; Merle Pedigo, who became a US Army chaplain and rose to the rank of colonel; Warner Fussell, who became president of Truett-McConnell College; Jack Kilgore who became chairman of the Department of Philosophy at Baylor University; Henry Turlington who became a missionary to China and Professor of New

Testament at Southern Seminary; T. C. Smith, who became Professor of New Testament at Southern Seminary and Furman University; John Walker, who became a medical missionary to the Congo; Winston Crawley and wife, who taught the Chinese class at the mission and later relocated to China as missionaries; Wayne Oates, who became Professor of Pastoral Care and Psychology at Southern Seminary and Professor of Psychiatry at the University of Louisville School of Medicine; and Carlyle Marney, who became a distinguished preacher and pastor. Marney was one of only three Southern Baptists (the other two being John A. Broadus and John R. Claypool) invited to give the Yale Lectures on preaching.

Meeting Charlotte

Charlotte Ford and Edith Stokely, both students at the Woman's Missionary Training School in Louisville, Kentucky, attended the Union Gospel Mission. As pastor of the Mission I observed that they would leave at invitation time when people would come forward and make their profession of faith in Christ and commitment to the church. When confronting Charlotte and Edith about leaving during the invitation, they informed me that they had to get back to the school and set the tables and help with serving lunch. Then I apologized for reprimanding them. Both were from prominent families in Tennessee. Edith was an heir to The Stokely Van Camp Company. Charlotte's father was production manager for The Reynolds Metal Company in Knoxville, Tennessee.

When our pianist at the Mission left for other service, Charlotte assumed that role. She had a college degree in music and often served as the organist at the Broadway Baptist Church. It was my responsibility to bring Charlotte to the Mission since I lived nearby at The Southern Baptist Theological Seminary. We fell in love and I proposed to her one day as we drove through Cherokee Park on the way home. We were happily married July 15, 1943. We had two stalwart sons (See Chapter Twenty-One on Vietnam).

Charlotte was a noble and courageous woman, an authentic Christian who gave birth to our first son in the old Haymarket Mission in a slum community. She ministered to the poor, the sick, and the suffering in that seedy section of Louisville.

An important outreach program of the mission was the "cottage prayer meetings" held in the homes of the poor, few of whom would attend a church. My wife, Charlotte Ford Barnette, who had a college degree in music and was assistant organist at Broadway Baptist, played hymns during these meetings on a battered old portable organ. People in nearby quarters would hear the music and singing, sometimes joining in with us and even finding their way to the mission.

Students from the Woman's Missionary Union Training School were active at the mission, either as volunteers or doing class-assigned field work. In addition to these, the mission enjoyed the services of a dozen or more volunteers from throughout the city.

The range of ministries, activities and other services provided by the Union Gospel Mission included: Sunday school and worship services; Wednesday night prayer meetings; choir practice; "cottage prayer" meetings; the Women's Club; weekday church school; daily vacation Bible school; "Sunbeams," a children's missions education program; work among the Chinese population; benevolence; counseling; cooperation with the courts and institutions dealing with juvenile delinquents; summer camps; softball; swimming; Boy Scouts, Girl Scouts and Cub Scouts; day nursery and playground activities; a library, game room and woodwork shop; employment through a lawn care business.

"Revival" meetings also were an annual event at the Union Gospel Mission. Two preachers who always won the people's hearts were Clarence Jordan and Carlyle Marney. Jordan preached 31 May–10 June 1942. He played the song "The Holy City" on his trumpet and the folks loved it. Fifteen united with Broadway Baptist Church. These made up the first core of solid Christians who developed into pillars of the mission fellowship. On 6–16 September 1942 Marney attracted large crowds out of which several were converted and others joined Broadway Baptist Church by transferring their membership from other congregations. Both played the same song, Marney on the trombone, and Jordan on the trumpet. As the revivals drew to a conclusion, our mission congregation would gather at Broadway Baptist for worship and baptisms. Our choir sang; I preached and baptized the new believers.

I was referred to by some as the "Bishop of the Haymarket."[1] But I was popularly known as "Brother Barnette." My ministry involved going down dark alleys, climbing stairways, dodging huge rats and sitting in smelly vermin-infested rooms while attempting to minister to people. One of the saddest things to see was the babies at whose flesh rats had been eating.[2]

Winos, drifters, drunks, bums, moochers, addicts and some of the best people in the world came to the mission for help. They all had tales of woe. I recall one child who came to the mission and begged me to go to his home because his family was being held hostage by the tenement owner. According to the boy, the man refused to let the family leave because rent had not been paid. The owner did, in fact, leave before I arrived to check out the situation; and shortly following, the family did the same.

One man came into the mission wanting a bed to sleep in for the night. I asked him what he had in his hip pocket. It was a pint of gin. I took it and placed it on the piano and told him to look at it. I asked: "Which do you want, God or gin?" Slowly he reached for the gin and staggered out of the mission.

In one tenement flophouse I discovered the former Commissioner of Alberta, Canada, persuaded him to attend the Mission and eventually baptized him. He told me that he made three mistakes and lost a fortune: he switched from raising cattle to sheep, bucked the labor unions and married a French woman. His brother lived in Louisville and was a multi-millionaire. They stopped speaking to each other after a falling out involving a challenge to a family will.

Around the corner from the Mission lived "Prof Hamilton," the tattoo man. He came from a prominent family in Bardstown, Kentucky. His clients were largely military people from Fort Knox who came in on weekends for "recreation" in the community. Prof showed me a large drawing of Christ's head with thorns and blood he had put on a Pentecostal Holiness preacher's body. He also showed me a picture of Leonardo da Vinci's painting of the Last Supper that he had tattooed on a woman's back. After traveling for years with the Barnum and Bailey circus, Hamilton had settled in Louisville to continue his trade or profession as a tattoo artist. I finally persuaded him

---

[1] See *Courier-Journal Magazine* (23 March 1952): 6–7.

[2] A photo of an eighteen-day-old baby's cheek, gnawed by a rat, appears in Louisville's *Courier-Journal*, Saturday, 15 April 1944, Section 2, p.1.

       A Pilgrimage of Faith

to attend the Mission worship services. He always carried a large roll of money and a pistol—even during worship. We took the offering in tin plates and he always dropped in a few coins. Folk began to listen for the sound of the coins in the plate when it passed by Prof. I urged him to put his money in a bank and warned that he would be robbed some day. He refused and would pat his pistol. He called me "Pal." One day he was found dead in his cubbyhole place.

One of the largest day nurseries in Louisville during World War II was in the mission house at 114 East Jefferson. The house needed repairs, especially in the nursery. Appeals to both the Protestant Board and Baptist Board for repairs went unanswered. Each declared the other body responsible for the matter. Frustrated, I went to see the chairman of the Protestant Board, Mr. W. E. Pilcher, who manufactured the famous Pilcher pipe organs. He saw that I was upset. His calm voice restored my hope that something would be done. He assured me that he would look into the matter. Sometime later, Mr. Pilcher appeared at a prayer meeting in the mission chapel. After I closed the meeting, he came to the pulpit and handed me a deed to the mission property—about half a block of real estate. On 23 September 1943 an official service was held to commemorate the transaction. The ball now was in the Baptists' court, and repairs were finally made.[3] Soon after, the name of the ministry became Central Baptist Mission.

The Randles Family

While the pastor of the old Haymarket mission in Louisville, I visited the Samuel & Mary Randles family and their three children. The parents and children were all blind or partially blind except the twelve year-old lad Elwood Eton. They lived on the second floor of an old tenement house behind a brewery. I secured Braille copies of Genesis and the Gospel of John for this family. On the fly-leafs of each copy I wrote: "Open thou mine eyes, that I may behold wondrous things out of thy law" (Ps 119:18). The next Sunday morning the twelve-year-old boy professed faith in Christ in the Union Gospel Mission chapel service. On the next Sunday, he led his blind mother to the altar. Then came the sister, brother, the father—all

---

[3] See Maude Abner, *The Story of the Union Gospel Mission* (Louisville: Mays Printing Co., 1944) 140.

joined the Broadway Baptist Church; but their worship and service to the Lord remained at the mission.

With the nurture, guidance and support of devoted Sunday School teachers, this family grew toward maturity in Christ. The lad who acted as eyes for the family became a lawyer and served for many years as counsel of a large business firm. The sister, Helen Rufena, graduated from Georgetown College with a major in music. I was there for her recital in German and Italian. Because of her inability to see, she could not get a teaching position. Friends made it possible for her to have an operation on her eyes at a hospital in Louisville. When the bandage was removed, she exclaimed: "I see faces forming!" She taught music in the Kentucky School for the Blind for many years. The younger brother, Raymond, after eye surgery, became professor of history for seven years at William Penn University. Later he entered a seminary to prepare himself to teach religion. He eventually earned a Ph.D. It was my joy to give the installation sermon when Dr. Randles became associate pastor at Fourth Avenue Baptist Church in Louisville. He also worked as an editor in the Kentucky School for the Blind.

"Wondrous things" out of the Word of God were revealed to this Haymarket family. Their eyes were opened to the things of God in Christ. Commitment to the light of the glory of God in the face of Jesus Christ transformed each one more and more into the image of our Lord.

A Ministry Concluded

On 15 September 1945 I submitted my resignation as pastor and superintendent of the Central Baptist Mission. Several reasons for that decision return to mind. Bureaucracy began to demand administrative details of everything—each visit, service, witness, conversion, etc. Neither Clarence Jordan, the founding spirit behind the enterprise, nor I were hung up on micro-management. Jordan left Louisville in 1942 to pursue the dream of a Christian Community that was inclusive of all races. He established Koinonia Farms in South Georgia near Americus, the same town in which Habitat for Humanity International would make its headquarters years later. My own growing vision for the Central Baptist Mission included a larger program, including a family center and gymnasium, a place in the country for retreats and camping, and perhaps even a houseboat for ministry on the Ohio River. I saw no hope for this sort of far-reaching program to develop. In addition, I needed to complete my doctoral dissertation and spend more time with my family.

My last sermon, given 15 September 1945 in the mission chapel, appears below:

Giving God the Glory

"I have planted, Apollos watered; but God gave the increase" (1 Cor 3:5–6).

Paul points out the fact that God blesses the growth of his work.

The real source is not human effort but a spiritual result. Reports often give the pastor or evangelist the glory for the growth of the church instead of God.

Many volunteer workers have served here at Central Baptist Mission. They have given sacrificially of their time and service. But, God gave the growth.

1. First year: 1941–1942.

On my first visit to the Haymarket I climbed a long flight of rickety stairways in an old tenement house and discovered a family named Adams. One family member was a young lady with a broken back who was lying in an improvised bunk. They lived in two small rooms and informed me that I was the first minister in twenty years that had been in their home. I went away with the conviction that there were hundreds of other people in that area who were without pastoral ministry. Some time later Miss Asenath Brewster, then in charge of the Union Gospel Mission, requested that I conduct prayer meetings in the mission's little chapel. I spoke at two prayer meetings and then on 17 September 1941 I was called to be the mission's pastor.

2. Second year: 1942–1943.

During this year we were able to develop a working relationship with Broadway Baptist Church, where Dr. Duke K. McCall served as pastor. Under this relationship, people could join the mission through baptism, by letter of transfer from another church, or by statement. Those who joined the mission would also be received as *bona fide* members of Broadway Baptist Church. Their commitment as to church attendance and service, however, was to remain at the mission.

During this year it was my happy privilege to baptize forty persons and to receive thirty-two by letter of transfer from other congregations. Also during this period we noted a steady growth in Sunday School and other activities of the mission.

3. Third year, 1943–1944.

During this period there was a program of intensive training and teaching. The buildings and grounds, formerly owned and operated by the Protestant churches of Louisville, were deeded to the Long Run Baptist Association. I had visited Mr. W. E. Pilcher, famous manufacturer of Pilcher pipe organs, and told him of my dilemma in getting repairs for the building. At that time he said that he would personally work toward the goal of getting the property deeded to Long Run Baptist Association. During a prayer meeting service a few weeks later, he presented the deed to the Union Gospel Mission to me. I, in turn, presented it to the association's Superintendent of City Missions.

4. Fourth year: 1944–1945.

During this past year there were again notable increases in Sunday School and church attendance. The mission has gained the respect of churches and educational institutions and social institutions in the city. We have been helped by many volunteer workers from the churches, from the WMU Training School and from the Seminary.

God has been giving the increase all along. Now the work is built upon a firm foundation and it will go on as long as we are workers together with Christ. This work is not built primarily around any personality, except the personality of Christ!

You people and this work will always be close to my heart.

Postscript: The Mission Fellowship

A group called the Mission Fellowship was later formed and is led by Myrtle Rosenbaum Cunningham of LaGrange, Kentucky. It meets annually and is composed of former mission volunteers and persons who made commitments to Christ in the early 1940s through that ministry. In all, about thirty-five folks who have had some significant relation to the mission across sixty years are on the roll. The meetings each year are a joy and an inspiration. Fellowship, food, testimonies and wonderful memories edify us all.

7

Alabama Bound

"I wish I were in Dixie…"
Daniel Decatur Emmett

After I had resigned as pastor of the Central Baptist Mission my family moved to a house on Duker Avenue, located just off Bardstown Road in Louisville. It was close to Deer Park Baptist Church and some larger stores. I began working on my dissertation in earnest and for financial support did supply preaching, as well as speaking at clubs and church organizations.

On 18 July 1946 I caught a train for Birmingham, Alabama. An offer had come to me about a teaching position in sociology at Howard College (now Samford University). I had a conference with the college president, Major Harwell G. Davis and James Chapman Burns, the Dean, relative to my teaching sociology at Howard. The offer was that of an assistant professorship in the Department of Sociology, paying $3,000 a year. After my first year, I was to be made full professor and head of the department. I was also promised time off with half-pay to pursue further studies at the University of North Carolina. As I understood it, my focus was to be on applied or clinical sociology, rather than provide merely a theoretical course in the field.

After talking the matter over with my wife, Charlotte, I decided to accept the position at Howard College. Harold Johnson was leaving Howard for Southern Seminary, so we exchanged houses. My family moved out of the Duker Avenue house and the Johnsons moved in. We spent our last night in Louisville with Wayne and Pauline Oates, seminary students, who lived in an apartment complex called the Greentree Manor. Across the years Wayne and Pauline have helped many persons in the midst of relocation by inviting them to spend the night in their home.

Tuesday, 10 September 1946 Charlotte, Johnny and I began our long drive to Birmingham in my old 1935 Chevrolet. We arrived in Nashville and spent the night with Victor and Edith Glass; both had worked as staff members at Union Gospel Mission. Victor later had become a teacher at the American Baptist Theological Seminary in Nashville.

We finally arrived in Birmingham on 11 September and settled into a tiny house consisting of just two rooms, a bedroom and a kitchen. Johnny slept in the kitchen in this house at 7529 Fifth Avenue, South. Written in my date book just after we arrived were these words:

> My heart is heavy. I don't know just why I am coming to Howard College to teach. My heart and head say "No! Don't do it." Circumstances say "Yes." Perhaps I have not followed the leadership of the Holy Spirit. Time will tell.

Charlotte informed me that another child was on the way. I was grateful, but our housing was so inadequate and we could not afford to pay for a larger place. Wayne was born in 18 May 1947. We brought him home from the hospital and he cried for one week straight because the doctor had given him the wrong formula.

Once in Birmingham, I immediately plunged into teaching and preaching in churches. The first church I visited as a supply preacher was at Uniontown, Alabama, 125 miles south of the college. Getting there was a long and dreary drive, but the honorarium helped pay for food for the family. My date book for Tuesday, 10 October 1946, records a typical day: I took my Criminology Class to the courthouse in Birmingham to hear some trials and to tour the courthouse. Later that evening I spoke to a group of young people at Moulton Hotel. So it went for the two semesters I taught at Howard.

At one point, I was charged with heresy by a student who was the secretary of an evangelist in Birmingham. She claimed I stated in a lecture that I did not believe in the virgin birth. She brought the issue before the Baptist Ministerial Association of Birmingham. I took a survey of the class with the student present, asking how many heard me say that I did not believe in the virgin birth. She was the only one in the class who seemed to have arrived at such a conclusion. She had to report to the ministers that she was the only one in a classroom filled with students who had heard me make that sort of remark. The matter was dropped. What I had said was that the famous preacher, Harry M. Fosdick of Riverside Church in New York City, declared that he did not believe the virgin birth.

Hokes Bluff Baptist Church, near Gadsden, Alabama, called me as interim pastor. They had built a new parsonage and owed several thousand dollars on it. I announced from the pulpit in March 1947 that we were going to "March in March" and pay off the mortgage. I proposed that on every coming Sunday worshippers march to the front of the church and place our money in the offering plates until enough was raised to pay off the debt. A deacon, smiling faintly, told me the idea would not work because that was "the way the Negroes do it in their churches." But we did it and celebrated with a "mortgage burning."

Almost half-a-century later, Hokes Bluff Baptist Church invited me to participate in the celebration of their sesquicentennial, one-hundred and fifty years of existence. Unable to attend, I wrote to them using 2 Peter 3:18 as my theme text: "go on growing in grace and in the knowledge of Jesus Christ."

Interracial Baptist Pastors' Conference

In early 1947 the Rev. J. E. Rouse, pastor of Avondale Baptist Church in Birmingham, and I were appointed by the Birmingham Baptist Association to the Committee on Social Concerns. Rouse called shortly before the association met and informed me that we were to make a report. I suggested that we attend the Black Pastors' Conference at the Sixteenth Street Baptist Church with the purpose of organizing an interracial Baptist pastors' conference. Rouse was a brave man. He took me up on what truly was a challenge to the *status quo* in those years. At first the pastors would not recognize us, though the chairman tried to introduce us. They would moan and stomp the floor when he tried to do so. Finally, a pastor jumped to his feet and almost screamed: "Brethren, this is the first time in the history of this organization that a white man has ever visited us. I think we ought to hear from them." You could hear a pin drop. Rouse spoke first on loving God and neighbor. He was a bit startled when a black man stood, expressed appreciation for what had just been spoken and requested to be allowed to come to Avondale Baptist Church and tell the people of that white congregation just what Rouse had told the black pastors.

When I spoke, I told them that we had not come to tell them anything or to do anything for them. "We have come," I said, "to see if we can better understand one another. I propose that we organize an interracial Baptist pastors' conference." The proposal was accepted and a framework for the new organization was in place by the end of the pastors' meeting. I was the new conference's first secretary. Rev. Luke Beard, pastor of the Sixteenth Street Baptist Church, was elected the first chairman or president. That church was bombed during the civil rights struggle of the 1960s, causing the death of four children.

As secretary of the group I invited Dr. Benjamin Mays, president of Morehouse College, to give the first message to the conference. He was a black man, had earned a Ph.D. from the University of Chicago, was recognized as an outstanding scholar by the Phi Beta Kappa society and was the author of numerous books. He was one of Martin Luther King, Jr.'s teachers and gave the eulogy at the civil rights leader's funeral. I was surprised at the large crowd that came to the Sixteenth Street Church to hear Mays, including Dr. Bowman, the white pastor of the First Baptist Church in Birmingham.

As reported in February 1948 (one year later) by the *Witness* of the Birmingham Baptist Association, "...through the organization of an interracial committee and the building of a fine fellowship [there was] laid a solid foundation upon which the committee this year has been able to build so well. Even sooner than was anticipated the Negro Baptist Center is now a reality."[1] The purposeful establishment of an organization to promote positive interracial relationships in the city's churches began to have positive effects in other institutions as well. For example, an extension agreement was later arrived at between Selma College—a black school—and the all-white Howard College. It was also arranged that a professor from Howard would teach classes at Selma.

While progress would be made later, I was in the meantime called in for a special conference with the president and dean of Howard College. They informed me that I was "teaching a dangerous subject." The

---

[1] See *Birmingham Baptist Association Witness* (February 1948): 2

A Pilgrimage of Faith

implication was that there was too much activism going on, too much of relating sociology to actual situations in the community.

The Jefferson County Negro Teachers Association

Members of Alabama's Jefferson County Negro Teachers' Association began to seek equal pay for black teachers who had the same academic preparation as white teachers. It became a hot issue in early 1947. I was invited to speak at the association's annual meeting held on 11 February of that year. My assigned topic to discuss from a sociological point of view: "Does the Negro Suffer from an Inferiority Complex?"

Only one other white person besides myself was present at that meeting. Several speakers addressed the audience. One young teacher told us that in his spare time he operated an elevator in the building in which we were meeting. He recounted an incident in which a white man got on the elevator and challenged, "What is on your mind, Sambo?" The young man had replied, "Nothing, Boss." He told his audience, "I wouldn't dare tell that white man what was on my mind. He would have killed me." We all knew this was no joke. It easily could have happened in those days.

I was the last person scheduled to address the meeting. When it was my turn to speak, I put aside my prepared remarks and delivered a spontaneous message. I declared that both black and white people experience a sense of inferiority to at least some degree. To illustrate the point, I reported that I had recently talked with Dr. Benjamin Mays, the president of Morehouse College, about speaking to the recently organized Interracial Baptist Pastors' Conference. Dr. Mays's superior command of the English language, I told my listeners, was so noticeable that I felt inferior in his presence.

I concluded by saying we are all people of dignity, made in the image of God. Further, I said, there is no place in a democratic society for discrimination on the basis of race. I declared we must all work together for justice and equality. With my parting words I reminded the meeting that it takes both the black and the white keys on a piano to bring out the full beauty of our national anthem. In the same way, it takes black and white people working together to win the battle for equality and justice. I received a standing ovation from the meeting participants.

More invitations to speak to black and white groups began to come, not all related to race relations. The Birmingham Discussion Group Council requested I speak on "Is there a Crisis in American Family Life?" I presented the statistical data on family trends from a sociological perspective. The program was broadcast on Birmingham's radio station WBRC. Other participants in the broadcast were Judge Emmett Perry, Rev. W. H. Mariman and Dr. Louise Branscomb.

By the end of my second semester at Howard College, President Davis would no longer speak to me. I had not heeded his warning to lessen my sociological activism in the community. Just a few years later in 1951, he telephoned and told me, "We made a mistake when we let you go." Dr. Davis led in developing a new campus for the school. Howard College became Samford University and is now one of the finest private schools in America. Deeply gratifying to me at the time of this writing (2004) is that my son, Dr. James R. Barnette, is Minister to the University and a teacher in the Department of Religion.

An Enduring Easter Sunday Lesson

On Easter Sunday 1947 I was scheduled to preach at Hokes Bluff Baptist Church near Gadsden. I thumbed a ride early that morning from Howard College in Birmingham. When I reached Attalla, I had to board a bus for Gadsden where a deacon was to pick me up and take me to the church. The bus was filled except for the rear seats, two of which were occupied by a couple of black persons. Passengers were dressed in their Easter Sunday best, many of them carrying Bibles.

I sat in the back with the African-Americans for the trip to Gadsden. I noted they moved as far away from me as possible. Shortly, the bus driver observed where I was sitting and announced that I would have to move. I ignored him. Again he barked at me, "You will have to move. It is against the law for you to sit there." I felt the hostile glare of the other white passengers, but still I did not move for there was not another vacant seat on the bus. The driver slowed the bus down and threatened to evict me if I did not move. Finally, I decided to stand and did so all the way to Gadsden.

To this day I regret getting up from my seat on the bus that morning. I think at that moment I became like the priest in the story of the Good

Samaritan. He passed by on the other side of the robbed and wounded man on the road to Jericho (Luke 10:30 ff.). Here were two persons robbed of their rights as human beings and a busload of priests, Levites and laypersons who passed them by because of prejudice and unjust law. We were all headed for Jericho, some to lead worship, some to preach and pray, some perhaps only to be seen on Easter Sunday in their new clothing and hats. Most saw no relationship between worship, ethical responsibility and action.

8

The Sunshine State

When ills betide and woes o'ertake, Florida, my Florida…
—Florida's first state song

Fortunately, before the fall semester of 1947 got underway at Howard College, I received a call from Stetson University in DeLand, Florida, inquiring if I would be interested in a teaching post in sociology. It turned out to be a Godsend. I went by train to DeLand and met with Stetson's president, Dr. W. S. Allen. He had anticipated all that I would ask. He added, "I would not offer you anything less than a full professorship in sociology." I was completely surprised. He pushed a contract toward me on the table. I told him that before signing I would like to talk with my wife and the chairman of the sociology department. He called for the chairman, who came immediately, seeming angry and frustrated. Perhaps he had his own candidate in mind for the position. I asked if he thought we could work together, adding that I would not take the position if he did not want me. Surprise flashed across his face and he smiled as he said, "Yes, I think we can work together."

So I joined two dear friends who were graduates of Southern Baptist Seminary as a colleague on the faculty of Stetson University; professors Pope Duncan and O. L. Walker, who had first called me about the position. I served there from 1947 to 1951. I began preaching in churches, speaking to clubs, schools, and political groups almost immediately upon my arrival in Florida. My family and I joined DeLand's First Baptist Church, where the Rev. Grady Snowden was pastor. These were happy years for my family and me.

Sociology at Stetson was largely considered a "crip" course. Many students took courses in the discipline thinking they would avoid demands for serious study as well as enjoy the assurance of a passing grade. In my first class, some of these students sat in a single row about half-way back in the room. Apparently, a bright guy in the first seat of the row passed information to the others. On one test, I asked the students to identify an obscure Russian sociologist, his theory, methodology and significance in the field. Their papers revealed that no one knew the sociologist. Neither did the all-wise student in the first seat, but he must have put down a name and passed it on. The rest of the students all had the same answer!

During the next class meeting I announced that there had been cheating on the test and that I would be in my office at a certain hour expecting the cheaters to show up. They did and confessed. I forgave them and warned that if it happened again they would be reported to the dean and dismissed from the class. So far as I know, the cheating never occurred again.

A number of my students did not keep up with their studies that semester. As the final exam drew near, they sent a committee to my home to inquire if I would tell them generally what questions and materials would be covered on the test. Replying that I would be happy to share the information, I told them the test would come from all the class lectures and the assigned reading. They were shocked and departed disappointed. The word got out quickly, sociology at Stetson was no longer a "crip" course. Happily, class enrollment began to increase.

While in DeLand, I participated in the Big Brother Movement, the founding of the Family Counseling Agency and joined the Lions Club. I also completed my doctoral dissertation and graduated in 1948 from the Southern Baptist Theological Seminary with the school's first black, doctoral candidate to complete the Ph.D. in theology. Garland Offutt was the first black Th.M. and Ph.D. graduate.[1]

I loved teaching in a small denominational college like Stetson. Students generally were responsive. Even those who were not happy in my classes were kind, courteous, open and frank. My life was in danger only once that I remember. An older student brought a gun to class to shoot me. I assume my lecture that day calmed him down and perhaps saved my life. Years later when I visited New Orleans it was he who served as my a gracious host and guide, safely seeing me through the seamier side of that

---

[1] J. V. Bottoms was the first black person to receive the M.Div.

city where he functioned as a private detective. Despite a rough beginning, we had become good friends.

Professor and Pastor

From 5 March 1950 to 12 August 1951, while maintaining a full-time college teaching schedule, I also served as interim pastor of San Mateo Baptist Church in San Mateo. A tiny village near Palatka, San Mateo's streets were unpaved and its only business was the post office. The congregation itself was small and intimate.

One Sunday, a Mr. White came with his wife and two children and presented themselves for membership before the church at the conclusion of worship. Received gladly by the fellowship, Mr. White told how his family came to its decision to join San Mateo church. They had discovered a copy of John A. Broadus' *Baptist Catechism* in the bottom of an old trunk. The family had studied the catechism together, came to know Christ as Savior and Lord, and then acted to become members of the church.

Although seldom practiced, every Baptist church could be better informed and fortified in the faith by using a well-written catechism for new members. New members—whether previously unchurched or coming from other faith traditions—would benefit from a systematic presentation of the historic Baptist faith and an explanation of the religious life embraced by the congregations they are joining. Longstanding members of the church would also benefit from the regular review of those matters basic to Baptist faith and practice.

Race Relations

On 16 November 1949 I gave a speech on "Race Relations" to the annual meeting of the Florida Baptist Convention in Daytona Beach. It was a message against racism. It had been recently reported that blacks in a Florida town literally had been driven out of their community and their homes burned to the ground. Racial tension in the region was running very high. Hundreds of ministers and laypersons were present at the convention. I described the current problematic status of race relations, the biblical view of race and some practical things the individual local church, Baptist Convention and Baptist colleges could do to improve race relations.[2]

Upon concluding the speech, I took it straight to the recording secretary on the platform to be printed in the convention's annual report. He angrily rejected it and informed me that he would not print "that stuff." Finally, however, he relented and the message appeared in the 1949 *Florida Baptist Convention Annual*, 31–34. Comments pro and con on the speech were carried on the front page of the Daytona and Orlando newspapers.

A few days later the president of Stetson University informed me that one of his biggest clients (President Edmunds was a lawyer as well president of the college, duties for which he was paid one dollar a year) had identified me as a Communist and thought I should be fired. Dr. Edmunds asked, "Are you a Communist?" Reply, "No, Sir." He never again brought the matter up.

In April of the following year I spoke in Winter Haven to more than one thousand members of the Baptist Woman's Missionary Union Convention of Florida. My remarks were carried on the front page of the *Winter Haven News-Chief* under the headline, "Church Leader Calls for Racial, Political Equality."[3] Stetson again received demands that I be fired, for this speech as well as my Daytona Beach remarks. Dr. Edmunds refused to be swayed by the racism behind the demands.

In 1951 I announced my intention to leave Stetson following the spring semester to assume a professorship at Southern Seminary. Dr. Edmunds pleaded with me to remain at the Florida school. Dr. Edmunds rightly believed Stetson faced a bright future, and he wanted me to have a share in it. As testimony to the prestige the school was steadily gaining, he showed me a check for $45,000—an enormous gift at that time—from a wealthy person.

Notable Stetson Students

There were several students at Stetson who "stood out of the crowd." Bill Fisher, a member of the Jewish faith tradition, was studying to become a journalist. He rebelled against having to take a required course in religion.

---

[2] See appendix, Equality.

[3] "Church Leader calls for Racial, Political Equity, *Winter Haven Daily News-Chief*, Winter Haven FL, 33:59, 1, 5 April 1950. (See appendix, Haven.)

He informed me that he was transferring to nearby Rollins College, where a course in religion was not required. I responded by suggesting it was imperative a journalist know a great deal about religion. Further, giving him a book on the life of Jesus Christ, I asked him to read it. Some days later I saw Bill on campus and asked if he liked the book. He responded that he had learned much about Jesus he previously did not know. Then he added: "The more I read about Jesus, the fewer Christians I see on this campus." In the end, Bill took the course in religion, graduated from Stetson and became a successful journalist. For years afterwards, I received a card from him at Christmas.

Earl Joiner came to Stetson after serving in the military. He was among those troops who liberated the Jews left in Hitler's concentration camps near the end of World War II. What he saw in the aftermath of the Holocaust was so gruesome that for many years afterwards Earl could not talk about it. Following studies at Stetson, he pursued post-graduate work at the Southern Baptist Theological Seminary, completing two degrees. He became chairman of the Department of Religion at Stetson and was the author of many significant books, including *History of Florida Baptists*. He became a leading lecturer on the topic of the Holocaust and was recognized as one of the heroes of liberation by the Jewish community in Florida.

Adrian Rogers was a quiet student of strong conservative religious convictions. Since I was a professor at Stetson who served churches, they often called me to obtain the names of likely candidates among our student body to fill their pulpits for short or long term periods. I recommended Adrian as a pastoral candidate to a church in South Florida. Apparently, the small congregation was impressed by this articulate student of religion; they soon called him as pastor. Under his ministry, the church grew in membership. Adrian was eventually called as pastor of Bellevue Baptist Church in Memphis, Tennessee. Under his leadership across the years, the church's membership has grown into the thousands, by some estimates to more than 26,000 members. His televised ministry is very popular. The church provides programs designed to appeal to all age groups, including worship, religious education, recreation and retreats. Adrian Rogers was at the center of the fundamentalist takeover of the Southern Baptist Convention that began in earnest in the late 1970s.

9

Back to "The Beeches"

You can't go home again.
—Thomas Wolfe

I did anyway.
—Henlee H. Barnette

In February 1951 I boarded a train in Daytona Beach for Atlanta to attend a Baptist city missions conference. That was the first time I had traveled in a roomette, that is, as a first class carriage passenger. After the Georgia conference I traveled to Louisville for a conference with Dr. Gaines Dobbins, then acting president of the Southern Baptist Theological Seminary. He had invited me to consider a teaching post at the seminary.

Perhaps it was something of an omen. Upon my 8:30 A.M. arrival in Louisville, the first person I met on the street was a drunk. I was lodged in the seminary's guest house. My visit included extended conversations with my former graduate studies supervisor, Dr. Olin T. Binkley, under whose supervision I would work at Southern were I to take the position. It was proposed that I teach an introduction to Christian ethics and a course titled "Christianity and Social Problems," addressing issues related to urban sociology. I would be allowed a teaching fellow and after one year be able to teach a seminar for graduate students. Several faculty members encouraged me to return to Southern as a teaching colleague, including Dale Moody, Henry Turlington and Wayne Oates.

Dr. Dobbins began my employment interview by asking, "Where would one look for the greatest opportunity to do some creative work?" He noted that little had been done by Southern Baptist academics to address Christianity and its application to modern social problems. The financial details of the employment contract proposed are interesting in light of our economy in the early twenty-first century. My salary was to be $5,200 for eight months of teaching and would increase $200 every year until, at the end of ten years, it would reach approximately $7,000. The seminary would pay my family's moving expenses. In addition, a $2,500 loan for a lot on which to build a house was offered. Relief and Annuity—somewhat like unemployment insurance and a retirement plan—would be paid by the seminary. Our family health and accident insurance amounted to six dollars of annual coverage per person and provided a $2,000 payment to beneficiaries in case of my death.

Full time employment as a teacher at Southern Seminary required that faculty sign a historic document, the "Abstract of Principles," to indicate that one would teach in accordance with the general theological ideology under which the school was first founded. Baptists historically have been a non-creedal people, and I informed Dr. Dobbins of my sense of difficulty with signing the abstract, since it seemed a bit like affirming an established creed. He explained that the document was a body of principles offering guidance in matters of doctrine and theology, not rules demanding rigid conformance. Indeed, he went on, the abstract was a compromise between the seminary's founding fathers who themselves did not uniformly agree on all matters of theology. So, I signed on.

The next six months were the most agonizing of my life. I had accepted the seminary position, but doubts quickly began to gather. My family and I loved delightful DeLand. Charlotte and the boys were not enthusiastic about leaving the Sunshine State. Winters were cold in Louisville and in warm weather the area was legendary as the "sinus bend of the Ohio Valley." Returning to Southern seemed less than a wonderful prospect as our time to depart Stetson drew nearer.

The day we left DeLand was sad for the entire Barnette family. We left dear friends, a fine university, a delightful town and a great climate. Stetson's Dean Hopkins provided consolation in assuring me that I could return to my old job within two years if I changed my mind.

We moved into Southern Seminary's Foster Hall, a small apartment complex for staff and faculty. Dr. and Mrs. W. O. Carver were the first to visit and welcome us to the community. As a result, we formed and maintained with them a lasting and richly rewarding friendship.

On Tuesday, 11 September 1951, in 105 Norton Hall, the course "The Church and the Urban Community" was offered for the first time at the seminary. About twenty-five students were in attendance, including three blacks: B. J. Miller, J. V. Bottoms and Claude Taylor.

A few days later I participated in the ordination of Bill Macy at Lynn Acres Baptist Church.[1] Prior to the ordination service, the candidate was interviewed by a council made up of ordained ministers and deacons. I asked him a question that seemed to startle the committee: "What is your position on race relations?" They apparently had never before heard that one at an ordination council. From then on, my calendar was filled with teaching, preaching, marriages, funerals, student recruitment and representing the seminary at various events.

Shortly after my own arrival, Dr. Duke K. McCall, the new seminary president, was honored at a banquet in Faculty Center. Dr. Dobbins welcomed him by declaring that seminary founders Boyce and Broadus were builders and that later presidents also made their unique contributions. Whitsitt, he said, was an advocate for academic freedom, Mullins a needed mediator, Sampey a seer and Fuller fulfilled the founders' early vision for the school. McCall, Dobbins declared, would be the much-needed minister of education to lead the seminary community forward toward even greater academic excellence.

Southern Seminary's weekly chapel services were always a meaningful experience. Great spiritual leadership inspired students' faith and expanded their vision. For example, Dr. Wayne E. Oates, Professor of Psychology of Religion, once spoke on "Provincial Religion" using the text about Naaman who wanted two mule-loads of dirt from Israel to stand on in his own country so that he could talk to Israel's God, YAHWEH (2 Kgs 5:15–17). Application: We come from different places and bring with us our different perspectives on religion. God, however, cannot be constrained by our parochialisms; God is universal.

During the summer of 1952 I did further studies at Union Theological Seminary in New York City. I took two classes with Dr. John Bennett,

---

[1] Dale Moody preached a sermon during the service as if a thousand people were present in the church. It was based on the four chapters of Second Timothy. He gave it the title, "The Man of God." Its outline was: A Man of the Spirit (chapter one); A Man of Strength (chapter two); A Man of Scripture (chapter three); A Man of Sound Doctrine (chapter four).

"Ethical Relativities" and "Christianity and Communism." The latter started me on years of studying Communism. I attended lectures by the distinguished New Testament scholar, T. W. Manson, and also heard John Baillie of St. Andrews University in Scotland. After returning to Kentucky that fall, my life was filled with preaching most Sundays, classroom lectures, speeches or more informal talks to clubs, groups and youth organizations.

Family Tragedy

The truth of James 4:14—we do not know what tomorrow holds—became dramatically personal to my sons and me on Monday 20 July 1953 in the home-going of my wife, Charlotte Ford Barnette. Stricken suddenly at about seven in the morning, she took her flight to "that country from which no traveler returns" at three-twenty in the afternoon.

Charlotte was pregnant and had been feeling well. Her physical condition appeared to be perfect for the coming of the little one due in just a few days. Her spirit was jubilant and she was radiant with the expectancy that only a mother can experience as she anticipates the arrival of her baby.

On Sunday morning 19 July, Charlotte was up at 8:00 A.M., busy in the kitchen of our little campus apartment. She had breakfast on the table in a matter of minutes. All the time she was humming a hymn and occasionally urged the boys to get ready for the morning meal. We ate our breakfast as usual after sons John and Wayne "said the blessing" in unison. Charlotte remarked that she would not attend church anymore until the baby came.

By 9:00 A.M. the boys were dressed and ready for Sunday school. They were eagerly looking forward to riding home on the bus afterwards by themselves. I was scheduled to preach at Mill Creek Baptist Church near Fort Knox and drove there after leaving the boys at St. Matthews Baptist Church.

My sermon text and theme that morning was "Through a Glass Darkly." I sought to show that human knowledge is limited—limited in the areas of science, human relations, morality, suffering and tragedy. Special emphasis was given to the mystery of human suffering and tragedy. Several times following the morning service, I had the impulse to return home for the afternoon to be with Charlotte and the boys. But, that would have meant three more trips on the Dixie Highway—known for its treacherous driving history—from Louisville to Fort Knox in order to meet my evening preaching commitment. Besides, I had reasoned with myself, Charlotte had been feeling well and comfortable despite her advanced pregnancy.

I returned home at 9:30 P.M. to discover that Charlotte had called our physician, Dr. Ed Morgan, during the day. She had experienced sudden pains in her abdomen and thought they might be birth contractions. The doctor had examined her and concluded she was merely suffering the discomfort of stomach gas. He gave her a sedative and told her to call him again in the morning if she was still uncomfortable. That night she was up several times because of nausea. I recall that at about 4 A.M she told me, "I am comfortable now."

At 7:00 A.M. I awoke and saw Charlotte sitting on the edge of the bed. Immediately I was at her side. "What is the trouble, dear?" I anxiously asked. She answered, "I don't know." I put my arms around her. She was cold and perspiration covered her body. I helped her into a comfortable position on the bed and then quickly called Dr. Morgan. After I described her condition, he said he would be by to see her on his way from the hospital that morning. A few minutes later Charlotte suffered a convulsion. I called the doctor again and he came to our home in a matter of minutes. Taking one look at her, Dr. Morgan called an ambulance. Charlotte was given an injection of some sort that calmed her and she went to sleep. My wife never again awoke to see her sons or me.

At the hospital, Charlotte was placed in the labor room. A specialist was called and initially seemed to be optimistic about her condition. Nevertheless, a little later Dr. Morgan reported that Charlotte's condition was worsening and critical. I called her parents who were visiting in Alexandria, Louisiana. The Fords immediately left for Louisville. About 2:00 P.M. Dr. Morgan gave me another report, indicating the baby might be saved but that there was little hope for Charlotte. Next came the report that the baby's heart had stopped beating. Despite knowing that all was lost for the baby, I clung to the hope that Charlotte might live.

Shortly after learning of our baby's death, a neurologist brought me the grim report that Charlotte could not possibly survive and that she was expected to die within hours. At about 3:10 P.M. Dr. Morgan announced that it would only be a matter of minutes before she would expire. I followed him to Charlotte's room where five nurses were in attendance to her needs, and mine. My darling wife was already cold when I took her by the hand. At 3:20 that afternoon she was gone.

Throughout this experience, several friends remained by my side in the small hospital waiting room where the doctors' reports were delivered. Wayne Ward, my colleague at the seminary, and city pastors John Boykin, Eugene Enlow, and John Carter stood by me in the shadows until the bitter end.

Immediately following Charlotte's death, Dr. Morgan requested that I permit an autopsy. He explained that the results might help to save the lives of others suffering similar circumstances. I consented because I was certain that it would have pleased Charlotte. About 7:30 in the evening Dr. Morgan called and informed me that Charlotte had died as a result of a cerebral hemorrhage brought on in the convulsions caused by a toxic condition known as eclampsia. I remember the wrenching feeling that he should have detected the toxemia in his diagnosis on the previous Sunday when he had examined her.[2]

The most difficult thing I have ever had to do was to return home Monday afternoon and tell John and Wayne the shocking news. I called them into the apartment, washed their faces and asked them to join me on the studio couch. I opened the Bible and read John 14:1–4, "Let not your hearts be troubled…" Then I said, "Boys, Mom went home to be with Jesus this afternoon." Their little hearts were broken. John cried, "Oh Daddy, why? Why did Mom die? She was so good!" I explained that mothers sometimes die in childbirth due to poisoning of the kidneys. A few moments later he gazed at me with the most dazed look I have ever seen on a lad. Slowly he remarked, "I'm puzzled." Then he said very softly, "Let's be the kind of men Mom would want us to be."

Soon Dr. Cort Flint, Assistant Administrator to President McCall and a classmate of mine in seminary, came and spoke words of encouragement to us. He was the first of many friends who descended upon us from every direction. Turns were taken in answering the telephone which rang incessantly, conveying sympathy and offers of help.

---

[2] An expectant mother should be checked carefully for this and other dangers every week at least two months before the baby is born.

I was in a daze. People came and went. I remember little of what was said that afternoon and evening, but I remember the loving concern on so many faces. I do remember a few particularly poignant words spoken by honest friends who knew my pain in their own experience. Mrs. Ellis A. Fuller, widow of the former president of the seminary, shared something of my sorrow, for she had lost her companion. Professor Inman Johnson put his arm around me and prayed: "O Lord, be with this our brother in his hour of sorrow and suffering. I know what he feels now, because I too lost my companion. Be with him and the boys and help them to bear their burden. In Jesus' name. Amen."

Some words can seem meaningless in the hour of deep personal tragedy. While events were transpiring at the hospital, one person began to "preach" to me, quoting a number of Bible texts. He likely thought he was helping me, but in reality it was irritating. What meant most and offered most comfort to me was the supportive presence of friends; simple offers of practical help with a multitude of matters to which I was in no frame of mind to attend; brief messages that came from the heart and avoided stereotypical condolences.

Charlotte's parents, the Fords, en route from Alexandria to Louisville, called from Memphis about 9 P.M. Monday night. I told my father-in-law the terrible news. He gasped, "Oh, she's gone!" I heard his own wife's heartbreaking sobs in the background. I urged them not to continue driving the highways that night, but to continue the following day.

My family members arrived about 9:30 P.M. on Monday. Mother Barnette, (Dad was not physically able to make the trip), sisters Mazo, Evelyn, Colleen, and brothers Baines and Roy. Colleen's husband, C. A. Lowder, also came.

At about 9 A.M. Tuesday, Cort Flint, Wayne Ward and I joined Herbert Cralle, Jr., at the funeral home on Frankfort Avenue in Crescent Hill. First we went to Cave Hill Cemetery and selected a grave in the seminary plot. Charlotte's grave was to be between Dr. Ellis Fuller's and Dr. E. Y. Mullins's. Space was also to be reserved for me. Next we went to the casket factory and I chose a modest pale pink casket for Charlotte's burial. She would never have consented to anything elaborate or expensive.

Back home again, I had to select one of Charlotte's dresses for her burial. I chose, with the help of the Wards, a simple blue dress that my wife liked. A small string of pearls was also part of her burial outfit.

The Fords arrived Tuesday afternoon. When I told them that Charlotte was to be buried in Louisville, they became upset. The Fords had long been the owners of a cemetery in their hometown of Knoxville, Tennessee. I spoke with my older son John. He said it did not make much difference to him whether his mother was buried in Louisville or Knoxville. I consequently agreed that Charlotte should be buried at the Woodlawn Cemetery in Knoxville. Both the Fords and I were comforted by the decision. The Knoxville cemetery has more natural beauty than Louisville's Cave Hill. Additionally, Charlotte's grave would receive special care from the Fords who lived at its edge.

On Wednesday the black limousine from the funeral home called for me and the boys at about 1:30 P.M.. We rode to the funeral home in silence and shortly the funeral procession moved down Frankfort Avenue to St. Matthews Baptist Church. Charlotte loved the congregation at St. Matthews and had served as a very active superintendent of the church's primary department.

When we arrived at the church a lone figure, an elderly man, opened the limousine door for us. After the service, the same man opened the limousine door for us again. No words were spoken; he closed the door and tottered away. That "doorkeeper" was Dr. William Owen Carver, who was eighty-five years old and himself ill. He had ventured out to show his love and concern for a bereaved colleague and family. A few months later he died. His silent ministry was more meaningful to us than any words of sympathy.

Mrs. Carver and Charlotte had been close friends and often walked together. Both joyfully anticipated the new baby. I recently discovered a card Mrs. Carver had written to my wife after she had presented her with a baby's cap for the expected child:

> My dear Charlotte,
> Purl one
> Knit one
> Now the little hat is done.
> I hope it tells something of the

deep interest and congratulations
The Carvers feel for The Barnettes
on the coming event.
With love,
A.S. and W.O. Carver

The little cap was never worn.

The pall bearers—Drs. T. D. Price, Guy Ranson, John Joseph Owens, Dale Moody, Latrell Stanfield and Wayne Ward (all except Dr. Ward had been students with me at seminary)—carried the casket from the hearse. John and Wayne walked by my side as we followed the casket into the church, which was well-filled and had flowers of all kinds banked across the rostrum. Earlier that day, clouds hung heavily and threatened rain across the region. As the funeral service began, however, the sun broke through the clouds. Sunlight streamed into the church, helping to lift our sorrowful spirits.

Inman Johnson, Professor of Speech and Church Music in the seminary, began the service by singing "O Love, That Will Not Let Me Go." Wayne, our youngest, who had borne up under the strain to this point, burst into tears. I held him close to my side and he soon gained control of himself. John remained silent throughout the service. Rev. Eldred Taylor, interim pastor of St. Matthews Church, read passages of Scripture that I had selected: Psalm 23; John 14:1–6: Romans 8:31–39; 1 Corinthians 15:51–58.

Dr. J. B. Weatherspoon, my former graduate supervisor and the seminary's professor of preaching, led in a prayer that was a source of strength for us all. Dr. Verlin Kruschwitz, pastor of St. Matthews when we joined the church, gave the sermon. He had returned to speak again from his former pulpit out of love for Charlotte, the boys, and me. Following a last hymn, we slowly filed out of the church and were returned to our small apartment home.

Loading our car with the things we would need, the boys and I departed for Knoxville that same afternoon. It rained just ahead of us all the way to the Tennessee state line. A lovely rainbow—a unique sign of comfort—appeared before us for many miles along our journey.

We reached the Fords' residence that evening at about 10:30 P.M. A large crowd of friends was waiting there for us with plenty of good food prepared for any who might be hungry. This was traditional bereavement hospitality in East Tennessee.

On Thursday we were up about 9:00 A.M. Already calls were coming in, along with flowers for Charlotte's grave. By 1.00 P.M. a large crowd had gathered at the grave site. Five of my colleagues at the seminary were also present: Drs. Goerner, Ward, Ranson, McGlon and Stanfield. Dr. Charles Wauford, Charlotte's pastor who had baptized her years earlier, led us in prayer and a commital service. When it was concluded, we returned to the hospitality of the Fords' home.

After Thursday I lost track of time. Sleep failed me. The boys bore it better than I. Burning memories haunted me—especially during the long sleepless nights. I meditated much on Romans 8:28: "We know that in everything God works for good with those who love him, who are called according to his purpose" (RSV). One night I almost caught the meaning of the text for my circumstances. I learned it is easy to quote, but can be difficult to comprehend and accept.

On Sunday following Charlotte's burial, we attended South Knoxville Baptist Church where Dr. Nolan Howington was pastor. He preached a profound sermon on our anchor of hope in God. These were most helpful words, undergirding me when I needed spiritual support. Few others can preach like Nolan Howington.

John, Wayne, and I stayed with the Fords until the following Tuesday, 28 July 1953. Leaving Knoxville, we drove through the Great Smokies, which Charlotte loved so much. How I missed her as we ascended the mountains, smelled the cool refreshing air, saw bears and gazed down deep ravines. Despite her absence, I felt that she somehow must have shared the experience with us.

We arrived later that evening at my parents' home in Kannapolis, North Carolina. Days slipped by me unnoticed. Perhaps it was one week that we stayed there. Next, we traveled to the Baptist retreat center at Ridgecrest, North Carolina. Despite the fact that it was the beginning of Woman's Missionary Union week and the retreat was already heavily booked. J. Clifton Allen of the Sunday School Board secured a place for us to stay high up on the hill behind the center's Pritchard Hall.

I had promised the boys to take them to Mount Mitchell, the highest peak east of the Mississippi River. They insisted on going the very day we had arrived at Ridgecrest. The Blue Ridge Parkway was a wonderful road to travel. We drove to the top of the mountains, and then began to descend—still no Mount Mitchell. We passed within five miles of the peak—the highest mountain east of the Mississippi—but I had not seen it! We turned around some fifteen miles farther down the road and eventually found our destination. On the way back to Mount Mitchell, John suddenly asked, "Daddy, who is going to take care of us?" Before I could respond, he added, "I guess that we will just have to take care of ourselves." Wayne remarked: "Daddy, if we had planned the trip and used a map, we would not have missed it."

The boys and I climbed Mount Mitchell. It was cold and the wind was blowing at about forty miles per hour. Back at Ridgecrest and thoroughly worn, we had a good night's sleep. It was so quiet. That was the first real sleep I had had since Charlotte died. The next day began our journey home to Louisville.

Charlotte's death caused John to raise some large issues despite his young age. (Wayne, who was only seven, may have had his own questions. If he did, he kept them to himself.) The day after my wife died, John looked at me with great hurt, puzzlement and some anger in his eyes. "Daddy," he asked, "why did my mother have to die? She was such a good Christian." I tried to explain that in childbirth, mothers sometimes die. John turned and walked away without hearing the details of my lame explanation. His mother, indeed, had been a devoted follower of Christ. She was a brilliant person, having completed a college degree in music as well as having earned a theological degree. Charlotte was a faithful Sunday school teacher, always seeking to serve where the need was greatest, as she did with missions to Appalachia or as pianist and teacher in the Louisville Haymarket ministry.

Weeks after his mother's death, John asked me if Adam was the first man. I answered affirmatively. Then he replied: "According to science the cave man came first and he was a brute and stupid. But Adam was smart and named all the animals." I attempted some answer, but he walked away without hearing me. Shortly afterward he really stumped me: "Daddy, I have been reading the story of Noah and the Ark. According to the size of that boat, Noah could not have possibly gotten pairs of all animals in it." I was about to give him the usual Sunday school answer when he interrupted me and said, "Beside Noah would have had to go to the antarctic to get a pair of penguins." Again he turned and walked away. John's statements were posed as a challenge to me. I perceived that they were aimed at God as well, who my son thought was somehow responsible for the death of his mother.

I soon realized that we had to move to a new home. The heart of our present one had been cut out, and much of our own hearts as well. The boys and I were sharing a growing sense of depression. Our conversations had become minimal, and the boys lost interest in playing with each other or taking part in what had been their normal routines. We moved to a small frame house on the edge of the Seminary campus.

The seminary community kept us well stocked with food. Of course, I could fry eggs and bacon, and serve cereal. In our new place, however, I tried preparing a real meal for us. After the blessing, the boys gazed suspiciously at the food, looked at one another, and somehow found the courage to tackle it. After a few bites they sat still. Their inactivity told me "loud and clear" that what I had prepared was not edible. I dumped the mashed potatoes and other ingredients I had added to the meal into the disposal. The disposal became so gummed up that we had to have a plumber come and fix it!

The seminary allowed me to modify my schedule to meet the needs of a single parent—long before that was expected of employers in the United States. Fortunately, my eldest sister, Mazo, eventually came to live with us. She was a Godsend and provided indispensable help with the boys and our domestic matters for the next three years. With her help, I was able to maintain a busy schedule. This was healing in relation to my grief.

I enrolled John and Wayne in a Cub Scout troop. They had achievement projects to do. One of these was to cook a meal. Wayne decided to do his breakfast. He was proud of the fact that he had done his own toast, bacon and egg. We began eating breakfast. Wayne was struggling with the egg. It was so tough that he could not cut it with his knife. Finally he got a bite cut loose and chewed a bit on it, spit it out and sheepishly glanced up at me. After a moment he replied: "Daddy, the scout manual says only that you have to cook a meal, not that you have to eat it."

Somehow, I managed to get my course schedules and student work assignments completed for the fall classes at seminary. We slowly began to find a new kind of normalcy at home, and although they continued to display a sense of sadness, the boys did their chores and school work.

One day I went to the drug store for medicine and chanced to see some paperback books on a rack. I picked up one with the title: *Women's Illnesses* and turned to the section on eclampsia, the illness that caused Charlotte's death. I was stunned to read that in our day, with proper medical care, it was inexcusable for a woman to die of this illness.

For days after I was thrust back into the acute grieving stage. I blamed myself for not insisting that Charlotte see a specialist instead of a family doctor. This is what I had always urged in my lectures on marriage and the family. But she seemed satisfied with the care she was getting. I was later informed that her doctor had been the subject of discussion by the county medical association on two occasions relating to improper care. It took some time, but I was finally able to adopt a spirit of forgiveness toward the physician. It had become time to deal with issues at hand and let the past go.

A Professional Milestone: Faculty Address

Charlotte had died in July 1953. Just a bit more than one year following that devastating personal loss, I was faced with a significant professional responsibility at the Southern Baptist Theological Seminary. Each faculty member at Southern was required to deliver an inaugural address in the chapel before the assembled faculty, seminary staff, students and visitors. My assigned date for this important address was Tuesday, 21 September 1954. My subject was, "The Significance of the Holy Spirit for Christian Morality." The *Courier-Journal* carried comments in response to the speech. It appeared as an article in the seminary's academic journal *Review and Expositor*,[3] and was reprinted the following year by the Christian Life Commission of the Southern Baptist Convention in pamphlet form under the title "The Holy Spirit in Christian Ethics."

The address was generally well received. Philosopher Ralph Tyler Flewelling, editor of the *Personalist: International Review of Philosophy, Religion and Literature* at the University of Southern California, read the address and wrote me the following letter:

28 January 1955
Dear Professor Barnette:

---

[3] See *Review & Expositor* 51:1 (January 1955): 5–20.

You will probably not expect it from me as a mere philosopher but I wish to express my appreciation of your article, "The Significance of the Holy Spirit for Christian Morality" in the January *Review and Expositor*.

It seems to me to be of special importance, and in spite of the scandal which anything religious now enjoys in the common philosophical mind, it seems to me, as you suggest, that the doctrine of the "Holy Spirit" is the most significant and the most neglected doctrine in Christian theology.

Possibly I would go a little bit farther than you because I believe that the Holy Spirit is the actual presence of God within the human heart, not only as a source of ethics but as a source of all creative genius and of good. We will not settle the sorrows of the world until we enter the age of the Holy Ghost. To me it is one belief which confirms the doctrine of the incarnation.

I am happy to express my pleasure in your article.

Yours sincerely,

Ralph Tyler Flewelling

10

Road to Renewal

Weeping may endure for a night,
but joy comes in the morning.
—Psalm 30:5

In 1954, Helen Poarch enrolled in my Christian ethics class at the seminary. It was a large class and at first I saw her as just another student taking another course for credit toward a degree. I had to admit, however, there was a radiance about her and a smile that one could not easily ignore. At one point in the semester, she had been ill and absent from class. When she was well again, we chanced to meet on campus and I said in passing, "It is good to see that you are back in school." This is what I would have said to any student who had been absent from class due to illness, but that day I said it with a slightly stronger sense of interest.

One day Helen knocked on my office door. She stuck her head in and saw that I was dictating on one of those old fashioned cone record Dictaphones. She said she would come back another time. "I can put this down anytime," I said and motioned for her to come in.

I thought she had come to discuss her grade in the course. But she had come for some information on the upcoming Mullins Lectures, of which I was the committee chairman. I had only one bit of information regarding the upcoming lectures in my desk drawer, and it took me two hours to get it. We talked, time slipped away, and she missed a class. Finally, the mundane responsibilities of daily life at seminary forced their way into that office with us and the visit came to an end. But we knew that something had happened to both of us—a precious, ecstatic awakening that began to draw us together.

On another visit, Helen declared that she was beginning to think of me more as a person than a professor. I replied: "It is mutual!" I held her just briefly. Elsewhere I have tried to describe the indescribable emotion of that moment. Somehow, then and there, we knew for a certainty that we were made and meant for each other.

Naturally, overt courtship between a professor and a student would be received with some question in the seminary community. This would especially be true in the case of a twenty-three year old student and a forty-three year old widower professor. But, true love transcends all barriers. We subsisted on seeing each other in the halls of the school, on exchanged notes, and on long evening telephone conversations.

We had some early strong supporters on the faculty: Dr. Gaines Dobbins and Dr. Wayne Oates. "Prof" Johnson, who knew Helen's father and mother, also encouraged the relationship. Wayne and his wife, Pauline, developed a strategy whereby Helen and I could have some time together. Helen was to baby-sit the Oates's children and I would be allowed some supervised visitation during those periods. The children made sure we were both completely and appropriately entertained.

The first time we followed the "Oates Plan" was a bit of a disaster. I was to go by the women's dormitory, get Helen and then go to the Oates's home. In those days, a young man had to go to the main office of the women's dorm and request that the resident who was to be his date for the evening be called. I found myself standing in a line of students waiting for their dates' names to be called out over a loud intercom system. Students began to stare at me, wondering what I was doing there. For whom would I call? Once at the caller's desk, I asked for Miss Helen Poarch. The call was made several times and there was no response. Embarrassed and a bit angry, I wondered if I had been stood up. Then a voice was heard: "Helen is not here. She left with Dr. Wayne Oates." I departed as quickly as possible. A failure of communication had occurred. To save me the agony of calling for Helen at the student dormitory, Wayne had done it himself...but he forgot to tell me!

Faculty and students eventually became aware of our romantic interest. As expected, some less than charitable comments were made about us. Some simply were jealous of the relationship. Helen's companionship was being sought by the most eligible bachelors on the campus. And, too, I add humbly, not a few on the staff as well as in the student body manifested an interest in me. Some thought the relationship totally inappropriate. A few were not above having some "fun" with our unorthodox courtship.

Helen's mother, Mrs. O. G. Poarch, came to visit and to meet the popular, handsome young man she thought her daughter was dating at seminary. When Helen met her at the airport in my old Chevy with my two small, unkempt, sad-faced boys she was surprised—and then shocked when she learned that I was the suitor. Nevertheless, Mrs. Poarch attended one of my classes. Providentially or not, the topic that day was "Ten Criteria for the Wise Choice of a Mate." Mrs. Poarch thought the lecture ridiculous. She warned her daughter that I was too old for her, that she could never live and raise a family on a seminary professor's salary. Mrs. Poarch was from a well-to-do family in Knoxville, Tennessee. While she herself had married a minister, she enjoyed significant additional income from a trust fund.

The first visit I made to Helen's home in Buchanan, Virginia, was an unhappy experience. In fact, the tension was so great that during the night after all were asleep I decided to slip out and escape to Louisville. To my dismay the doors were locked. So I stayed all night. Thank God I did!

Helen's parents quickly made known their opposition to our relationship. Accordingly, we postponed any wedding plans, but we continued to see one another as opportunity allowed. When Helen completed her seminary studies she accepted a position as Assistant Dean of Women at Radford University in Virginia. In 1956 we met at her home in Buchanan. Her father, the Reverend O. G. Poarch, was a Baptist pastor in the town. Rev. Poarch invited me to preach on Sunday. After the sermon people came forward to greet and thank me for the sermon. Something in the events of that day caused Helen's mother to relent in her opposition to our courtship. After that she became warm and friendly toward me.

I must say that Rev. O. G. Poarch was the "parson" of Buchanan. The first time I visited the Poarches, I walked down town and asked what the banker thought of Preacher Poarch. Reply: "Brother Poarch does not own an inch of this town, but it all belongs to him." He was a man of God, characterized by integrity and compassion.

On 6–7 June 1956 I was back in Buchanan for two reasons: to marry Helen and to lecture at nearby University of Richmond. The family had accepted me. Rev. Poarch desired to go with me to Richmond not so much for my lectures, but for the lectures of the other person on the lectureship—the renowned Christian philosopher, Dr. Elton Trueblood. I charged Rev. Poarch with wanting to accompany me to keep me from bolting the marriage. A bit of humor began to emerge between us. On our return there was more. I insisted on stopping at Appomattox where Lee surrendered to Grant. My future father-in-law heard me say that I had the feeling I, too, was surrendering-not in war, but my freedom in marriage. We laughed.

On Friday 8 June, Helen and I were married at 4:30 P.M. in the parsonage of the Baptist church. It was a simple and beautiful wedding. Helen's mother played the piano. Her father officiated, pronouncing us man and wife. Her sisters were bridesmaids and a close friend was the best man. There was joy all around. We honeymooned in DeLand, where I taught at Stetson University's summer school session. (By the way, I eventually became the Poarch's favorite son-in-law…or so they would tell me!)

Helen brought healing to our sons, John and Wayne. When we first met, the boys still seemed depressed over the death of their mother. After Helen had given Wayne some attention and played with him, he suddenly started running around, even swatting me on the behind. I asked, "What is wrong with that boy?" Helen quietly told me that he was just becoming the little boy that he should have been all along.

None of us could get through to John. The trauma of his mother's death and the loss of a much anticipated sibling had been very hard on him. We never saw him crying during Charlotte's illness or after her death. Years later we learned that he in fact did cry. There was a large clump of bushes at the corner of the next apartment where we lived. It was John's secret crying place. He would go there and weep for his mother. Our neighbor witnessed it many times, but never told us.

An emotional breakthrough for John did not occur until 1959 when we were at Cambridge, Massachusetts. I was studying at Harvard on sabbatical leave from Southern Seminary. The family accompanied me for the extended period, and we enrolled the boys in area schools. Soon thereafter, Helen asked John how the Cambridge Latin High School compared with Kentucky high schools. John's answers were always brief and to the point. He never volunteered information nor did he ever raise any complaints. To Helen's inquiry he responded, "They seem to be pretty dumb here." We soon discovered that John had been put in a class of underachieving children. If Helen had not raised the question he would have remained in that class, bored to death but without complaint. It was discovered that John's IQ was so high that he was consequently placed in five honors courses. After that, John began to open up to Helen and others. Today he is a man who freely and easily engages others in wholesome conversations and friendship.

Helen loved all our children and helped to bring them up in the nurture and discipline of the Lord. Her impact upon John, Wayne, sons of my first wife Charlotte, and Martha and James, my children by Helen, is seen in their own characters which reflect the basic values of intellectual honesty, personal responsibility, hard work, common sense, sensitivity to others in need, respect and regard to their parents, peers and other persons. Her influence on my own life for good has been immeasurable.

Brilliant and beautiful, Helen expressed a spirit of humility, compassion and passion for truth and justice. She possessed many of the qualities of the ideal woman in Proverbs 31: "Strength and honor are her clothing...her children rise up and call her blessed." I often said to her, "Many women have done excellently, but you surpass them all" (Prov 31:29).

Helen also possessed a delightful sense of humor. When I came home from the office one day, I wanted to say something about her spirit. So I quoted from the King James translation of the Bible: "Who can find a virtuous woman? For her price is far above rubies." She asked, "Who is Ruby?"

Helen loved classical music and once played the violin in a small orchestra. She taught me appreciation for great music, art and literature. We had thirty-six happy and meaningful years of marriage.

At age fifty-eight Helen became a victim of cancer. For two years she suffered bravely through surgery, radiation treatments and chemotherapy. After just a few months of remission, the cancer again returned and with it, her suffering. I informed the provost of the seminary that I wished to resign my position as Senior Professor of Christian Ethics so that I could devote all my time to Helen's care.

It is always so painful to remember the last days of a dying loved one. The medications, trips to doctors and clinics, the various treatments—these make the experience that much more difficult. During those sad final days, I stayed close to Helen. We often quoted together one of her favorite passages from the Book of Romans about God's care and love in Christ: "God is for us and nothing can separate us from the love of God in Christ Jesus" (8:37–38). When she finally became so weak that she could not articulate the words, she just moved her lips.

Helen died peacefully on 26 April 1992. The memorial service was a celebration of her life. She was buried in the seminary's new plot at Cave Hill Cemetery where one can look straight ahead and see the steeple of the seminary chapel in which she loved to worship. Looking to the left, one can see Barrett Junior High School where she taught. The inscription on Helen's gravestone is: "Neither death nor life... shall be able to separate us from the love of God in Christ Jesus our Lord."

11

Conference with Khrushchev

We will bury you.
—Nikita Sergeyevich Khrushchev

During the summer of 1957 I toured the Soviet Union with a group of Americans under the leadership of Dr. Jerome Davis, who spoke Russian fluently. Formerly Professor of Christian Ethics at Yale University, Davis was now director of an organization called Promoting Enduring Peace. We shared a cabin on the good ship *Pobeda* (Victory) and were on the Black Sea when he asked me, "Whom do we want to see when we arrive in Moscow?" I suggested that we start at the top. By that I meant, "Let's see if we can get a conference with Nikita Khrushchev." He immediately typed a letter to the Soviet leader, making pen and ink corrections afterwards, requesting a conference. I did not think that anybody in the Kremlin would ever read it. When we eventually reached Moscow, however, we discovered that Mr. Khrushchev had agreed to meet with us.

Upon our arrival at the Kremlin, we were surprised when Mr. Khrushchev met us at his office door and offered us a cordial greeting. Right then and there Khrushchev also revealed his sense of humor. Earlier in Leningrad one of our companions, a tall and lanky student at Oberlin University, had been arrested for taking pictures of people who objected. His film had been confiscated by the police. I advised him that even in America I would not want my picture taken by a total stranger and suggested he first ask, "Your photo, please?" Khrushchev looked at the slender fellow and declared: "You are the skinniest fellow I have ever seen come out of a rich capitalist country. Don't your parents feed you? I am going to keep you in the Soviet Union and fatten you up before I let you go back to the United States."

We all shook hands with Khrushchev, almost in disbelief that we were really there. Photos were taken and our host appeared to be enjoying himself. We gathered around a long table loaded with drinks and cigarettes, none of which we consumed. We asked Mr. Khrushchev twenty-three questions we had prepared beforehand.[1]

At the time of our visit there were no American students studying in any of the Soviet Union's Universities. We asked under what conditions he would be willing to participate in an exchange of students, and how many that would involve. Perhaps as many as five thousand? He said, "No, that would be too many as we would have to pay for their stay in the United States and that would be too expensive." But we argued, "You have a rich country." He agreed, but declared that what was lacking were US dollars. Our response: "Then we will pay for your students and you can pay for ours." Khrushchev was blunt: "All right, please. Some think that our students will turn to capitalism. Perhaps some may, but this would be no tragedy and would not shake our country even if some decided to stay in your country. The same thing could happen with your students here, even though I am sure you would send the strongest supporters of capitalism. This in no way stops our desire for these exchanges."

Then we asked: "Do you want all kinds of exchanges?"—meaning in the areas of culture, technology, agriculture, and such. Khrushchev's firm response: "Yes. Certainly."

As soon as the conference was over Dr. Davis called the United States State Department and informed Lincoln White, State Department Press Officer, about Khrushchev's stated willingness to engage a specific formal proposal for exchanging students between the two countries. On 26 July 1957 Mr. White, in a news conference, called on the Soviet Union to make a specific formal proposal to initiate a student exchange program between the Soviet Union and United States.[2]

This was the beginning of cultural exchanges which had been brought to a halt during the early years of the Cold War. One of my former students, Andy Blaine, was among the first to take advantage of the opportunity to attend a Soviet university under the new agreement. It is my personal

---

[1] See *Review and Expositor* 56/3 (July 1959): 250–59. (See appendix.)
[2] "Bid to Students by Khrushchev, Favors Exchange," *New York Times* (27 July 1957).

conviction that this program of exchange between our two countries was the beginning of the end of the Cold War. Khrushchev himself said that trade and exchange make for peace between nations.

John Crutcher, former senator from the state of Kansas, a US Postal Commissioner, and fellow traveler with us, later wrote: "The cultural exchange program between the Soviet Union and America was initiated by our visit with Nikita Khrushchev in July 1957."[3]

Of special interest to me were visits to the Baptist Church in Moscow. Here I met Ilia Orlov, the distinguished organist of the church, who was also a dentist and an ordained minister. Former First Lady Eleanor Roosevelt once devoted a newspaper column to him. I also met Rev. Jacob Zidkov, the church's senior pastor. In his office I observed a marble bust of the famous preacher Charles Haddon Spurgeon, whose writings were popular among Protestant ministers. Also, I noticed that Rev. Zidkov had placed on his desk a copy of a religious paper carrying one of my articles. One of the first questions he asked me was: "Are you a Spurgeon or Fosdick Baptist?" (Fosdick, considered a liberal preacher in those days, was at the Riverside Baptist Church in New York City. Spurgeon was a well-known conservative.)

Memories of the Soviet Union linger still. The Baptist churches there had impressed me. In spite of strict government control, they survived. In Moscow I asked Pastor Zidkov's son, Michael, what I would have to do to gain membership in the church. First, he responded, I would have to attend for two years. Following that I would have to make formal application for membership. I would then be examined about faith and doctrine. I would, of course, have to confess Christ as Savior and Lord. Tenets of required belief included that God was in Christ (the incarnation); that Jesus was born of a virgin, lived, taught the true way of life, was crucified, rose the third day and is coming again. I asked Michael, "You don't really believe that, do you?" His immediate answer: "Da, da, da!" (Yes, yes, yes!) Finally, the pastor's son disclosed the final requirement faced by a prospective member of the Baptist church in Moscow. Each candidate would be asked: "Are you ready to die for Christ?" I remember telling Michael, somewhat jokingly,

---

[3] See personal letter dated 2 March 1990, appendix, p. 269ff. See also a letter to Khrushchev in the appendix.

that an honest answer to that last question would thin out the membership of my home church.

In Karkov, Ukraine, Senator Crutcher and I spent a half-day searching that city for the Baptist Church. Rev. Porchevsky was its pastor. Back in the USA, I wrote an article on "Baptists Behind the Iron Curtain." Pastor Porchevsky was furious with what I had written. There was, he declared, no "Iron Curtain" in the Soviet Union.

We enjoyed visits to many museums as well: the Tretyakov Gallery, the Lenin Museum, and the Heritage Museum, all with fabulous collections of art. We also toured the Peterhof Museum outside Leningrad where Peter the Great built his castles. One evening a friend and I attended the Bolshoi Theatre in Moscow. That was an unforgettable experience!

A Russian schoolteacher sadly confided that most of the people in the USSR were pressed into one lower economic class with little prospects of rising above those circumstances. I found the people lived in fear of speaking out against the government. "I am not a politician," they would say in order to avoid bringing trouble their way. But they were curious about the United States and wanted to know all about Americans.

Generally speaking, life in the Union of Soviet Socialist Republics (USSR) struck me as drab, sad and melancholy. Spies followed us everywhere. People in that part of the world had been reduced to pawns of the government. While in the Soviet Union, I experienced an ever-growing longing for "the land of the free and the home of the brave." Returning home on the ocean liner Queen Elizabeth—as opposed to our travel in Soviet ships, trains, and airplanes—was a welcomed luxury. As we approached New York Harbor, I stood on deck and took eight snapshots of the Statue of Liberty. Feelings of freedom and joy came over me.

Upon our return to the United States, I discovered that some religious fundamentalist leaders were identifying me as a communist. They apparently believed that anyone who could gain access to the most powerful man in the Soviet Union was *ipso facto* a communist. The administration of the Southern Baptist Theological Seminary never mentioned the charges made against me. I am grateful for their trust in me.

I engaged in lectures and wrote articles about the Soviet Union and Poland—at that time under Soviet rule and which we had visited during our travels—with a focus on the church, mainly Baptist. It had been a special challenge to preach at the Baptist church in Warsaw. My interpreter turned out to be a communist who had no idea what I was saying about the Bible. Finally, he had to be replaced. This was all my fault. It was my responsibility to secure an interpreter, and I unwittingly selected a committed Polish communist. Two books came from my studies in the USSR. Also there were television appearances.[4] We were in the middle of the Cold War with the Soviets, and the few people who visited the Soviet Union were in demand by the media.

Scrutiny by the FBI

Following my return to the United States in 1957, the FBI began investigating me and continued to do so until 1974. The bureau's interest appeared to focus on a small book I wrote on communism and on my relationship with Dr. Jerome Davis. Some of my mail arrived already opened. I was audited by the Internal Revenue Service.

In the spring of 1969 FBI investigation intensified when my son, Wayne, became a draft-resister in protest against the War in Vietnam and left the country for Sweden. Unannounced, two FBI agents appeared at my home to interrogate my wife and me. They came again a few weeks later. Helen and I both became angry. I told the agents never to come to my home again. If they wanted to interview me, I said, they would have to make an appointment and meet me in my office at the seminary.

On 19 November 1970 I received a note from David A. Walters, Special Agent with the FBI, declaring that he had tried unsuccessfully to contact me at my office. While I cannot say how many FBI agents listened in on my classroom lectures, I do know that at least one agent stood outside my classroom door while I was speaking. He took me in tow for another round of questioning when the class was over. On another occasion, an agent came to my office to interview me. As he began the now-familiar line of questions I interrupted him and said, "These are the same old stupid questions I have been asked over and over again." I then uncovered a tape recorder on my desk and asked, "You don't mind this conversation being taped do you?" He became immediately angry, jumped out of his chair, grabbed his coat and declared that the conference was ended. I pressed my

---

[4] The 16 April 1957 *Louisville Times* reported my guest appearance on "Small Talk."

advantage, making the point that it was only fair I tape the conversation since the FBI taped my telephone calls. Maybe he felt a bit of sympathy for me at that point, because he simmered down and we proceeded with the interview.

In 1971, I was on sabbatical as a visiting professor in the environmental engineering department at the University of Florida in Gainesville. Helen and the children decided they wanted to live in DeLand. So, I commuted the seventy miles to the university by bus, often spending the night at the Baptist Student Union in Gainesville. We had been in DeLand about three weeks when an FBI agent knocked on our back door. I told him that he should have come to the front door. He insisted he could not gain access to the front door through the locked screen door. That screen door, however, had no lock. Helen appeared and launched into the agent with such a severe—but proper—"talking to" that I actually began to feel sorry for him!

Back in Louisville following the sabbatical leave, I received more visits from the FBI. Marion Barnett, a student at Southern Seminary, informed me that in April 1973 an FBI agent—Thomas Fitzgerald, the same man who had stood outside the classroom eavesdropping on my lectures only two years before—called him after mistaking his name in the directory for Henlee Barnette. I resorted to my foundational pedagogical principle—listen both to those with whom you agree and disagree—and invited the regional supervisor of the FBI to address my Christian ethics classes. My students at least had the opportunity to learn some valuable things about the agency.

Seven years into Wayne's exile, a court ruled that he had been illegally drafted, because he had never been sent the proper paperwork. The Attorney General of Kentucky welcomed him back to the USA without prejudice or condition. Wayne and his wife Ann returned home 10 March 1974, bringing with them my six-year-old granddaughter Jennifer, whom we had never seen. Shortly afterward, the FBI advised me that the agency had put an end to its efforts to investigate me—after seventeen years.

12

Crisis at the School of the Prophets

What is the cause of fighting and quarrelling that goes on
among you?
—James 4:1 (TCNT)

From 1956 to 1959, I served as the first Acting Dean of the School of Theology at the Southern Baptist Theological Seminary. The seminary had grown, and now included schools of theology, religious education and church music. The latter two had full-time deans. I was to serve until a theology dean could be secured, and being the first dean for that school, I had few precedents to follow. Hence, I requested input from the theological faculty to help me with the new responsibility.

Shortly after assuming my role as acting dean, I was walking in Norton Hall with my friend and colleague, Professor T. D. Price. He looked down at me (he was six feet, four inches tall) and said "Barney, do you know what an acting dean is? An acting dean is a mouse with the aspiration to be a rat." Dr. Price had a dry sense of humor and, probably because he did love me, he did not spare me the occasional friendly barb. He was, to be sure, a part of the unanimous faculty vote that had resulted in my taking the position.

In the meantime, tensions arose over the right of the faculty to make major decisions affecting the seminary's curriculum, as well as those touching on employment and promotions of faculty members. Some faculty, especially those educated in the Northeast's Ivy League schools, desired that Southern evolve as more of an independent divinity school rather than as a seminary bound in close relationship to the denomination's churches.

By 1958 the tension became open conflict. Thirteen professors joined together for the purpose of demanding full participation in the administration of the academic affairs of the School of Theology, including the right to choose the dean. As Acting Dean, I was never invited to the numerous meetings that took place between the thirteen and the seminary's administration. My responsibility was to keep the school of theology functioning despite the ongoing dispute between some on the faculty and the seminary's president. On 11 March these thirteen faculty members brought formal charges against the president in a "Supplementary Report" delivered to a committee of seminary trustees who had been constituted to investigate the troubling situation. The group's report was specific. It concluded, "[President McCall] by word, act, and temperament, has lost our respect, confidence, and trust. We therefore, appeal to the Trustees to help us resolve our difficulties."

The charges leveled included a purposeful failure by McCall to allow faculty a meaningful role in the conduct of the seminary's affairs, specifically in the choice of a dean for the School of Theology. The thirteen desired William Morton, Professor of Archaeology, to assume the position. Dr. McCall favored Dr. H. C. Goerner, Professor of Missions. Goerner ultimately declined the president's proposal and took a position with the Foreign Mission Board of the Southern Baptist Convention.

Plagiarism was also included among the charges brought against Dr. McCall. The Sunday School Board of the Southern Baptist Convention, through Broadman Press, had engaged Duke McCall to write a book of Sunday School lessons titled *Broadman Comments*. He discovered he did not have time to do the research for the lessons. He paid several professors to do that part of the work for him. It was to be, in the minds of some of the retained professors, "starter data" from which the president would get ideas and reshape the materials to reflect his own thinking. When the book was published, some of the thirteen who had been paid to be Dr. McCall's research writers, alleged that their background materials had been published almost verbatim under the president's name. Hence, they charged him with plagiarism.

I had also contracted with Dr. McCall to do research for the book related to the problem of justice in life. I was paid for my efforts and happy to do so. While a paragraph here and there appeared largely to be mine, it did not seem objectionable. Disagreement also arose over another book about the centennial history of the seminary. Dr. McCall had been named as the project's final author. Dr. William Mueller had understood that the book was to be his responsibility. Dr. McCall, however, noted that three or four others had also been assigned work for the volume.

The trustee committee received the Supplementary Report, but sided with the president in the dispute. The unhappy professors then sent the report to all fifty-five trustees. In a cover letter, they demanded the matter be settled according to their preferences and additionally informed the trustees that "if we receive no specific proposal from the Board of Trustees, you may expect to receive our resignations."[1]

While the board stood by Dr. McCall in the matter, they instructed him to do all he could to effect reconciliation. The date 12 June 1958 was set for a plenary meeting of the trustees in Louisville to hear the president's recommendations and to give the professors a full hearing as well.

When the meetings began, the thirteen professors refused to retract their charges against Dr. McCall and he reported failure to accomplish reconciliation. President McCall and Dr. Allen Graves, Dean of the School of Religious Education, came by my office that day and reported that they had agreed to accept the resignations of the thirteen. Dr. McCall asked if I was in agreement. My answer was in the affirmative. The Board of Trustees, however, dismissed them on 12 June before the resignations could be accepted. Duke McCall did not, as often is charged, fire the thirteen faculty members; it was a decision and action taken by Southern's Board of Trustees.

The professors who had been dismissed were:

Thomas O. Hall, Jr., Old Testament
John M. Lewis, Christian Theology
J. Morris Ashcraft, Biblical Theology
W. L. Lumpkin, Church History
J. Estill Jones, New Testament
William H. Morton, Biblical Archeology
Guy H. Ranson, Christian Ethics
T. D. Price, Church History
John J. Owens, Old Testament

---

[1] Chauncey Daley, "The Southern Baptist Seminary Controversy," *Western Recorder* (5 June 1958): 6.

Heber Peacock, New Testament
G. Hugh Wamble, Church History
Henry E. Turlington, New Testament
T. C. Smith, New Testament

Drs. Hall, Lewis, Lumpkin, Jones and Turlington eventually accepted calls to pastoral positions. Drs. Morton, Price, Smith and Wamble took positions in other Baptist colleges and seminaries. Dr. Peacock became a translator for a Bible society. After teaching at Midwestern and Southeastern Baptist Seminaries, Dr. Ashcraft became the acting president of a new Baptist Seminary in Richmond, Virginia. Dr. Ranson went on to teach at Trinity College in Texas. Of the thirteen, only Dr. Owens eventually returned to his former position at Southern.

Immediately after the thirteen faculty members were let go, Dr. McCall told me, "It is your task to replenish the faculty." After numerous sessions with the remaining faculty, we came up with the names of competent individuals to serve on the faculty and recommended to the president that they be considered. I invited each of the candidates to the campus for a couple of days during which they met the faculty and employment negotiations took place with the president. Twelve new faculty, two former faculty, and an additional five specialized instructors were employed.

Dr. Joseph A. Callaway was chosen to teach Old Testament and Archeology. The Archeological Museum of the seminary is named in his honor.

Dr. C. Allyn Russell was called to teach Church History. He would later become Chairman of the Department of Religion at Boston University.

Dr. J. J. Owens was persuaded to return to his former post as an Old Testament professor. Each year since, I received a note from him thanking me for encouraging him to come back. He was a superb teacher, scholar and the author of four massive volumes on the Hebrew Bible.

Dr. Ray Summers, New Testament scholar and formerly a professor at Southwestern Baptist Theological Seminary in Fort Worth, Texas. He eventually became Chairman of the Baylor University Graduate School.

Dr. Willis Bennett, a Christian ethicist, came to Southern from the pastorate of Red Springs Baptist Church in North Carolina. Bennett became Provost of Southern Seminary.

Dr. Earle Ellis, who is now recognized as a leading New Testament scholar and an authority on the Gospel of Luke.

Dr. William Hull came to Southern as a New Testament professor. He published significant academic works, as well as more popular books and articles for ministry. Hull also served Southern Seminary as Provost.

Dr. Jerry Vardaman joined Dr. Calloway as a teacher of Old Testament and Archeology. He would later direct the Cobb Institute of Archeology at Mississippi University.

Dr. Samuel Southard became a member of the Department of Psychology of Religion and Pastoral Care. He became a respected author, writing several books about pastoral care.

Dr. Leo Garrett, Historical Theology, came from Southwestern Baptist Theological Seminary. A well known academic contributor to his field, Garrett later returned to the Fort Worth seminary as a Distinguished Professor.

Dr. James Cox came from the pastorate in Johnson City, Tennessee. He was for years the publishing editor of the hugely popular (*Doran's*) *Ministers Manual*.

Dr. Hugo Culpepper was added to the Missions Department. He was a distinguished missionary, administrator and teacher.

Dr. Penrose St. Amant became Professor of Church History and Dean of the School of Theology. I had informed Dr. J. Washington Watts, Acting President of New Orleans Baptist Seminary, that I was contacting Dr. St. Amant about joining the Southern Seminary faculty. I thought it was the courteous thing to do. He wrote back, charging me with "robbing" his seminary of its faculty. From the inception of the seminary at New Orleans, Louisville's Southern Seminary had provided it both with presidents and many faculty members. I thought it high time that the New Orleans seminary should come to aid of its Mother School.

Dr. Clyde Francisco, Professor of Old Testament, returned to Southern after having taught for a period at Southwestern Seminary. He had originally departed Southern because of perceived theological differences with many of the thirteen professors who had just lost their positions in Louisville.

W. Morgan Patterson arrived to teach Church History. Page Kelley came to teach Old Testament Interpretation. Instructors were added to the teaching staff, most being doctoral students. Henry Durham, Ronald

Deering and Clayton Sullivan taught New Testament courses. Robert Cate and Matthew Pierce Matheney, Jr., took on teaching course in the Old Testament. Deering eventually became the seminary's librarian. The others became professors in seminaries and universities.

My efforts to persuade Drs. Heber Peacock and Henry Turlington (New Testament) to return to their former posts at Southern failed. My "magnificent recruiting failure" was Dr. Robert Bratcher. He was formerly a missionary professor at the Baptist seminary in Rio de Janeiro, Brazil, and then later a translator for the American Bible Society. Bratcher declined the offer to join the faculty at Southern because he had misgivings about President McCall. It is of note that he later translated the *Good News New Testament*. Had he accepted a faculty appointment in Louisville, I doubt he would have been able to produce the New Testament translation which was published in the millions.[2]

I also invited Dr. Frank Stagg to join the faculty. He declined in 1958, leaving open the possibility for a future time. He became a part of the Southern Seminary teaching community in 1960s.

With the faculty largely replenished and the new dean on board, I took a great deal of satisfaction in my role in the recovery of the seminary's hope for the future. My task completed, I resigned as Acting Dean of the School of Theology. In the interim, I had been awarded a Faculty Fellowship by the Commission of the American Association of Theological Schools to do research at Harvard University.

---

[2] For more data on the rebuilding of the faculty of Southern Seminary see:

Louisville Times (18 July 1958) Section 2, p.1; *Courier-Journal*, (13 July 1958) Section 1, p.1; *Courier-Journal* (17 July 1958) Section 2 p.1; *Western Recorder* (17 July 1958) p.4; *The Tie* (September 1958) 3.

For President Duke K. McCall's views on the crisis, see *Duke McCall: An Oral History* with A. Ronald Tonks, Baptist History and Heritage Society (Nashville: Brentwood and Fields Publishing Inc., 2001.)

13

Harvard Highlights

One of the next things we longed for and looked after was to advance learning and perpetuate it to posterity; dreading to leave an illiterate ministry to the churches, when our present ministers shall lie in dust.
—Founding of Harvard in 1636

Helen, John, Wayne, Martha and I moved to Sacramento Street in Cambridge, Massachusetts, in the fall of 1959. This was a poor section of the city, and it was the most we could afford. The children entered Agassiz and Cambridge Latin High School. Helen and I took German courses in Harvard Yard. I studied with great teachers: Paul Tillich (Religion, Art and Science), Amos Wilder (New Testament), James Luther Adams (Ethics) and heard other distinguished scholars lecture on special occasions.

A special highlight of the experience was attending worship at Harvard Memorial Church. Pastor George Buttrick was one of the most well known and influential American preachers in the twentieth century. In addition, there were the occasional sermons of Drs. Paul Tillich, Robert McCracklin (Riverside Church, New York City), Reinhold Niebuhr and his brother H. Richard Niebuhr. Tillich and Dean Samuel Miller also gave lectures on the arts.

Dr. Buttrick's pastoral ministries and preaching filled the once nearly empty church to capacity with worshippers each Sunday. It was most impressive to see Dr. Nathan Pusey, President of Harvard University, rise from the congregation, walk to the podium and read from the Hebrew Scriptures, followed by Dr. Buttrick who read the Christian Scriptures.

Dr. Tillich had class in Harvard's old Emerson Hall where Ralph Waldo Emerson, William James the psychologist, and other notables gave lectures in their day. Twice a week we listened to Tillich, but I fear few of us comprehended much of what he was saying. His assistant came one day each week to explain what Tillich had said.

As an aside, at that time a New Orleans Baptist Seminary professor had been fired for publishing a book titled, *Saved By His Life*, in which he referred to Tillich, and for referring on a positive note to the Harvard teacher in his own class lectures. Upon my return from the sabbatical in New England, a professor at Southern asked if it was true that I had studied with Tillich. I confessed I was guilty. My colleague wanted to know what effect the experience had on me. "None," I replied. "I never did find out what he was talking about!" I still chuckle when recalling that exchange! I am grateful for Tillich's concept of the Protestant Principle and for his efforts to state biblical truths in modern categories.

Back in our humble quarters on Sacramento Street, I was attempting to write my first book on a tin-topped table. When I finally finished it, I was disappointed and went to the kitchen to tell Helen that it was a failure. I returned to the table, threw the manuscript in the waste can, and got back up from the table to leave. Helen had followed me to my place of defeat, ordered me to sit back down and "do it right." I guess I did as I had been ordered. Broadman Press published the book in 1961. It has been translated to Chinese, Korean and, I am told, other languages. It has gone through several English editions. In 2004, after more than forty years, *Introducing Christian Ethics* is still in print and not a word has been changed. It recently came out in paperback.

While at I was at Harvard a search committee from Baylor University issued me an invitation to serve as Chairman of the Department of Religion and to develop there a graduate school of religion. Helen pointedly reminded me that I did not like administrative work. Again, she was more than right. Nevertheless, it was with great reluctance that I turned down the gracious invitation. It proved, however, to be a wise decision. My remaining years at the Southern Baptist Theological Seminary were exciting and enriching for my family and me.

The Harvard experience is unique and, relatively speaking, only a few people have the opportunity to enjoy it. By recounting some of the events from my first week there, as well as other highlights from my year at the school, I hope to share something of the marvelous depth of that rich academic environment.

Convocation Week 1959

Harvard University was founded in 1636, only sixteen years after the Pilgrims landed at Plymouth Rock. Henry Dunster, a Baptist, was the school's first president. On the wall at the main entrance to the university is inscribed:

> After God had carried us safe to New England, and we had builded our houses, provided necessaries for our livelihood, rear'd convenient places for God's worship, and settled the civil government: One of the next things we longed for and looked after was to advance learning and perpetuate it to posterity; dreading to leave an illiterate ministry to the churches, when our present ministers shall lie in dust.

Harvard Divinity School's 1959 convocation week exercises stand out in my mind as the most exhilarating academic experiences of which I have been a part. At the beginning of the week's events, the new students assembled as a body to be initiated into the academic community's life. Dean Samuel Miller gave us warm and thorough introduction to the school. Incidentally, Dr. Miller was the first Baptist ever to hold the position of Dean of the Divinity School. He was a scholarly man who carried himself with great dignity and grace. He reminds me a great deal of Dr. Sampey in his appearance. He welcomed the new students to this community of learning to share in the battle of ideas and the adventure of rigorous and arduous academic pursuits. He quoted poet William Blake: "Stars and souls are threshed from their husks." Dr. Miller noted that there must be some threshing of our souls from the husks of prejudice and the sloughing off of unauthentic aspects of our lives if we were to come to understand our own truest identities.

Registrar Conrad Wright next offered the assembled student body some facts about the composition of the newest crop of learners at the Harvard Divinity School. Among us were forty-six beginning B.D. students, twenty-seven graduate students pursuing Th.M., Th.D. and Ph.D. degrees, and eleven unclassified special students. The new class included forty-three married students with forty-one children and three more on the way! Fifteen students were from New England, thirty from the Northeast to as far west as the Mississippi, thirteen from below the Mason-Dixon Line, sixteen from states west of the Mississippi and eight from foreign countries.

The divinity school required that students engage in rigorous academic work and participate in the more pragmatic experiences of ministry through assigned fieldwork. Dr. Paul Lehmann (Department of Theology) made a few comments to that regard. He said that fieldwork tended to make students "prematurely wise" in their own conceit about church work. He went on to affirm that fieldwork would help committed students avoid intellectual sterility.

On that first afternoon we reconvened at Wellesley Human Relations Clinic where Dr. Erich Lindemann, head of Harvard's Psychiatric Clinic and one of the leading psychiatrists in the world, led us in a discussion concerning "The Church and Resources in Preventative Therapy." I have met few persons with keener minds. In the course of his remarks, Dr. Lindemann observed that in the giant Massachusetts Hospital Outpatient Clinic only twenty per cent of patients under care had a *bona fide* medical problem. He asserted that four-fifths of those being treated had mental, not medical, problems!

In the evening we gathered at the Divinity School to attend a faculty forum dealing with "Faith and Idolatry: Promise and Menace of American Religion." Dean Miller set the stage by noting that American religion had an exuberance to it, but that it is spent on programs, organization and promotion. These, he said, do not lead to meaning at the deeper levels of life. Instead, American religion was largely characterized by ambiguity and idolatry. Professor Heiko Augustinus Obermann, a brilliant young historian from Holland, defined church history as the exciting and ongoing story of the tension between authentic faith and idolatry. He defined idolatry as the revolt of man against the invisibility of God. He suggested that when authentic religion fails to have a healthy impact on culture, the culture has an unhealthy impact on the church. He spoke of the "Americanization" of the Christian gospel, offering three reasons why religion in America tends to be idolatrous: (1) It attempts to make God visible, to domesticate the Divine; (2) it is characterized by an easy tolerance that is not grounded in an authentic and non-negotiable sense of conviction; (3) it identifies salvation with self-realization—that is, persons' efforts to find God in themselves and the propensity to identify salvation with the development of one's potential by one's own strength.

Professor G. Ernest Wright of the Old Testament Department dealt with the historical dimension of idolatry, noting that whatever infringes on the sovereignty of God is idolatry. He further opined that American churches have become great ecclesiastical institutions run by bureaucrats dealing with everything but real religion. He nevertheless concluded that in spite of the idolaters within the church, God is still able to use the church for God's own purposes. For that reason, declared Dr. Wright, he himself continued to remain a person of the church.

Dr. James Luther Adams of the Christian Ethics Department had an encyclopedic mind. He told of a Southern evangelist who gave an invitation at the conclusion of the service. In describing the horrors of hell, the evangelist said that there would be weeping and gnashing of teeth at the judgment. A man near the front said that he didn't have any teeth. Whereupon the preacher declared that teeth would be furnished. Then Dr. Adams proceeded to put teeth into the discussion. He said that idolatry is related to power and configurations, that it seeks to abstract a segment of the finite and bestow on it the quality of the infinite. He laid much of the blame for idolatry in American churches on an urbanized middle class mentality that is largely unaware of life's real tragic elements. He also linked idolatry to a devotion to pigmentation and the pursuit of power and property.

Dr. Paul Tillich, the famous Harvard philosopher, spoke of idolatries at the intellectual level—idols are not always graven images. I must say that he exhibited expertise with the concepts of the demonic and the ambiguous! Rather than addressing the "menace" of American religion, Dr. Tillich chose a positive path and dealt largely with the "promise" religion offers our society. He outlined that promise in three segments: (1) American religion has a future-directed mentality or attitude in terms of conquering the world for God. While it has taken as its pattern models of the Kingdom of God on earth and visions of Utopia, it nevertheless, has real value because of its future-directed perspective. (2) It reflects openness both in terms of space and mind. He noted that the conquest of the great American plains of the West became a symbol for all religious life in America. He was impressed as well with the "inner-openness" of the American mind in general—ready to listen to others speak about their anxiety, guilt and doubt whether from a religious or secular orientation. (3) Finally, the American religious experience was characterized by what he called a "new beginning." Its churches did not have to overcome the old, suffocating class structures that in previous centuries existed in Europe.

An interesting and exciting discussion of preachers' idolatries followed. Dr. Sam Miller noted that preachers tend to identify current cultural ideals with timeless Christian ideals. The result is that the church has no depth of spiritual value and, in this age, turns to the standards of "big business" to find a sense of validation: bigger buildings, more complex programs and ever-increasing membership rolls.

As the convocation week came to a close, Dean Miller gave a lecture titled "Art: Mirror of Faith and Idolatry." After he spoke, he led us on a tour of the university museums. Dr. Miller noted that art seeks to get back behind the surface to the deeper reality of things. It is there that artists seek revelation. Like theologians, artists often do not know what to say about reality. Artists, he explained, seek to reflect in their work that which has been revealed to them as participating in things that are eternal. Hence, we have Euclidian geometric figures, psychologically thematic works, paintings such as Picasso's stirring canvasses or even creative doodlings. All make an attempt to communicate something that has been revealed about deeper truths and authentic reality.

I will not soon forget our visit to the art collections from the European Middle Ages, reflecting the search for order or "humanity-made-whole." Dean Miller suggested that Middle Age's search for such order is especially evident in three manifestations: (1) in literature, such as Thomas Aquinas's *Summa Theologia*; (2) in architecture, such as in the rush to build cathedrals; (3) in much of the art of the time. Is this not also the task of present-day theologians—to pull together the fragments of life into a great and meaningful whole or harmony?

Notes from Around the "Yard"

Students at Harvard were generally cordial, especially those from the South. Most that I met took their studies very seriously. They had to in order to meet the exacting academic performance standards of the university's various schools. Perhaps some divinity students suffered under the press of complex theological and philosophical studies. The majority, however, were able to maintain perspective and humor in the midst of their academic trials. As evidence of such, the following creative verse was posted on a bulletin board at the Divinity School:

"Cry of the Junior"
Stiff, stagnant academicity,
Frozen forms and symbols,
Verbiage incomprehensible,
C'est la theologie!

Eschatology, exegesis,
Phenomenology, aphorism,
Allegory, category,
Das ist theologie!

Kant, Kierkegaard,
Feuerbach, Schleiermacher,
Rauschenbusch, Kattenbusch,
That's theology!

Transcendentalism, speculativism,
Hermeneutics, homiletics,
Evolution, revolution,
Intellectualism?....Hell!

Professor James Luther Adams was my professor in Christian Social Ethics. A brilliant scholar, he was known as the "intellectual clearing house of Harvard." He translated many of Paul Tillich's works, most notably *The Protestant Era*. Dr. Adams also published a small number of his own writings. Among these was a small volume, *Taking Time Seriously*, in which he discussed the priesthood and prophethood of the believers. Dr. Adams argued that the roots of contemporary democracy were to be found in the teachings of the radical reformers and the primitive church.

I took all the courses I could with Professor Adams, but I missed his most widely known course on volunteerism. I owe much to Professor Adams in terms of developing my own passion for learning. I was privileged to maintain friendly correspondence with him for years after my stay at Harvard. His death on 26 July 1994 was a significant loss to the scholarly world and its academic enterprise. We often corresponded. He attended a meeting of the American Association of Christian Ethics on the campus of Southern Baptist Theological Seminary in 1962. Because of a mix-up in schedule Adams had to leave early. This was a great disappointment for him. In a letter dated 30 January 1962 he writes: "What a pity that, on my one visit to Southern, I had to make such a quick getaway. And this meant I didn't get a chance for a talkfest with you….It was a delight indeed to get acquainted with that charming lady, Mrs. Barnette."

During the year in Massachusetts I renewed my friendship with Rollin Armour, a former student in my class in Christian Ethics at Southern Seminary. He completed his doctoral program at Harvard that year and began the process of searching for a teaching position. He interviewed for an assistant professorship in Church History at the Southern Baptist Theological Seminary but was rejected upon "crossing swords" with at least one member of the search committee. When he told me the discouraging news, I picked up the telephone, called a friend at Stetson University in Florida and recommended Rollin as a fine teaching candidate. Dr. Armour spent several years at Stetson and then was called to the chairmanship of the Department of Religion at Auburn University in Alabama. From there he moved to Mercer University (Macon, Georgia) where he served in the capacity of dean. Not an unimportant aside, his doctoral dissertation was of such good caliber that it won the prestigious Brown Prize and was published by Harvard University Press.

Another highlight at Harvard was getting to know Dr. Samuel Miller, Dean of the Divinity School. He was a gracious and brilliant man who welcomed Helen and me in his home along with other students. He loved art and took us on tours of museums, carefully explaining artists' purposes and methods. Dean Miller's hope was to reconnect the Divinity School to the churches and set the Divinity School in that direction before retirement.

I have followed the fortunes of Harvard for more than forty years. It is perhaps the richest University in the world. During a recent fundraising campaign, the amount given to the institution came to one-and-a-half billion dollars. I also have had the privilege and opportunity to provide input to the school's Presidential Search Committee when a new leader was being sought in 2000 and 2001. I shared my thoughts about academic and institutional leadership in the following letter:

September 18, 2000
Dr. Robert G. Stone, Jr.
Harvard University Presidential Search Committee
Loeb House, 17 Quincy Street
Cambridge, Massachusetts 02138

Dear Dr. Stone:

At your request I am listing the qualifications I think essential to presidential leadership of Harvard University in this new millennium.

1. Our new president must have a vision of what Harvard University should be in a radically changing culture. "Without a vision the people perish," so says the ancient prophet, and so will universities that lack a vision. It must be a vision of wholeness, inclusiveness, seen from many angles of vision.

2. Harvard's president must be aware that it takes more than a vision to lead a great university. He or she must have energy and boldness to flesh out the vision in concrete ways.

3. Accomplishing this goal demands a person of competency who can articulate the vision clearly, comprehensively, accurately and cogently.

4. Another quality is the power to see things through, the will to get things done and the energy to finish the job. Such power is related to being possessed by a compelling cause; in the president's case, complete devotion to shaping a university of academic excellence and ethical action.

5. The president must be a person of compassion, sensitive to the needs, hurts and hopes of all souls in the Harvard community. Compassion without justice is pure sentiment. Justice must extend to all for the enrichment of the quality of life in the university and the world community. The circle of compassion embraces all of God's creatures and creation.

6. In this ever-changing digital age a wise president will lash the university to those realities that "changeth not," that provide stability and soundness for academic excellence. In short, it will be the task of the president by precept and practice to keep the university anchored in spiritual realities and moral principles of practice.

May Harvard continue to be an academic community of faith, learning and action.

Sincerely,
Henlee Barnette, Ph.D.

Through the years I have been an active member of the Harvard Club of Kentucky. We provide a book for each student entering Harvard from our district. We also enjoy distinguished speakers from the school and good fellowship at our regular gatherings.

Home Again

In the fall of 1960 we moved back to Louisville from Cambridge. We had come to love that area: Boston, Cape Cod and Concord. Soon we were busier than ever. I introduced several new courses in Christian Ethics and continued to serve as Book Review Editor for the *Review and Expositor*, a responsibility I maintained through 1966. It is a matter of some satisfaction to me that the criteria I set for book reviews and the review section organization are still in use by the journal nearly forty years later.

In 1961 I was elected to the Board of Directors of the American Society of Christian Ethics, which was comprised of leading scholars in the field in America. In 1961 I invited Dr. Martin Luther King, Jr. to lecture to the Christian Ethics classes at Southern Seminary. His visit was, to say the least, historic.

In the midst of the swirl of academic life, Helen and I were blessed with a son: James Randolph. He was born on 21 March 1961 at the Kentucky Baptist Hospital in Louisville. These days, Jim is Minister to the University and a teacher in the Department of Religion at Samford University in Birmingham, Alabama.

14

Race Relations

Of a truth I perceive that God is no respecter of persons.
—St. Peter (Acts 10:34)

In both the 1950s and 1960s important actions in race relations occurred in the seminary and beyond. The Southern Baptist Convention (SBC) met in Chicago 28–31 May 1957 in the International Amphitheater. About 12,000 persons attended the sessions. After being introduced to the convention by Arkansas Congressman Brooks Hays, the new president of the Southern Baptist Convention, I spoke to the report of the Christian Life Commission of the Convention calling for the guarantee of African Americans' civil rights. The Rev. W. M. Nevins of Lexington, Kentucky, rose to his feet on a point of personal privilege to deny my implication that those opposed to integration were acting in an unchristian manner. Rev. Nevins declared: "I love the Negro and would fight to defend his rights, but I am opposed to amalgamation of the races to which integration inevitably leads. I would like to ask for unanimous consent to have all reference to integration stricken from the convention records of the year."

As he left the platform audible shouts of "no" followed him. The convention accepted my complete speech for the record and proceeded with its business. That was a significant step forward for Southern Baptist life in race relations. Reports of the incident appeared in the print and broadcast media, including the *Dallas Morning News*, the *Charlotte Observer* and the *Chicago Daily Tribune*.[1]

As I left the meeting, Dr. James Baker Cauthen, president of the SBC's Foreign Mission Board, stopped and thanked me for the speech. He believed

---

[1] *Chicago Daily Tribune* (1 June 1957): I-8.

it an important contribution to the board's own endeavors at improving relations between blacks and whites on the mission field.

This procedural and practical victory for race relations at the Convention level also spurred efforts to integrate the faculty at the Southern Baptist Theological Seminary. On 23 September 1967, in a joint faculty meeting, President Duke K. McCall announced that the seminary trustees' Executive Committee had discussed the employment of a black person as a fulltime member of the faculty[2]. The president noted that two of the seminary's schools had already proposed such an addition. The Dean of the School of Religious Education, Dr. Allen Graves, had suggested it in conference and members of School of Theology had proposed the same in writing. Dr. McCall also noted the Trustees had declared, "No one will be elected to the faculty because of race or rejected because of race." The president told us that action by the seminary to integrate the faculty was to be pursued with great care. But many of us felt it could be delayed no longer.

The Christian Ethics Department quickly proposed that Dr. George Kelsey, Dean of Drew University Divinity School, be invited to the seminary campus with a view to election to the faculty. He was a Baptist, well-informed in the area of Christian Ethics, having earned his Ph.D. in that subject at Yale University Divinity School. His dissertation was about Southern Baptists and issues related to ethics.

As a student at Yale, Kelsey had visited our campus while doing research for his doctoral dissertation. I had invited him to use my office in Norton Hall. During that time, if he had wanted to eat in a restaurant Kelsey would have had to travel to Louisville's West End Louisville, the black community, to be served. Restaurants in the East End, where the seminary was located, were segregated.

Dr. Kelsey was officially invited by President McCall to come to Southern Seminary for a conference on 4 February 1968. He ultimately declined the seminary's offer of a professorship in Christian Ethics, choosing instead to remain as dean at Drew Divinity School.

---

[2] Duke McCall had previously approved the appointment of Emmanuel Dahunsi—a Nigerian student at the seminary in the 1950s—as an instructor in New Testament studies.

Other efforts were made to bring a black professor on board in the Christian Ethics Department. George Thompson, holding a Ph.D. from the University of Chicago, and Pastor Emmanuel McCall were interviewed, but without success.

Black Church Studies

One of the attractive and successful programs at the Southern Baptist Theological Seminary has been Black Church Studies. It has influenced numerous blacks to attend the school. Today (2004) the seminary faculty includes a full professor of Black Church Studies.

On 14 October 1969, I proposed formally to a Historical/Theological Division committee of the seminary that we include in the Christian Ethics Departments two courses addressing Black Church Studies. The committee, consisting of Drs. Rust, Garrett, Mueller, Ward, Moody, Patterson and St. Amant unanimously approved the proposed courses.

The proposal was presented to the entire faculty 30 October 1969. One course was to be "The Black Church and Social Justice," taught by the Rev. Emmanuel McCall, whose crendentials included the B.D. and M.Div. from Southern Seminary, and the D.D. from Simmons University. We also recommended another course titled "The Black Church in American Society." Recommended to teach the course was Rev. Wilbert H. Goatley, who had earned the B.D. at Southern and the D.D. from Simmons. He was as well a respected authority on Black Baptist history.

Although we were careful to follow each step in the process of designing and requesting the new courses related to Black Studies, we were charged by some decision-makers with not following the rules as required. There were also complaints raised that Emmanuel McCall and Goatley were not academically qualified to teach the courses. The proposal was initially rejected.

Despite the first setbacks, a program in Black Studies finally was established at the school. Dr. Emmanuel McCall was retained as a teacher. His primary course offering, a January Term course—"The Black Church and Social Justice"—was a great success over the more than twenty years that he taught it. Emmanuel McCall did more than any other person to attract black students to the seminary.

Southern Seminary, slow to sponsor Black Studies, was not slow to find enormous public relations value in the program. After it was launched and began to gain strength, an attractive brochure was printed to promote the seminary and its Black Studies offerings. The brochure's cover sported bold white letters on a solid black background. Inside were photos of black students and excerpts of their testimonials about what the seminary meant to them. The piece also described the valuable resources available in terms of scholarships, student services, competent faculty, a superior library, and of course, Black Church Studies.

By 2003, Black Church Studies at Southern Seminary has grown into an academic department and is directed by a full professor, Dr. T. Vaughn Walker. He is an African American and pastor of a black Baptist church. He holds B.S., M.S., M.Div. and Ph.D. degrees. The seminary's Black Church Studies curriculum includes six courses related to the Black Church.

Civil Rights and the Seminary Community

Most students at Southern Baptist Theological Seminary in the 1940s and 1950s favored racial integration in American society, and especially in churches and theological institutions. In March of 1950 the results of a student opinion poll taken at Southern showed that of 714 students, 94.7% favored admitting blacks to seminary classes. When I arrived in 1951, I met no faculty members opposed to the admission of blacks to the school.

As early as 1947 I began to participate in the civil rights movement that was growing across America. It was my privilege to be a founding member of the Kentucky Christian Leadership Conference (KCLC), an affiliate of the Southern Christian Leadership Conference (SCLC). The organization was brought to life in Louisville on 15 April 1965 at Mount Lebanon Baptist Church.

Dr. Garland Offutt, the first African American to graduate with a Ph. D. from Southern Baptist Theological Seminary (1944), presided over a called meeting to organize the KCLC. Dr. Offutt stated that Kentucky needed a Christian civil rights organization. Immediately, the Rev. W. J. Hodge, then president of the National Association for the Advancement of Colored People of Kentucky (NAACP/K), rose to his feet and responded that a local Christian civil rights organization already existed, namely the state affiliate of the NAACP. As the discussion progressed, the Rev. A. D. Williams King, Pastor of Louisville's Zion Baptist Church and a brother of Dr. Martin Luther King, Jr., explained the relationship of an affiliate organization to parent SCLC. He sought as well to allay the fear of potential conflict between the SCLC and the NAACP.

Following some lively discussion, the group voted to proceed forward and establish the Kentucky Christian Leadership Conference. Dr. Offutt was elected temporary chairman and Mrs. Jasper Ward became the organization's first secretary. Dr. Offutt was authorized to appoint seven persons to a nominating committee that was to present a slate of prospective officers at a future date.

Dr. Offutt appointed the Rev. King chairman of a committee to draw up a constitution for KCLC. W. J. Hodge and I were also on the committee. This group met at the Zion Baptist Church and drew up a constitution. I insisted that a statement be added to exclude communists. A comprehensive statement was included that disallowed membership to members of subversive organizations. The first constitution was more of a "working draft." A number of changes were made over time as the organization got on its feet and better understood its mission.

Among the projects—most of them successful—engaged by the KCLC in the struggle for equality are included:

> 1965—Desegregation of hospital in Georgetown, Kentucky
> 1966—Desegregation of state-wide public accommodations
> 1967—Open Housing (Louisville)
> 1968—Open Housing (state-wide)
> 1968—Partnership in the Poor People's Campaign

The KCLC maintained a philosophy of nonviolence in the quest to establish broad-based civil rights for all Americans. In May of 1968, as it had in many other cities throughout the nation, tensions related to race issues spilled over into the streets of the city Louisville. The KCLC's office was located near the epicenter of the violent civil unrest. During six days of turbulence, the office remained open twenty-four hours a day as a center in which leaders met endeavoring to restore the peace. Officers and board members of the KCLC walked the streets and urged the crowds to disperse.

The KCLC worked with both black and white organizations interested in restoring harmony to the community, including Louisville's law enforcement and police forces. The KCLC also facilitated a meeting between the city's Board of Aldermen, Safety Director and Chief of Police and key representatives from within the black community. This was the first official meeting of the sort between city officials and the black community. It served to establish a productive and open line of communication between the city and its African American constituency.

Personal Glimpses

I received letters from many irate readers of my articles related to the civil rights movement published in various periodicals. The following letter is a typical sample of the responses received following the publication of one piece in which I called for racial integration in the local churches:

> Dear Sir:
> I help pay your salary, and I want you to know I strongly resent your segregation article published in Ohio Baptist Messenger (12 March 1964 issue).
> Publication of such tripe does no service to the cause of Christ as represented by Southern Baptists. Wise Southern Baptists long before your time knew that it was not practical to integrate white churches with colored people. From many talks I feel sure that self-respecting colored people don't want into white churches, and neither does self-respecting white people want to get into colored churches. Those wanting integration of churches are for most part Negro political groups and a few fuzzy white thinkers like you.
> You quote several Scriptures presumably showing that churches should be integrated. Had there been any quotes on integration, you would have used them, but I know as well as you that there are none. You do not seem to know, as I with little effort found out, that God created people into different races and nationalities. It is very reasonable to me that this was done for a purpose, and it is also reasonable to me that if God had wanted all people in the same church He would have made them more nearly alike. The hundreds, and likely thousands of different denominations, testify to created differences, all worshipping God in manners peculiarly suited to them.
> What you are doing can only divide Southern Baptists. Presumably you are aware of some of the Baptist leaders in the past like Campbell, Graves, Whitsett, Norris, Elliott and others who have tried to divide Southern Baptists, and the damage they did to the cause of Christ. You and a few others

are trying to do the very same thing and I hope you have the same success as they did, but hope that you are not able to accomplish the damage they did.

If you cannot see the impracticality of what you are doing, I suggest you resign your job and get off my back and a lot of other people's backs who struggle to pay your salary. You might offer yourself as a pastor for some colored church. Due to secular publicity you are getting some colored church might just take you. Then, try to integrate your church with white people. When you get into that hornet's nest, I believe you will see the impracticality of what you are advocating. Such stuff is Caesar's work. You remember what Jesus told the Pharisee about "rendering unto Caesar." When men like you get into Caesar's political business you are out of your field and inevitably will get burned.

I am writing in effect to the Editor of *Ohio Baptist Messenger* what I have written you.

To his credit, the letter writer did sign his name following the customary—if somewhat ironic—conclusion greeting phrase, "Yours very truly."

My response to the letter was as follows:

Dear Brother:

Forgive this belated reply to your letter of 19 March in which you expressed strong resentment against my article, "Southern Baptist Churches and Segregation," which appeared in the *Ohio Baptist Messenger*, 12 March 1964. Since you have written a similar letter to the editor of the *Ohio Baptist Messenger*, and because you helped to "pay my salary," I am sending this response to you.

I am grateful to all who help pay my salary. But I want to make it clear that no one is paying me to think like they think on all issues. As a Baptist, my conscience will not permit me to allow anyone to tell me what I must think or write. Now if I make statements that cannot be supported by the gospel of God, I deserve to be "called on the carpet." What I stated in the article is, I think, in the spirit of Christ and in keeping with the Scriptures.

Since you are so concerned about your part in my salary, I have engaged the services of a CPA who figures that your contribution to my salary through the Cooperative Program of the Southern Baptist Convention amounts to about three cents a year. That is true if you are an average giver. Hence, I am enclosing a check for $1.00, which will reimburse you for the past ten years and take care of the salary problem for the next twenty years with a bit left over.

Speaking of salaries, I think you brethren out in the hinterland should know that until a few years ago, seminary professors were still on depression salaries. They are not much better off now. It would be a fine thing if some of you brethren would insist that teachers in our seminaries be paid more adequate salaries, so that they would not have to engage so much in other activities to meet their financial responsibilities and to make it possible for some of their wives to give up their work outside of the home.

Editor L. M. Davis of the *Ohio Baptist Messenger* is a Christian, a Baptist and a man of integrity. He is editor of a Baptist paper that prints different points of view. This is true to the Baptist position, for no one Baptist can tell another what he has to believe or not believe about moral issues. The moment he does, he ceases to be a Baptist and assumes the role of God or a pope.

Now why can't we disagree without being disagreeable? As a Christian brother, I want to express my sincere appreciation for your letter. While I don't agree with your position on race, I will be the first to insist that you get your opinions aired in one of our state papers. I see that Editor Davis has already published your views on this matter in the Ohio Baptist Messenger. This is as it should be, for as Baptists we have the right to hear both sides of the question.

May the Lord help us to grow in grace, the grace of understanding and mutual respect.

Yours in Christ,
Henlee H. Barnette
Enclosure: Personal Check, $1.00

My correspondent wrote again. His second letter was just as interesting.

Dear Sir:
The letter I wrote you 14 March 1964 required no reply. When a letter came in from you about 13 May, it laid around the house until 31 May. Having to take a plane trip from which there are some chances of one not coming back, curiosity overcame me and your letter was opened and read. Only [because of] the fact that you enclosed some of your ill-gotten gains in your letter trying to make me a Judas Iscariot do I now go to typewriter to return same to you. I don't aim to have you put off such on me. You can answer to God for how you got it, not me.

It may be added here that I work for government, which is in fact the taxpayer and you and I enjoy no tax exemption privileges that you as a minister do. My loyalty and best efforts are and have been directed to yours and other people of this country's good. If my loyalty to this country ceases or is divided with our enemies, then you know what will happen to me in the sight of God and in your sight. If I took your tax money under such circumstances, I can well imagine what you would think of me.

Turning the thing around, you are, with some others, trying to divide Baptists. That is not loyalty to Baptists. Still you complain about not getting enough money for the divisive things you are doing. The laborer is worthy of his hire and you doubtless have just lit in a place where the pickings are poor. There are other places beside the Seminary where the money is bigger and I sincerely hope you find one. I hardly think it will be pastoring a colored church as I suggested, but with the rep you have picked up from getting into print, doubtless the money will flow freer now.

For your benefit I suggest that the Lord God has supplied all the money I have ever needed and I haven't had to put my wife out to work in competition in the market to support her and our family. Had I not put God first in my life and stewardship, the above would not have happened, I believe.

One last thing, "disagree without being disagreeable." We have no argument at all there. I disagree with friends in the faith at times and we are still friends, still Baptists. If I started putting my mouth in papers and books making them look like dogs, as you have done, our friendships would dissolve pretty quick. I wish you no success in what you are trying to do, and if you do not resign from the Baptists and go with those who are raising the current political struggle, it is plain to be seen that the cause of Christ is to take another setback it can ill afford to take.

Despite his apparent distaste for the likes of me, he nevertheless again remained "Yours very truly!"

Participation in the Civil Rights Movement

What follows is a brief chronological listing of my more significant speeches and other endeavors in support of or related to the American civil rights movement from the late 1940s through the 1960s:

1947   Organized Interracial Baptist Pastor's Conference, Birmingham, Alabama, at Sixteenth Street Baptist Church.

Spoke at Jefferson County, Alabama, Negro Teachers Association in favor of equal pay for black and white teachers in public schools.

Published an article on race relations in *Windows* magazine of the Southern Baptist Woman's Missionary Union.

Speech on race relations before the *Florida Baptist State Convention*, Daytona Beach, Florida. (See appendix.)

Speech on racial equality at Women's Missionary Union Convention, Winter Haven, Florida. (See appendix.)

1953   Speech on "Church-related Colleges Dilemma" at American Baptist Seminary (a school for blacks) in Nashville, Tennessee, during the Southern Baptist Convention of Theological Students.[3]

Speech on race relations before the Southern Baptist Convention meeting in Chicago, Illinois.

Participated in the inauguration of Willie Lawnse Holmes as tenth president of Simmons University, conducted at the Zion Baptist Church, Louisville, Kentucky.

1961   As chairman of Christian Ethics Department of the Southern Baptist Theological Seminary, sponsored the visit of Dr. Martin Luther King, Jr., to the Louisville school where he spoke in chapel and various classes.[4]

1961   The Alabama State group at Southern Baptist Theological Seminary, of which I was chairman, drew up a petition to the mayor of Louisville urging desegregation of public facilities.[5]

1961   My class in Christian Ethics involved in letters to the *Courier-Journal* and *Louisville Times* calling for equitable treatment in public services and employment.

1964   Freedom March on Frankfort, Kentucky (Capital) with Dr. Martin Luther King, Jr., Jackie Robinson and others for desegregation of public facilities and related issues.[6]

---

[3] Books at the American Baptist Seminary were ancient; many had Roman Numerals for pagination. At the 1957 Southern Baptist Convention in Houston TX, I spoke before the convention for about five minutes and pled for members to send books to the seminary. A couple of years later I encountered the president of that school. He informed me that so many books arrived they were still trying to find places to put them.

[4] Reported in the seminary catalog twenty-three years later: "We're Out to Change the World," *Catalogue* 1984–86, p. 16. Also see *Review and Expositor Vol. 93* (Winter 1996): 77–126.

[5] It was given to Dr. Martin Luther King, Jr., to present to the mayor. A layman's group of Alabama learned about it and demanded a copy of those who signed it. (Previously in the discussion group, a student stated: "Let's do it now, for when we get back to Alabama we will not be able to do this.") The laymen desired the names of the Alabama students so they could prevent them from becoming pastors in that state. The demand was not honored and the *Courier-Journal* did not publish the petition in deference to the students' well-being.

1965   Kentucky Christian Leadership Conference organized 15 April 1965 at the Mount Lebanon Baptist, Louisville, Kentucky.

1965   Operation Selma (a fundraiser) at Broadway Temple A.M.E. Church.

1967   Open Housing Workshop.

1967   Sold tickets for and attended NAACP banquet, Sheraton Hotel, Louisville, Kentucky.

1967   Operation Open Housing and march on Louisville's City Hall.

1967   Member, Interfaith Committee of Clergyman on Open Housing

1967   March on City Hall for Open Housing with Rev. A. D. Williams King.[7]

1967   Proposed the addition to the faculty at Southern Seminary of Dr. George Kelsey, an African American teaching at Drew Divinity School.

1968   Led a memorial at Southern Seminary's Chapel for Dr. Martin Luther King, Jr., following his assassination in Memphis, Tennessee, on 4 April 1968.

1969   Proposed courses on Black Church studies be included in the curriculum at the Southern Baptist Theological Seminary.

---

[6] My motives were as follows: The march on Frankfort was a religious one. It was announced that the march would have a religious character. Some leading pastors, including Baptists, were there. The same choir sang when I preached at the Kentucky State College the previous Sunday. The whole atmosphere of the march had a religious tone. It was also a moral march. Marchers were there in protest against discrimination and segregation of human beings in places of public accommodation in Kentucky.

[7] By 1967, Rev. A. D. Williams King had still not been invited by the administration at Southern Seminary to speak in chapel. When it came my turn to speak, I invited him to take my place. He also spoke that day in my Christian Ethics classes.

15

A Day in the Life of a King

Injustice anywhere is a threat to justice everywhere.
—Martin Luther King, Jr.
("Letter from a Birmingham Jail," 16 April 1963)

With respect to the struggle for civil rights in America, the highlight of the 1960s at Louisville's Southern Baptist Theological Seminary was the visit of Dr. Martin Luther King, Jr. on 19 April 1961. I had proposed that Dr. King be invited to give the Julian Brown Gay Lectures on Christian Ethics, and the invitation had been subsequently issued. The Christian ethics lectureship had been established and endowed by Mr. Julian Brown Gay, who was resident of Montgomery, Alabama, the heart of the segregated South.[1]

In his chapel speech, King spoke about "The Church on the Frontier of Racial Tension." There were as well many other tensions in the world at that time. President John F. Kennedy was beginning to deal with what would blossom into the Cuban Missile Crisis. American intelligence suspected that Soviet leader, Nikita Khrushchev, had begun to build in Cuba missile bases capable of launching nuclear warheads against the United States. Aerial reconnaissance verified this as fact in October 1962. Two days before King arrived on campus in Louisville, the ill-fated invasion of the Bay of Pigs, Cuba, had begun. In East Germany, the Berlin Wall was being built against the concerted objections of the United States and the free West.

In America, racial tensions were mounting. Prior to King's Louisville visit, he had successfully led the Montgomery Bus Boycott (1956). Public

---

[1] See *Review and Expositor* 93/1 (Winter 1996): 94, 112, which carries the story of King's visit.

schools were being pushed toward integration following the US Supreme Court's ruling in Brown vs. Board of Education (1954). Boycotts, sit-ins, marches and other forms of protest against discrimination and segregation were spreading across the South and reaching into other regions of the United States. Organizations advocating racial equality were increasingly well organized. Among these were the Southern Christian Leadership Conference (SCLC). The Student Nonviolent Coordinating Committee—established in Raleigh, North Carolina, just three days before King's Southern Seminary lectureship—was sponsored by the SCLC.

Racial tensions in Louisville were also running high. Protest demonstrations aimed at integrating public facilities were occurring in the downtown area. On 15 April, four days before King arrived, black students conducted sit-in protests at ten eating places. Four of the establishments began serving blacks immediately, while three others followed suit only after prolonged protest action. Two of the targeted restaurants closed rather than integrate. Demonstrations in the city continued during King's stay at Southern Seminary. On 20 April more than 140 black persons were arrested while demonstrating in restaurants or at lunch counters.[2]

Dr. Allen Graves met Dr. King at Standiford Airport on the morning of 19 April and brought him to the seminary. Here King was introduced to other members of the lectureship committee: Drs. Nolan P. Howington, Willis Bennett, Wayne Ward and James Leo Garrett, Jr. In my office that morning, King, Graves, Howington and I talked for a while and were photographed by Otto Spangler, a student employee in the Seminary's Public Relations Office. I presented King with a copy of my book, *Introducing Christian Ethics,* and he graciously thanked me for it. He hinted that he had already read it.

From my office, we made our way to the chapel to hear King speak at 10:00 A.M. The chapel was packed and many people had to stand around the walls. A reporter from the *Courier-Journal* estimated that 1,400 people were present for the occasion.[3] "The Church on the Frontier of Racial Tension" was the subject of King's address. In summary, King declared that integration was not merely a political problem but a moral one. The old

---

[2] See *Courier-Journal* (21 April 1961): I-14. Such was the political and social climate and context surrounding King's visit.

[3] Ora Spaid, "Dr. King says 'Segregation is dead'" *Courier-Journal* (20 April 1961): 14.

order (racial segregation) is passing away, he said, and the church must help make the new order possible. First, the church must develop a worldwide perspective: we must learn "to live together as brothers or we will perish as fools." Moreover, he counseled, the church can reveal the true intention of the African American to society by clarifying the ideological roots of racial prejudice. It must be made clear, Dr. King stated, that the black man's basic aim is to be the white man's brother and not his brother-in-law. It is, King insisted, incumbent upon the Christian church to develop a program of action to attain the moral goals of integration. Wherever there is economic injustice, segregation within the church itself, and racial discrimination, the church must act. Creative love (*agape*)—redemptive good will toward all people—is the type of love that must guide the church and Christians through the time of transition.

After chapel Dr. Howington, Frank Stanley, Jr. (son of the editor of the *Louisville Defender*, a newspaper for the black community) and I accompanied King to the Student Center in Norton Hall which was under the direction of my sister, Mazo Barnette. Here we had coffee and cokes. Dr. John Claypool, pastor of Crescent Hill Baptist Church in Louisville, joined us. A picture of the group appeared in one of the local newspapers. (Ora Spaid, The *Courier-Journal*, 21 April 1961, 14) Claypool received some flack from his flock as a result of this incident.

Fortunately, following his chapel speech, I had a few minutes to talk personally with King about the role of the seminary in the civil rights movement—what we had done thus far and what more we could do. I stated that we had included the issue of racism in some of our courses in Christian ethics. I noted that Dr. J. B. Weatherspoon began to offer undergraduate courses in "Christianity and Race Relations" in 1939 and that blacks had been coming to the seminary since the early 1940s. Also, I indicated that I had been pushing for a black professor in the Christian Ethics department. He appeared genuinely impressed and encouraged me in these efforts.

Dr. King had been scheduled to meet with the combined Christian Ethics classes at Southern. More than 500 students, faculty, staff and visitors met to hear and share dialogue with him. Before the dialogue began, Dr. King gave a brief discourse on the methodology of his movement for racial justice. Of the three characteristic ways of dealing with oppression—acquiescence, violence and nonviolent resistance—he elaborated especially upon the last. Nonviolent resistance, King declared, has positive elements: 1) it has the possibility of working for moral ends through moral means; 2) it is a spiritual movement rejecting the materialistic and ethical relativism of communism; 3) it is based on the Christian ethic of love; and, 4) nonviolence presupposes that there is a basic potential for goodness in everyone and the possibility of authentic transformation. Dr. King noted that human beings also have the potential for evil. He knew this from his own suffering at the hands of his enemies.

Following his comments on nonviolence, Dr. King fielded questions from the students. Questions were asked ranging from boycotts to the right of property owners to choose whom they serve. King answered the inquiries calmly, convincingly and clearly.

Responses to King's presence and message were negative and positive. Faculty, staff and students had received him warmly. Editors of state Baptist papers were divided. Kentucky and Texas Baptist editors were positive and supportive. The seminary's trustees appeared not to be of one mind.[4]

Some churches, thirty-one in Alabama and on a lesser scale elsewhere, so designated their financial gifts to the denomination as to prevent their monies providing benefit to Southern Seminary. Some Baptist colleges canceled invitations to seminary faculty to speak or lecture. Among other invitations that were withdrawn, I had an invitation to a lectureship at Samford University cancelled.

When King was assassinated (4 April 1968), I was at Duke University listening to lectures on hope by Jürgen Moltmann and others. From behind someone passed a note to me and I passed it on to the person sitting in front of me. Finally the note reached the speaker at the podium who read its message to stunned members of the conference: "Dr. Martin Luther King, Jr., has been assassinated." A moment of silence was observed by members of the conference.

Memorial services for King were being held in his honor all across the nation but none had been scheduled at Southern Seminary. When it came my turn to speak in chapel a few weeks following his death, I made my comments a memorial to King. I observed that America had produced three

---

[4] For Dr. Martin Luther King, Jr.'s impression of the Southern Baptist Theological Seminary in 1961, see our correspondence in the appendix.

great prophets: Abraham Lincoln (brought up a Baptist), Walter Rauschenbusch (Baptist social reformer and historian) and Martin Luther King, Jr. (Baptist preacher and civil rights leader). I caught some flack for my message. Two pastors wrote, "It is blasphemy to put Abraham Lincoln and Martin Luther King, Jr., in the same category." King, they additionally complained, could not be compared to a biblical prophet. Apparently they didn't know who Rauschenbusch was! My response to these criticisms appeared in *The Gadfly*, a Southern Seminary student newspaper[5].

> Specific parallels between Martin Luther King, Jr., and the Old Testament Prophets have been drawn by Dr. Henlee H. Barnette, Professor of Christian Ethics at the Southern Baptist Theological Seminary in Louisville. Barnette offers the following comparisons:
> –Like Amos, King stressed justice in economics, politics and social relationship.
> –Like Hosea, he stressed love.
> –Like Jeremiah, he advocated an unpopular view in war time.
> –Like Isaiah, King counseled rulers and kings.
> –Like Moses, he conceived of himself as a leader to guide his people out of bondage and slavery.
> –Like Jesus, King advocated nonviolence and a setting aside of laws when they conflict with human need.
> –Like Micah, he believed in democracy.
> –And, like all the prophets, King had human weaknesses

Baptist papers also carried the chapel address and readers' various responses.[6] The vitriol was intense on the part of some. A couple of milder examples from letters I received will suffice to give expression to the general disgust, fear and hate for King by some religious responders. Written by a man in Memphis, Tennessee: "I am amazed at this article entitled, 'Martin Luther King—A Major Prophet.' So you class him alongside one of our greatest presidents! Amazing! Disgusting!" And this from a man in Rockwell, Maryland: "I read your article 'Martin Luther King in Retrospect.' I could only come to one conclusion, and that is, it's a shame

---

[5] *The Gadfly* 6/14 (23 April 1968): 5.
[6] For example, see "Martin Luther King—A Major Prophet," *Arkansas Baptist News Magazine* 67 (16 May 1968): 11.

A Pilgrimage of Faith

we have such poorly informed men teaching young men who will some day be teaching our children and grandchildren."

Epilogue

From 19 April 1961, the day of Dr. King's visit to the Southern Baptist Seminary, until his death, King led numerous protest movements, was jailed several times, met with presidents, wrote books, letters, articles and witnessed the crumbling of the walls of segregation. Space permits only brief mention of some important contributions Dr. King made to the American civil rights movement and related issues, but the impact he had our nation's history as well as on my own faith journey demands acknowledgment here.

In 1963, King opened the campaign of protest against segregation in Birmingham, Alabama, was jailed, and wrote his "Letter from Birmingham Jail" while imprisoned. On 28 August of that year he delivered his "I Have a Dream" speech to 250,000 at the Lincoln Memorial in Washington DC. He was present at the White House on 2 July 1964 for the signing of the Civil Rights Act by President Lyndon B. Johnson. Later that year, on 18 September, King had a private audience with Pope Paul VI at the Vatican.

In December 1964 Dr. King was awarded the Nobel Peace Prize in Oslo, Norway. On 4 April 1968 he was killed by a sniper while standing on the balcony of the Lorraine Motel in Memphis, Tennessee.

Great persons may also have feet of clay and Martin Luther King, Jr., was no exception. For years the FBI sought to tarnish his reputation by branding him as a communist and womanizer. Communism had no appeal to King. He was a socialist only to the extent that he sought basic economic change for a more equitable redistribution of wealth in the United States. He was a "Christian Socialist" in the same sense as were theologians Karl Barth, Paul Tillich, Dietrich Bonhoeffer and Walter Rauschenbusch.

As for King's womanizing, it is true that he had extramarital affairs. Until after his death, not too much about this part of his life was reported in the media. Contemporary students of King's life boldly report his sexual escapades.[7] Even his closest friend, the Rev. Ralph Abernathy, has written freely and frankly about King's extramarital affairs in recent years.[8] King's reputation was further tarnished when it was discovered that he was guilty of plagiarism in some of his college papers and his doctoral dissertation at Boston University.[9]

In spite of these revelations about Martin Luther King's private life, the Southern Baptist Theological Seminary has honored him in several different ways over the decades since his death:

> 1. Martin Luther King, Jr. Day. This has been a service in his memory held in the Seminary Chapel in April or as near the date as possible to the date on which King spoke there in April of 1961. Nationally known African Americans have been regularly invited to speak on that occasion. In 1993, Kevin Cosby, an African American graduate of the seminary and a prominent pastor in his own right, spoke to the group.
> 2. Black History Day. Observed in February of each year; it has more recently been referred to as African American Day.
> 3. The Martin Luther King, Jr. Fellow. This position was established in 1987 by the seminary administration. It provides employment for black students in the school's Admissions Office.
> 4. In 1987 a course was established at Southern to study the life and work of the civil rights advocate. The course was titled "Martin Luther King, Jr. and the Black Church."
> 5. Martin Luther King, Jr. Holiday. A day in January as near as possible to King's birthday given as a holiday to all faculty, administration, staff and students. It is a paid holiday for all full-time seminary employees.

Martin Luther King, Jr. was human and therefore was not perfect. He would have himself vigorously rejected any claims to the contrary. Nevertheless, his remarkable accomplishments in terms of racial justice

---

[7] For example, see David J. Garrow, *Bearing the Cross: Martin Luther King, Jr. and the Southern Leadership Conference* (New York: William Morrow and Company, Inc., 1986) 374–76, 638–39.

[8] Ralph Abernathy, *And the Walls Came Tumbling_Down: An Autobiography* (New York: Harper Perennial, 1989) 435–36, 470–75.

[9] See Peter Waldman, "To Their Dismay, King Scholars Find a Troubling Pattern," *Wall Street Journal* (9 November 1990): I-A1, A6; and, Claybourne Carson, senior editor, *The Papers of Martin Luther King, Jr.* (Berkeley: University of California Press, 1992) 49–50.

overshadow his failings. He will be remembered in history as a twentieth-century prophet and liberator.

Postscript

In a letter to me, former seminary president Dr. Duke K. McCall affirmed that he told me that having Dr. King on our campus cost the seminary between two and five hundred thousand dollars in money withheld by individuals and churches. Somewhere I responded: Money well-spent. Now Baptists are proud that King was on their seminary campus. Even the fundamentalists who took over the seminary in the 1990s love to use that historic visit as a public relations tool to benefit their own aspirations for the institution.

16

Protest Action

Therefore to him that knoweth to do good
and doeth it not, to him it is a sin.
—James 4:17

Thank God for whistle-blowers, protesting the injustices they see. During the long history of the church there always have been protest movements. When Luther posted his Ninety-five Theses on the Wittenburg church door, it was a protest against corruption in the church and a call for reform. In America there is a whole history of protest and calls for social reform in education, economics, business, religion, politics and in social relations. Across the years, I have taken a full part in protests against many socially accepted injustices and moral wrongs.

In the 1960s protests were frequent among students, religious and secular. Protests against the military involvement of the United States in Vietnam were common on American campuses and in many of our urban centers. At one time, US Navy Rear Admiral James Kelley spoke in the chapel at Southern Seminary. In his remarks, he implied that it was God's will for the US military to be in Vietnam. At that time I was teaching a course at the seminary on Christianity and Revolution. Some members of the class met in front of the chapel with signs protesting our participation in the Vietnam conflict. Many seminary students were shocked as they came out of chapel and saw some of their own engaging in the act of protest. Some denounced the protesters, threatening to do them bodily harm.

The protesters managed to arrange an impromptu meeting with the admiral. They discovered him to be a person with whom they could talk. The meeting concluded with an amicable spirit. Some of the protesters later were reprimanded by the administration. One or two were deemed to be mentally unstable. A few others were pressured to withdraw from the seminary and they transferred to the Louisville Presbyterian Seminary, about a quarter of a mile away.

On another occasion a Military Mobile Chapel was parked in front of the seminary chapel. Members of the same class picketed the vehicle and targeted the chaplain's assistant in charge of the vehicle with their protest as well. The chaplain's assistant was shocked by their action, becoming frustrated and angry. I invited him to speak to the group in our classroom setting, to which he agreed.

In the classroom, our guest declared he had decided that if some students wanted to make damn fools of themselves, it was okay with him. He said he had visited the campuses of the many leading seminaries in America, but that this was the first time he had encountered a protest group. He also told us that he never left a campus before the scheduled time, except at Bob Jones University. There he said that so many students tried to get him saved that he could not take the pressure. The students and he spent some time in dialogue. We agreed to disagree peacefully and with dignity.

More Protest

When President Nixon was inaugurated in January 1973, it was alleged in many Baptist state papers that Dr. Paul Simmons and I were there protesting. Unfortunately, we did not make it. Both Dr. Simmons and I were in Richmond, Virginia, attending a meeting of the American Society of Christian Ethics. Indeed, both of us had planned to protest Nixon's inauguration. The president of the society, however, placed me on the nominating committee, and we did not finish our work in time to catch the bus that took the others to Washington. The editor of one of the Baptist papers assumed that we would be there, so that's how the story went to press.

Reaction from some pastors and laypersons was swift. The president of the seminary called Dr. Simmons into his office and claimed that the story may have cost the seminary $100,000 in Cooperative Convention funds. Dr. McCall declared that if the allegations were true, Dr. Simmons would never receive tenure. Simmons truthfully explained that he had not been present at the protest as the article had reported.

Dr. McCall next requested that I come to his office. He had received a letter from a prominent pastor in Little Rock, Arkansas (Rev. W. O. Vaught, Jr., pastor of the Emmanuel Baptist Church), declaring that professors who pulled such stunts should not be on the seminary faculty. I explained why I did not make it to Washington and that I did not consider the counter-inauguration protest "a stunt." The meeting was brought to an end and I went back to work.

I did take on some of the radical right movements across the years. At one time I spoke on "The Anatomy of Extremism."[1] The John Birch Society had been working to gain followers at Louisville's Broadway Baptist Church. It was announced that I was going to speak about the Birchers at the church. A large crowd came, including the Birchers who used the old "diamond strategy" to dominate the discussion that would follow my remarks. Four Birchers planted themselves at four diagonally oriented corners of the congregational meeting and when it came time for dialogue, each one around the congregation spoke up quickly to make it appear many anticommunists were present. I explained to the church that they were witnessing a common strategy to control public meetings employed by the very communists the Birchers so earnestly sought to root out of American life. While the meeting was going on inside, other Birchers were outside putting literature on parked cars and riding around the church waving Confederate flags. One physician in the congregation said, "If I had any hankering after joining the Birchers before, I don't have it now."

I once met John Birch's parents at Toccoa, Georgia, where I was lecturing. We talked and I got the impression that they were not too happy with their son's name attached to that movement. His parents claimed that their son John was not a "Bircher," rather the fundamentalist anticommunist group needed a hero and adopted John Birch, a brilliant advisor to Taiwan's Chiang Kai-shek. John was killed by Chinese communists.

Often I protested against appropriating tax money for religious causes. In 1987 there was an effort to appropriate tax money for sex education in religious schools. The lawyer for the Baptist Joint Committee requested I

---

[1] This appears in a book edited by Elmer West, Jr., *Extremism Left and Right* (Grand Rapids: Eerdmans Press, 1972).

provide some thoughts to be used in a brief before the Supreme Court of the United States. Among other things, I noted:

> It is a foregone conclusion that the various religious groups who are recipients of tax dollars are going to teach their own views on sex education, pregnancy, and abortion without providing equal emphasis on options and alternatives. Further, it is obvious that tax funded religious organizations will use such funds for the promotion of their own theologico-ethical teachings on sexuality. Clearly this would be an advancement of particular religious doctrines and a violation of the Constitution.[2]

Southern Seminary Social Workers Sit-in

In 1995 the Carver School of Social Work at Southern Baptist Theological Seminary was on its way to being closed by the seminary's fundamentalist-controlled administration and trustees. Dean Diana Garland, the school's dean resigned after a dispute over faculty hiring with the seminary president, Albert Mohler, Jr. Dean Garland's resignation appeared to be purposefully set up by the president when she recommended a candidate to the faculty who would not participate in systematic discrimination against women and homosexuals in the workplace. The social worker's code disavows any form of discrimination against persons for reasons of gender or sexual orientation. Members of the Carver School began a protest of the president's actions outside of his office in Norton Hall.

For some reason, I happened to wander down the hall and saw protesters sitting on the floor. I inquired as to what it was all about. They informed me of their cause. I offered to sit down with them if they would help me get up when that time came. Two of the students helped me to a sitting position. My spot on the floor in the hallway was strategic. I could see directly into the president's office. Students, faculty and some trustees came by. Some avoided eye contact, but others greeted me. Eventually the Executive Director of the Long Run Baptist Association came along. I spoke so all could hear: "Here comes the Bishop of the Association." As he

---

[2] Statement for a brief to be used by Oliver Thomas, Attorney for the Baptist Joint Committee Public Affairs (BJCPA) before the Supreme Court of the U.S. Written 12/7/87 by Henlee Barnette

approached me, he began to bow down on his knees as if to do obeisance. Then he said, "Out there they call me the 'son of a bishop!'" Then he rose and entered the president's office—for what I have never discovered.

That humorous exchang help to allevinte the gloom the students felt, and tears began to vanish. We talked and prayed. Then it was time for me to go. I had identified with the students and provided my witness. Two strong students helped me to my feet and I ambled away.

The Carver School of Social Work, with 117 students enrolled, was officially closed in 1997. Students, families, faculty and friends involved were deeply hurt. One student came to me for advice and I recommended that he transfer to the University of North Carolina because a degree from Southern would be tainted. He took my suggestion and presently holds an effective social work position in North Carolina.

Pharmaceutical, Community, and Other Arenas

Across the years I have corresponded with politicians and all manner of civic and industrial organizations to speak to a variety of important issues: corruption in government, the Living Will, bailing out the "Savings and Loan Association," white collar and corporate crime, the cost of prescription drugs, foreign aid to countries, religious persecution and denying freedom of worship.

One of the issues that disturbed me most was the continually rising cost of prescription drugs. I urged senators, house members—national and state—and pharmaceutical companies to control the cost of these essential products. I noted that it is unethical and unconscionable to profit unduly from the illness and suffering of people. Why is it that drugs for people who are most seriously ill cost the most? Consumer costs for drugs to help the dying are astronomical. The pharmaceutical industry knows the dying will pay whatever is demanded of them to escape death or ease the transition.

I wrote President Clinton of my concern about the cost of drugs and sent copies to my senators and congressmen. Here is the letter.

January 20, 1993
President Bill Clinton
The White House
Washington, DC 20500

Dear Mr. Clinton:

Pursuant to your promise to contain and cut health costs, millions of us senior citizens and other age groups hope you will do something about the unbridled greed of drug companies.

Senator David Pryor is working hard on the problem, but apparently getting little or no help from other representatives. He continues to expose the unconscionable and unethical way pharmaceutical companies are profiting on drugs. For example, the drug Levamisol is sold to farmers as a sheep de-wormer for six cents a tablet. But a human with cancer must pay six dollars per tablet. And to add insult to injury most of the research on the drug was done by the Federal Government at the taxpayer's expense.

I have personally protested by letter to drug companies. What happens? The CEO does not even have the courtesy to respond but passes the letter on to a well-paid PR person who piously talks about how concerned they are, how they are working hard to keep drug prices down. Costs keep soaring.

Those of us out beyond "the Loop" feel that members of Congress no longer care about what happens to us common folks. Hence, we are looking to you and your administration to make radical changes in our health care system.

Respectfully yours,
Henlee H. Barnette
Senior Research Professor

Cc: Senator Mitch McConnell
Senator Wendell Ford
Congressman Mazolli
Congressman Jim Bunning

It has always been a matter of frustration to me that most politicians answer constituents' letters with pandering form letters, currying favor but accomplishing little of substance. Pharmaceutical and other health care related companies provide no stronger indication of concerned response, despite public relations teams that issue beautiful letters declaring the industry's concern for the health and welfare of their customers.

In the 1970s and 1980s parking at the seminary became a critical problem. Over three thousand students were enrolled in the school. Students were parking on the streets around the seminary campus to the extent that local residents were unable to park in front of their own homes. Seminary administrators twice sought to solve the problem by building a parking lot on three vacant lots that belonged to the seminary adjacent to the main campus. It happened that these lots were across the street in front of the Barnette residence. A petition against building the proposed parking lot was drawn up and signed by all the community property owners in the area in 1977 and again agreed to in 1984. Helen and I had been the first to sign and we enlisted the rest of those who lived in our section of the community.

I presented Southern Seminary President President Roy Honeycutt the petition representing the opposition of the community to the proposed parking lot. Our argument was that the proposed lots would irrevocably change the residential nature of our community. In any event, the small size and location of the new lot would not resolve the school's parking problem. I include this episode to indicate that we tackled issues in our own backyard in relation to economic, racial and political problems. Parking space was developed on the campus of the seminary which solved the problem.

Petition in Opposition

The undersigned do hereby Petition the Southern Baptist Theological Seminary to refrain from attempting to change or remove, in any way, the restrictive covenants previously placed upon property located at the corner of Godfrey and Meadowlark Avenues which would alter the residential character of said neighborhood, which has existed for the past sixty years.

The undersigned represent owners of property within Stilz Subdivision and our signatures appearing hereon unequivocally express our *total opposition* to the use of said vacant land for any purpose other than residential use, and our signatures further express a sincere request that the Seminary refrain from any and all overt acts to alter, disturb, lift, or remove restrictive covenants in any manner. Any indication of approval hitherto expressed, either vocal or written, is hereby rescinded.

I presented the petition representing the opposition of the community to building the parking facility to President Roy Honeycutt as follows:

29 June 1984
Dr. Roy Honeycutt, President
Dear Roy:
Attached is our response in 1977 to the proposal to put a seminary parking facility on the lots at Godfrey and Meadowlark. It is the feeling today of the majority of the people in the community. Once you waive a

deed restriction it may set a precedent for other enterprises—beauty shops, etc. This would eventually downgrade the quality of life in the community.

The request we received today is almost identical with that of 1977. We hope that the parking facility will not be built at the proposed spot. It will change nothing. Those parking farther out will simply take the place of those sixty persons parking on that lot.

Respectfully,

Henlee Barnette

I included this episode to indicate that we tackled issues in our own backyard in relation to economic, racial and political problems. Parking space was developed on the campus of the seminary which solved the problem.

From most of the politicians and pharmaceutical people, I received form letters indicating they agreed with me and that some task force or committee was working on the problem. Nothing concretely was done and to this day the costs of prescription drugs continue to rise.

In the late 1940s as a member of the Christian Life Commission of the Southern Baptist Convention I attended one of its conferences meeting at Ridgecrest, North Carolina. We had secured Benjamin Mays, President of Morehouse College, a Ph.D. from the University of Chicago, Phi Beta Kappa and author of a number of books, to join the conference and to give some insights into the troubled American race relations situation. We soon discovered that Dr. Mays, a black man, was not permitted to eat in the dining room at Ridgecrest because of his race. The chairman of the Christian Life Commission, Dr. Hugh Brimm, moved with Dr. Mays to the Montreat Presbyterian Assembly at or near Black Mountain, North Carolina. The remaining members of the committee of the Christian Life Commission remained at Ridgecrest because rooms for the rest of us were not available at Montreat. On another occasion several Africans who had been won to Christ by Southern Baptist missionaries met at Ridgecrest. Because they were black they could not eat in the dining room. The problem was "solved" by having them eat out on the grounds. A petition was drawn up to those in charge of Ridgecrest Assembly, calling for the immediate integration of the place of retreat and Christian inspiration. Our protest and petition eventually helped to bring about the racial integration of the Southern Baptist retreat at Ridgecrest.

In the 1950s I represented Southern Baptist Seminary at the Louisiana Baptist Convention, meeting at the St. Charles Avenue Baptist Church in New Orleans. When the session was over, I caught a streetcar for my downtown hotel. I sat about three seats from the rear of the car and observed a large black beam of wood across the seats in front of me. The conductor told me to move up in the car so as to sit in front of the beam. I did not move. He moved the beam behind me and we went downtown. Blacks were required to sit toward the back of the car behind the adjustable beam.

Doing My Job

Dr. Eric Rust was appointed Professor of Philosophy of Religion at the Southern Baptist Theological Seminary in 1953. He had recently arrived from England where he taught at Rawdon College. I stood with him as a witness when he and his wife, Helen, and their children applied for US citizenship at the Federal Building in Louisville.

On occasion the president of the Southern Seminary received letters objecting to my ministry, even calling for my dismissal from the faculty. Dr. Rust became upset on such an occasion and came to me saying that the president had received a letter from a powerful pastor and trustee calling for my dismissal as Professor of Christian Ethics. I said: "Eric, calm down. If the president doesn't get at least one letter a month demanding that I be fired, I don't feel like I am doing my job."

Christianity is a way of life undergirded by faith in God. I once said this in a sermon. A deacon of the church approached me and informed me that he had been a deacon in that church for twenty years and never thought of Christianity as a way of life. Christian ethics demands moral action on all issues that depersonalize humanity. My job, my calling, was—and continues to be while I have breath—to tackle any and all forces that dehumanize God's children.

17

Heresy Hunters

*A man may be a heretic in truth; and if he believes things only
because his pastor says so, or the assembly so determines,
without knowing the other reason, though his belief be true, yet
the very truth he holds becomes his heresy.*
—Milton, "Areopagitica"

Heresy, in the next generation, becomes orthodoxy
—Henlee Barnette

Since the beginnings of Southern Baptist life in America, heresy hunters
have been busy among them. The Southern Baptist Theological Seminary
has: long been a favorite target of those who find a heretic under every
institutional Southern Baptist mattress. Among the notables attacked as
heretics was Professor Crawford Howell Toy, who came to Southern
Seminary as Professor of Old Testament in 1869. He was forced to resign
ten years later because he affirmed "higher criticism" in relation to the study
and interpretation of the Bible. Higher criticism is the approach to
interpretation of the Bible that relies on academic disciplines—such as
literature, history, archeology, economics, linguistics, sociology, psychology
and any number of other scholarly fields of investigation—to grasp better
and understand the character, content, and context of the scriptures. Use of
higher critical methods is today common practice among most competent
biblical scholars, whether they are inclined toward the progressive or
conservative schools of religious thought. Following his ignominious
departure from Southern Seminary, Toy joined the Harvard University
faculty in 1880 as Hancock Professor of Hebrew and other oriental

languages. Here he was and still is esteemed highly for his scholarly competence and personal integrity.

William Heth Whitsitt was elected to the Chair of Ecclesiastical History at Southern Seminary in 1872 and became the institution's president in 1895. He created a controversy among Southern Baptists when he reported in an encyclopedia that "believers' baptism" by immersion was restored by English Baptists in 1641. This got Whitsitt into an ecclesiastical wasp's nest. Many Southern Baptists believed that an unbroken succession of Baptist churches, beginning with the followers of John the Baptist, could be traced to the present from the apostolic era. His article challenged that opinion. Whitsitt was forced to resign in 1899, but soon afterward was elected Professor of Philosophy at the University of Richmond in Virginia. Ironically, most Baptist historians since those years have fully accepted Whitsitt's position.

Among others who felt the wrath of the heresy hunters in the last half of the twentieth century included Frank Stagg (New Testament), Glenn Hinson (Church History), Eric Rust (Christian Philosophy), Dale Moody (Systematic Theology), Molly Marshall (Southern's first and last female Professor of Theology forced out for alleged heresy). In the Christian Ethics Department, Paul Simmons and I were attacked by heresy hunters on a repeated basis. The most outrageous attack on Dr. Simmons was brought by a trustee of the seminary. He charged that Simmons was an advocate of the absolute right to abortion on demand. It was, of course, false. Paul Simmons never held such a position.

In May of 1955, during a season of "heresy hunting" at Southern Baptist Theological Seminary someone came up with the well-intentioned idea that accusations could be countered by professors' writings on the great doctrines of faith to show how orthodox the faculty truly was. I was assigned the topic: "Why I Believe In Hell." I said I believed in hell for three reasons: 1) Jesus taught it; 2) People who give it to other people ought to get some of their own; and, 3) I'd been there.

The fall-out from that little effort was something to behold! Jehovah's Witnesses tried to convert me. Some Baptists demanded that I be fired. One brother from Arkansas wrote a hot letter, declaring that he believed in an eternal fire and brimstone hell and that he was "a damned good Baptist." He concluded, "Yours in Christ," and signed the letter. Needless to say my article wrecked the preemptive public relations scheme. I was courting Helen at the time and someone put the article on the bulletin board at the seminary, extending the title with the letters e and n. It read, "Why I Believe in Hellen."

A brother related to an organization called The Baptist Faith and Message Fellowship, Inc., wrote me a letter in 1977 stating that it had been reported that some seminary professors believed that the Bible contained errors. He wanted to know my view on the matter. He asked me "three very simple questions" to be answered by a "yes" or "no." They were: Do you believe that God inspired every word of the "original manuscripts;" that there were no errors in those manuscripts; that Adam and Eve were the first human beings? The conclusion of the letter clearly shows that the writer was searching for heretics at the seminary and he wanted me to disclose who these were. I responded to the inquiry in a three sentence letter:

> Dear Brother,
> Some chairman of a heresy hunting committee has written me an unbaptistic letter implying that I must subscribe "to certain views about the Bible". He signed your name to it. I thought you would appreciate knowing about it.
> Sincerely,
> Henlee H. Barnette

I never again heard from that particular heresy hunter. My response gained a certain amount of notoriety among the students at Southern. Some time later, a carbon copy of the letter brought a high price when auctioned off to raise funds for a student summer missions project.

In 1986 a special committee formed by Southern Seminary trustees was appointed to investigate concerns of the Southern Baptist Peace Committee about specific seminary faculty members. On 13 March 1986 the faculty (I was serving as a visiting professor at that time) met with the president of the seminary, Dr. Roy Honeycutt. We were informed that Adrian Rogers, a member of the Peace Committee, wanted to add names of certain faculty members, including mine, to a "heresy list." He was angry about an article I wrote, "The Baptist Brouhaha and Biblical Authority," in which I was critical of him for failing to use his position as the convention's president to unify rather than further divide Southern Baptists. In 1979 Rogers had proceeded to appoint only fundamentalists to the SBC's Committee on Committees. In turn, that body proposes the likely candidates who will be appointed as trustees to the seminaries and other denominational agencies.

Rogers—pastor of the influential Bellvue Baptist Church in Memphis, Tennessee—also objected to my previously published article, "Coarchy: Partnership and Equality in Man-Woman Relations."[1] He took strong exception to the idea of equality between men and women.

These instances were not the first time my path and Adrian's had crossed. It may be recalled that in previous years, I had recommended him to his first pastorate. In 1979 Adrian Rogers was elected as President of the Southern Baptist Convention. It was under his leadership that the fundamentalist Baptists began to take over the convention and force moderate Baptists out of positions of influence in denominational life. A doctrine of "inerrancy of the Bible," itself a heresy, was used as a political tool in the takeover. I was impelled to respond by publishing an article in a Baptist State paper. Dr. Rogers became upset and requested that I answer some questions. In addition, Rogers called the editor of the *Western Recorder*, Dr. Chauncey Daley, and chastised him for publishing the article. Other Baptist editors also received threats and criticism for publishing my article, as they had in previous years when they had published my various articles on the Vietnam War, race relations and other topics.

Rogers and I had one final exchange of correspondence, included below:

Adrian Rogers, Pastor
Bellevue Baptist Church
70 North Bellevue Boulevard
Memphis, Tennessee 38104
23 June 1981

Dr. Henlee Barnette
The Southern Baptist Theological Seminary
2825 Lexington Road
Louisville, Kentucky

---

[1] *Review and Expositor* 75/1 (Winter 1978). I had to defend my article before the trustees. Apparently they could find no fault in what I had written and dropped the matter from the docket.

My dear friend:

I have just read an article by you in the *Western Recorder* that has grieved my heart. I want to check and make certain that I am understanding you.

You said, "If ever discovered (the original manuscripts), they probably would not be perfect documents because they would reflect the culture and theology of the authors. Only God is perfect. All else bears the mark of imperfection."

Now this gives me a deep problem, especially when we speak of the Bible as being a perfect treasure and truth without any mixture of error. How do you reconcile such a statement? It is this kind of thing that keeps us constantly off balance. On the one hand, we affirm the "Baptist Faith and Message" statement and then on the other hand, we have statements such as this one that you made.

Am I understanding that you feel that the theology of the original manuscripts is not necessarily the theology of God, but may indeed be the theology of the authors? That is what your statement seems to clearly say.

Also, you stated, "The past President of the convention abused this power by appointing a committee made up of almost totally radically conservative members."

We have often heard the conservative side being accused of making broad sweeping statements of condemnation. Do you know all of the godly persons who have served on this committee? I think that your statement concerning them is almost slanderous. Unless you know them and know where they stand, I think that you owe to them and to me an apology.

Dr. Barnette, I have loved and respected you through the years. You have been a friend to me. But I must ask you to clarify what you have done.

I will await your reply. I love you in Jesus' Name.

Adrian Rogers

16 July 1981
Dr. Adrian Rogers
Bellevue Baptist Church
70 North Bellevue Boulevard
Memphis, Tennessee 38104
Dear Adrian:

Forgive this belated reply to your letter of June 23 which was addressed to Southern Seminary. I was retired from there four years ago and joined the University of Louisville school of medicine faculty. Since I do not have a mailbox at the seminary, your letter was received via a circuitous route.

I shall attempt to present my views in regard to your questions concerning certain statements in my article on "The Baptist Brouhaha and Biblical Authority."

1. Regarding reconciling the "probably" (my word) imperfect autographs with the "Baptist Faith and Message's" statement about the Bible being "a perfect treasure," "and truth without any mixture of error": I feel the perfect treasure refers to "divine instruction," not to the literal letter of the Bible and the truth without error refers to its "matter," that is, its basic doctrines which are infallible and inerrant. The incarnation of God in Christ is the infallible and inerrant Word. This is the "matter" or truth without "mixture of error."

2. Regarding the autographs reflecting the culture and theology of the authors: Amos and all the other prophets and New Testament writers, as you well know, reflected their cultural backgrounds and particular theologies. Theology is faith's attempt to understand itself. It is the conceptualization of our experiences with God. John's *Logos* theology reflects the Gospel's encounter with Greek thought and an anti-Jewish bias. Paul reflects his rabbinical training and his theology of justification by faith. Some of Paul's theology about the role of women in the church is culturally and historically conditioned. (Do you allow women to speak in your church?)

I can't believe the Bible came to us as did the Koran—allegedly—to the Muslims or from mechanical secretaries who gave us perfect autographs. To me there is something phony about a perfect book coming through imperfect men.

It is my conviction that the Bible as we now have it is so close to the autographs that we don't need them.

3. Regarding the "abuse of power" by the past president of the convention: At the time you appointed the Committee on Committees, our convention was becoming polarized over the doctrine of "inerrancy of the Bible." You had a golden opportunity to serve as a reconciler by appointing a balanced committee. Instead, many of us believe that you purposely appointed a conservative committee which, in turn, appointed a conservative committee on boards which proceeded not only to appoint largely conservative members to the agencies and commissions but also "bumped" some fine, qualified "moderates" (eligible for another term) from agencies. Fortunately this less-than-reconciling action was corrected by the convention at Los Angeles.

I do not consider being called an "ultra conservative" bordering on slander. I consider myself to be a radical ultra-conservative on the fundamentals of the Christian faith: Jesus as the incarnate Word of God, the Atonement, the Resurrection, the Coming Again of our Lord, Judgment, et cetera. But I hope I never use these beliefs to coerce other people to my way of thinking or to seize ecclesiastical power over my brethren who may differ with me over some minor theological interpretations.

You recall that I took note of "moderates" who have been "politicking" for power in the convention for a generation. Their power manipulations are as obnoxious to me on this point as that of fundamentalists.

Lately I have come to the conclusion that God is going to use your presidential actions for His glory in bringing about a more balanced representation in the convention enterprise.

My dear friend, it grieves me genuinely that my article grieved you. My intent was to try to put the polarization in perspective and urge moving "*beyond* the divisive arguments about inerrancy to the demands of the kingdom of God in terms of evangelism, religious education and missions." Though we may disagree on what I consider to be minor theological matters, I have rejoiced in your ministry of the Good News across the years and share with you a deep love for and commitment to our convention and our Lord.

Faithfully,
Henlee H. Barnette
Clinical Professor
Department of Psychiatry and Behavioral Sciences
University of Louisville, School of Medicine

Unfortunately, there is no more correspondence between Adrian and me. Tension between moderates and fundamentalists became so great as to become a barrier between us. Once I sent him one of my new books. There was no response. What really upset him was an article I published in the *Review and Expositor* 75/1 (Winter 1978) about equality for women. I had to defend it before the trustees. Apparently they could find no fault and dropped it from the docket.

Returning to the faculty meeting in 1986 with President Honeycutt: In his Southern gentleman's way, Dr. Honeycutt encouraged faculty under investigation to stick to our convictions. He assured us that the written responses we provided to explain our interpretations of the Bible would be quoted correctly in his report to the Trustee Academic Committee. I met privately with Dr. Honeycutt and Dean Willis Bennett a few days later. They assured me of their support, commended me for the response I had provided to allay trustees' concerns about the soundness of my biblical views, and offered further assurances that I had not increased their own burdens.

Dean Willis Bennett also requested that I write a response to the trustees' special concerns about my article which was published in the *Review and Expositor* (Winter 1978) eight years before. Their "concerns" related to my interpretation of Genesis 1, "Adam" as a generic term; woman being equal with man; Jesus as being a "feminist;" and the interpretation of Paul's teaching on man being head of the woman. I answered seriatim explaining the Hebrew and Greek from the best dictionaries and scholars.

The Academic Personnel Committee eventually made its report to the Board of Trustees, who in turn unanimously concluded that the faculty members cited (eleven in all) had written and taught "in accordance with, and not contrary to the Abstract of Principles." The report continued: "We further conclude that all faculty members should be commended for their sincere quest for truth and should be encouraged to continue such quest in the years ahead." Unfortunately, that quality of freedom, openness, scholarship no longer prevails at Southern Seminary because fundamentalists have since gained complete control of the school, enforcing an institutional environment that totally dominates the legitimate pursuit of knowledge and effectively stifles the authentic pursuits of academic freedom.

Diaspora of the "Heretics"

As a result of the takeover of the Southern Baptist Theological Seminary by denominational fundamentalists, seventy faculty members departed. Most of these left during the first three years of the presidency of Albert Mohler, Jr., due to an atmosphere of oppression and a loss of academic freedom. According to the pastor of Crescent Hill Baptist Church, long considered by many "the seminary church," thirty families were lost to its membership as a result of faculty departures. I spoke personally with many of these, listening to the sad stories of distress and personal suffering they and their families endured at the hands of the new wave of fundamentalist administrators, trustees, faculty, and students. Most of the disaffected faculty left as a matter of conscience. It was a costly choice for the younger professors, especially punishing to their families. Children were uprooted from schools, separated from playmates, friends and happy surroundings. Some older faculty, nearer to retirement, decided to try and finish their careers at Southern gracefully.

A few teachers acquiesced to the litmus tests of orthodoxy imposed by the new fundamentalist president: inerrancy of Scripture (a heretical view of the Bible cloaked in religious dogma, used as a political tool to solidify the fundamentalists' power), absolute anti-abortion and homophobia.

Dr. Molly Marshall, a professor of theology, and Dr. Paul Simmons, a professor of Christian Ethics, were forced from the faculty. Marshall took a professorship in another seminary and Simmons accepted a position teaching ethics in a medical school. Dr. Diana Garland, Dean of the School of Social Work, was fired because of the seminary's policy of discrimination in employment. She refused to withdraw the nomination of a man for the faculty who believed a woman had a right to serve as pastor of a church. She had received a $280,000 grant from the Lily Foundation to study the family. Diana became head of the School of Social Work at Baylor University and took the grant money with her. She has continued to publish significant literature on the family.

Thirty staff members likewise left the seminary to preserve their integrity. Dr. Paul Debusman, a brilliant reference librarian, was dismissed in an unchristian and shameful manner. He had been with the seminary for thirty-five years and had only a few months to serve before he would retire. Paul wrote Tom Elliff, president of the Southern Baptist Convention, a personal and appropriately respectful letter to object to comments made by the denominational leader in a seminary chapel service. Elliff had stated that he doubted that he would have been invited to speak in chapel when the moderates were in control of the seminary. Debusman noted that many fundamentalists had spoken in chapel and named several of them. Within two weeks after Debusman wrote the letter he was called before the dean of the seminary who fired him for "insubordination" without any discussion of the issue. Debusman was allowed to return to his office to retrieve personal belongings only under the watchful eye of a chaperon assigned by the administration, ostensibly to protect the seminary's property and interests! Paul was given one month's severance pay, offered no extended insurance coverage for the sudden period of transition and no seminary paid insurance normally provided to retirees and denied the bonus staff members earned after thirty-five years of service. I know of no respectful secular organization that would so callously deny due process to a loyal employee of such sterling integrity—as was Dr. Debusman—and dismiss that person by trumping up false charges of insubordination. My objections to the shabby treatment of Dr. Debusman by the seminary went unanswered by the dean, while the president hid silent behind the skirt of legal advice regarding discussion of the matter.

Paul Debusman's character speaks volumes despite the fundamentalists' wish to silence the man. The firing unleashed a flood of letters to editors and articles by former students and colleagues from across the thirty-five years in which he tirelessly and selflessly served the school in its academic mission to prepare men and women in the best way possible to fulfill their callings as servants of the gospel. These former students and colleagues with one voice praised his integrity, humility, competence, intellectual honesty and service. The outpouring of love for the man and the expressed sorrow, shock, and revulsion over his abrupt dismissal meant nothing to the seminary's authoritarian fundamentalist administrators and denominational rulers. They permit no challenge to their person or authority, not even when issued in Christlike and brotherly fashion. As long as control is not wrested from them, being dead wrong about an issue matters very little to these folks.

In comments to the press and the president of the Southern Baptist Convention, I suggested that there was a way to rectify the terrible injustice done to Dr. Debusman by the seminary's administration and its overlords in the denomination. They could: 1) Provide him a decent severance stipend; 2) Grant him his thirty-five years of service bonus and the recognition he so richly deserved; 3) Ask his forgiveness. Citing passages that provide instruction for the resolution of conflict among Christians (such as Matt 18:15), and appealing to an inerrant mode of ethical Christian behavior (not at all the heresy that is the false doctrine of Scriptural inerrancy!), I also wrote a personal letter to Tom Elliff seeking redress to the wrong done Paul Debusman. It will come as no surprise to the reader that my protests fell on deaf ears.

I must add here that Dr. Duke K. McCall, President of the Southern Baptist Theological Seminary (1951-1982) stood by his faculty against recurring and baseless charges of heresy. He believed in academic freedom and responsibility. So did Dr. Roy Honeycutt, Dr. McCall's immediate successor. Their tenures marked the golden age of the seminary, an age brought to an end by denominational fundamentalists who for their own purposes took the institution over in the early 1990s.

Finally, I offer below some practical suggestions for dealing with heresy hunters:

1. Be sure to have your facts well in hand. I can speak more freely when not inhibited by unfamiliarity with the facts.

2. Be brief and to the point. Most anything you say will be twisted (fundamentalists are noted Scripture-twisters) and used against you.

3. Be clear and cogent.

4. Take the charges as an opportunity to teach and win over the heresy hunter.

5. Except in rare cases, do not respond to personal attacks or when baited by pious cliches.

18

Debate on Morality

Justice is Christian Love using its head.
—Joseph Fletcher

In the 1970s America was engaged in a cold war with the Soviet Union and a hot war in Vietnam. We lost the war in Vietnam and our troops came home 12 August 1975. On 9 August 1974 President Richard Nixon resigned under threat of impeachment. He was charged with obstruction of justice related to the Watergate scandal.

During these times I was active in a variety of arenas, including preparations for and participation in a debate with Dr. Joseph Fletcher. The debate itself took place 16 March 1970 at the Atlanta American Motor Hotel. Sponsored by the Christian Life Commission of the Southern Baptist Convention, the theme of the forum was "Toward Authentic Morality for Modern Man."[1] Dr. Fletcher, author of *Situation Ethics: The New Morality* (1966) was a professor of social ethics at Episcopal Theological School, Cambridge, Massachusetts. I was a professor of Christian Ethics at Southern Baptist Theological Seminary, Louisville, Kentucky.

Dr. Fletcher was the founder of biomedical ethics. In 1954 he published *Morals and Medicine*, arguing the case for active euthanasia, for full disclosure to dying patients of their condition, for artificial insemination and sterilization of those unfit to be parents. *Situation Ethics* brought him notoriety as an ethicist. In all, he wrote and published eleven books and 350 articles. Fletcher was also a founder and participant in many organizations dedicated to improving the quality of life of all persons. He lectured on

---

[1] My initial response to Dr. Fletcher's situationism was printed under the title "The New Morality: Reconnaissance and Reply" in *Proceedings 1970 Christian Life Commission Seminar: "Toward Authentic Morality for Modern Man,"* (1970): 16–18.

medical ethics at the University of Cambridge, England, and at the University of Virginia where he served as a professor until his death at the age of eighty-six in October 1991. He was, in every sense of the word, a pioneer in the field of biomedical ethics.[2]

Dr. Fletcher and I stayed at the same hotel prior to our March 1970 debate. He came to my room to borrow some shaving cream. That meeting allowed us an opportunity to talk, and he told me a bit about himself. His parents separated when he was nine years old. His father was Catholic and his mother Protestant. Joseph was brought up as an Episcopalian. As a boy in West Virginia, he became conscious of the injustice to coal mine workers. In college he became "radicalized" after reading George Bernard Shaw, Henry Mencken, John Reed and similar authors who moved him intellectually toward democratic socialism. The Episcopal Church provided him the opportunity to nurture, develop and give expression to his growing commitment to social justice.

Fletcher described his theory of situation ethics as doing the most loving thing when engaging moral decision-making. He argued that our Christian obligation calls for lying, adultery, fornication, theft, promise-breaking, even perhaps sometimes killing. All depended upon the situation being faced. He claimed we are to live by the law of love, never by the love of law. He outlined three methods of moral decision-making: legalism, antinomianism and situationism. According to Fletcher, legalism is living by the rules; antinomianism is anti-law; situationism is love alone and is the principle.

Situationism holds that love (*agape*) is the one absolute norm. Exponents of this view live by an ethic described as an open-mindedness of loving concern. All laws, principles, guidelines and commonplace conventions are to be set aside if love is thus better served in a given situation. Fletcher provides numerous illustrations to prove his point. Jesus laid aside the law of the Sabbath to meet human need. Such was the case when his hungry disciples entered a field, plucked, shucked and ate corn in violation of the Jewish Sabbath work prohibition laws (Matt 12:1–8). The legitimate needs of humanity are above law. According to Fletcher, the atomic bombing of Japan in World War II was the most loving thing to do

---

[2] See *New York Times*, "Obituaries," (30 October 1991).

because it otherwise saved the lives of perhaps a million soldiers and civilians. That event also brought the Japanese to the surrender table. Fletcher calls this logic "Agapeic calculus."

In written articles and in our public debate, I attempted to clarify the semantic problem that characterized the new morality or "situation ethics." I noted the important distinction between the more popular—and purely secular—impromptu ethics and Fletcher's situation ethics that were grounded in a theological framework. The latter has some biblical rootage and is primarily an attempt to arrive at a methodology for putting into practice the Christian concept of love. Fletcher's model is encapsulated in the following: "Christian situationalism is a method that proceeds from (1) its one and only law, *agape* (love), to (2) the *sophia* (wisdom) of the church or culture, containing many "general rules" of more or less reliability, to (3) the *kairos* (moment of decision, in the fullness of time) in which the *responsible self in the situation*, decides whether *sophia* can serve love or not."[3]

For Fletcher, agapeic love is the *only* intrinsic good, the *only* absolute. God is absolute and thus God is here reduced from person to principle, that being *agape*. And "love alone" becomes ambiguous and needs moral law. Love transcends law but does not abrogate the moral law.

Fletcher claims that law is set aside where love is better served, noting that Jesus set aside the law on several occasions (Matt 12:1–8, Luke 13:10–17, John 5:1–18). But on each cited occasion it was the ceremonial, not the moral law, that Jesus challenged. He thereby "fulfilled," that is, radicalized and deepened the law, making even the "lustful look" to be adultery and "anger" equivalent to murder (Matt 5:21–48)

The character of love is summed up by the Apostle Paul in terms of moral law:

> You shall not commit adultery, You shall not kill, You shall not steal, You shall not bear false witness, You shall not covet, and any other commandment is summed up in this sentence, "You shall love your neighbor as yourself." Love does no wrong to a neighbor, therefore love is the fulfilling of the law (Rom 13:8–10).

---

[3] Joseph Fletcher, *Situation Ethics*: *The New Morality* Philadelphia: Westminster Press. 1966), 33.

Love needs moral law to give it direction, structure and concreteness. This saves love from subjectivism and sentimentality. The moral education of children finds little or no place in situation ethics. But children need to be taught the principles of right and wrong, for they do not always do the most loving thing. They must be taught it is wrong to steal, lie and cheat. When my oldest son was in elementary school, he came home one day and proudly announced that he had practiced the Golden Rule. He explained that a friend did not know the answer to an examination question. John helpfully supplied the answer. "Because," he said, "if I had not known the answer, I would have wanted him to give it to me." This action, he thought, was "doing unto others as you would have them do unto you." In other words, he thought in that situation he was doing the most loving thing!

The Apostle Paul was realistic in recognizing that moral teaching must be given to persons at various levels of moral understanding. He set forth a minimum morality for the morally immature (Eph 4:25–32, 1 Thess 4:1–12). Those who reach the rarified atmosphere of *agape* are not, however, somehow exempt from the "Do this-es." The apostle's list of concrete behaviors remain a part of love's expression.

Despite its significant shortcomings, situation ethics does make a contribution to ongoing research in Christian ethics. Fletcher's book, *Situation Ethics: The New Morality*, was a theological bomb dropped squarely on the field of ethics. It became a catalyst for the renewal of vital, exciting and relevant work concerning the nature and function of ethics in both the secular and religious spheres.

Fletcher was in great demand as a lecturer in ethics among business groups, fraternities and prestigious clubs. At the Pendennis Club in Louisville, Kentucky, he noted "It is better to love people and use things. The worst sin is the reverse, to love things and use people." He declared that unmarried love is superior to married "unlove." He went straight to a church for his next lecture. (See the *Courier-Journal*, 3 December 1966, B-1)

Dr. Fletcher and I became and remained friends until his death. We corresponded regularly and exchanged ideas freely. I shared with him the story of an event that occurred in 1804 in Jefferson County, Kentucky. At a community "log-rolling," members of the Long Run Baptist Church got into a discussion as to whether or not a man would be justified in telling a lie under any circumstance. An illustration was posed. "Suppose a man has five children. The Indians come and kill four of them, the fifth one being hidden nearby. The natives ask the father if he has another child. Would he be justified in telling them he had not?" The dispute grew so hot that the church membership actually had a falling out. The "lying party" moved four or five miles west and constituted the Flat Rock Baptist Church in 1805.[4] Fletcher loved this story and used it many times in his lectures, always identified himself with the "Lying Baptist Church."

I was influenced by the works of Fletcher which were kin to the works on ethics I had already read: Emil Brunner, *The Divine Imperative*, Rudolph Bultmann, *Jesus and the Word*, Dietrich Bonhoeffer, *Ethics*, and Karl Barth, *Church Dogmatics*, 2/2 and 3/4.

My major contribution to the academic discussion of the "new morality" was a volume titled *The New Theology and Morality*, (Philadelphia: The Westminster Press, 1967). Dr. Fletcher informed me that he used my book as a text in his Christian Ethics classes at the Episcopal Theological Seminary in Cambridge. Reports from other professors praised the book and found it helpful.

Chapter two of *New Theology and Morality* was chosen by Dr. Harvey Cox of Harvard University to appear in his anthology, *The Situation Ethics Debate* (1968). The chapter offers a comprehensive view of situation ethics as understood by twenty-eight scholars and a reply by Joseph Fletcher. In his introduction, Cox wrote the following about my essay: "Much more judicious is Henlee Barnette's careful systematic analysis of situationism, an investigation that is able to give credit where it is due and thus to make its critical comments much more plausible."[5] Quite a compliment given that Southern Baptist ethicists and scholars are not always held in the highest esteem by the more elite members of the academy.

---

[4] J. H. Spencer, *A History of Kentucky Baptists From 1769–1885*, 2 vols., Cincinnati, Ohio: J. R. Baumes, 1885, 2:335–336.

[5] Harvey Cox, editor, *Situation Ethics Debate* (Philadelphia: Westminster Press, 1968) 15.

19

Ecology

To love is to will and to work for the well-being of all of God's creatures and creation.

Across the nation in the early 1970s, millions of people demonstrated their concern for the welfare of the earth. Lectures about the ailing ecosystem were among the most popular in colleges, churches, seminaries and public places. School children, corporations and politicians got on the bandwagon to "save the earth." So many US congressmen took part in the first International Earth Day activities on 22 April 1970, that even congressional business was suspended.

In 1970 a group of Southern Baptist Theological Seminary students organized an Ecoclub. I became the group's faculty sponsor. The Ecoclub collected papers, cans and other items to be recycled. The seminary also observed Earth Day. I was chosen to provide the first prayer on the first Earth Day in the chapel. Its text follows:

O Father, the earth is thine and the fullness thereof, the world and they that dwell therein.

Thou hast given us this earth as our home.

We praise thee for its natural beauty: the sunshine and the rain, the hills and the valleys, the streams and the seas, the winds and the waves, the fields of grain, the flora and the fauna.

We confess that we have not been good housekeepers of this lovely dwelling place. We have failed in our stewardship for we have fouled the air, poisoned the land and the lakes, polluted the streams and filled the air with ear-splitting sounds and sonic booms.

O Lord, we have made such a mess out of this planet that now all mankind is threatened with extinction.

Grant to us the wisdom and the will to take better care of the only earth we have.

Grant us the courage to so rearrange our priorities that our natural resources may be conserved and the quality of life for all be enriched.

May the sort of dedication, energy and expertise which we have expended to put a man on the moon be utilized to make it possible for man to continue his existence here on earth.

May the billions of dollars and the thousand of lives now being sacrificed in a wasteful war of destruction and death be diverted to the saving of life and the survival of mankind in peace.

Bless the youth of our land who protest against the destructive exploitation of nature.

May this "earth day" be the beginning of a sustained and concerted effort on the part of all of us to create a cleaner world so that future generations will enjoy the beauty of the earth.

Through Christ who came to give us life in abundance.

Amen.

In concert with the growing concern over ecological issues, I offered a course specifically designed to address the looming ecological crisis. It was, I believe, the first such course offered in a Southern Baptist seminary. A social ethics seminar for doctoral candidates, it dealt with "the roots and causative factors of the present ecological challenge, and suggestions toward developing an ecological strategy for survival." Two years later I began offering a course in ecology for M.Div. students. Dr. Glen Stassen, my colleague on the faculty, taught the course at both levels after I retired in 1977.

I was a visiting professor in the Department of Environmental Engineering at the University of Florida in Gainesville (1971). Why? Dr. Tom Odum had written a book titled *Environment, Power and Society*. In the book's final paragraph he describes the failure of churches and seminaries to deal with environmental problems. "Let us," he challenges, "inject systems science in overdoses in the seminaries and see what happens" (310). He concluded with this question: "Prophet where art thou?" I wrote Dr. Odum and said: "Here I am." He was astounded that a theologian would actually rise to the challenge! I told him I wanted to spend a sabbatical year with him at the University of Florida studying the ethics of the environmental problem. He invited me to study with him in a seminar of about twenty graduate students. A world famous environmentalist, he was absent from the seminar on several occasions. At one moment he might be helping the Vietnamese grow back the mangrove trees destroyed during the war in that country, or he might be found on Crystal River in Florida trying to save the manatee.

On one occasion, he gave a lecture in which he itemized some needed guidelines to deal with the environmental crisis. When he had finished, I raised my hand and told Dr. Odum that all of those guidelines were in the Bible. He just sat there and looked at me; the rest of the class felt a bit uneasy. I elaborated on the principles that had biblical precedents and cited various of the related passages. Dr. Odum dropped his head on the table and thought for a while. He finally raised his head and exclaimed: "Well, I'll be damned." After that we became good friends, and he invited me on several occasions to be a guest in his home.

During that time I finished writing a book titled *The Church and the Ecological Crisis* (Eerdmans Publishing Company, 1972). Southern Seminary's Norton Lectures in the fall of 1971 had been scheduled to be delivered by *New York Times* writer, James Reston. At the last moment, he was unable to give the prestigious lectures as planned. The faculty of the seminary voted to request that I give those lectures and focus on the drug crisis and the church, since I had also just completed a manuscript on the subject. The book dealing with drugs had just been published two or three months prior to the lectures, so the faculty agreed that I could instead deal with the ecological topic. *Christianity Today,* a religiously conservative magazine, criticized the book as bad theology and bad ecology. But Norman Cousins' prestigious magazine, *World View/Saturday Review of Literature* (2 January 1973), gave it an excellent review. Among other things the reviewer wrote: "This is a lucid, scholarly appeal for the development of an ecological ethic... The book contains as clear an explanation of fundamental environmental problems and challenges as appears anywhere in similar brevity."

While on sabbatical at the University of Florida, I also taught a course at Stetson University in Deland: "Ecology: Socio-Religious Dimensions," a substitute for "Human Ecology" listed in the curriculum under sociology. My lectures dealt with the ecological crisis, causative factors, strategies for optimum pollution control and the role of religion as a motivational force in the search for a better quality of life. I noted the need for a theology of ecology. This is where the church can play a leading role as a motivational force in the ecological crisis.[1]

We are suffering, I declared in class lectures, from being "consumerholics," a term I coined for addiction to consumption. We have a bulldozer mentality and operate on a cowboy economy: "Go in, consume, destroy and move out." We did not merely study ecology; students put theory into action with a number of community improvement projects. These included an evaluation of the city sewage system and a study of pollution in the nearby St. Johns River. Three class members planted 400 slash pines between DeLand and DeLeon Springs. Other students cleaned up two truckloads of trash that had accumulated on a corner lot in DeLand. .[2]

The fundamentalist-instigated exodus of faculty members from the Southern Baptist Theological Seminary in the early 1990s, including the departure of my former ethics colleague Dr. Glen Stassen, left some doctoral candidates without required supervisory professors. One such group, studying ecology, asked me to supervise their remaining work. Although by

that time I was on the faculty of the Medical School of the University of

---

[1] See my book, *The Church and the Ecological Crisis* (Grand Rapids: William B. Eerdmans Publishing Co., 1972) Chapter 5. Theology has much to offer that can help humanity understand itself more fully and its responsibility to care for God's creation. There is today a need for a first-rate book on eco-theology, to include a theology of the inorganic. God is creator of all things, organic and inorganic. The first duty given to the first human being was "to tend and keep," that is, protect, God's creation (Gen 2:15).The universe is sustained by God's creative power, without which creation would return to chaos (Job 34:13–15; Ps 104:29–30). God loves what has been created. In the first book and chapter of the Bible, God declares as good everything that was made. God cares for and rejoices in this creation that is the product of God's will (see Gen 1; Matt 10:29–30; Ps 104:30; 147:4). This means we must care for the earth, for it is the Lord's.

[2] The *DeLand Sun News* published a front page piece about the course and its results (15 February 1972). The *Stetson Reporter* (18 February 1972, p. 3) covered the course and the projects, stating that the class was "worthwhile."

Louisville, I agreed on one condition: the classes were to be held at my house. That settled, the course was completed and the students graduated.

20

Politics

Politics are too serious a matter to be left to the politicians.
—Charles DeGaulle

Across the years I have lectured, preached, written articles and parts of books, demonstrated, and protested against numerous forms of social, economic, and environmental injustice. During the late 1960s and throughout the 1970s, my interest in local and national politics was especially keen.

My acquaintance with politics began in 1916 when my father was elected register of deeds on the Republican ticket in Alexander County, North Carolina. At that time we were living on Sugar Loaf Mountain. We moved to the county seat town of Taylorsville so my father would be close to his office. I must have been about five years old and delighted in going to his office and playing with gadgets and looking at the huge volumes containing deeds of the people of the county. I suppose my father would have been in politics for many years if it had not been for the objections of my mother. She disliked the drinking and the fighting that characterized those who were involved in the political system.

Each election year while I was a professor at the Southern Baptist Theological Seminary, I would make up a list of candidates I believed most suitable for office and passed it on to the seminary community. Only one faculty member ever objected and I never sent the list to him again. I considered my election year memos as offering a civic service, an effort to "get out the vote."

I also published memos encouraging all eligible voters to register for upcoming elections:

To: Faculty, Staff, Students
Date: 7 August 1964
From: Professor Barnette
Subject: Voter Registration
My Fellow Americans:

A presidential election is coming up 3 November 1964. Last day of registration in Kentucky is 5 September. If you have not registered to vote, please go to the Armory Building at Sixth and Walnut and do so before 5 September. Registration takes place on the third floor.

To register and vote one must have been in the state one year, the county six months and the precinct sixty days.

For further information on voter registration call 584-8277.

To vote by absentee ballot write to: County Clerk of your county back home. Better do it now in order to get registered before 5 September.

Yours for democracy,
Henlee Barnette
Paid Political Advertisement!

State and Local Politics

Through the years I have supported many candidates for public office. In 1969 I was active in support of Todd Hollenbach, a candidate for County Judge in Jefferson County, Kentucky. Kentucky state Senator Henry Beach, Stuart Alexander and I met for the purpose of helping to plan Hollenbach's campaign. We held a big rally in the Louisville district of St. Matthews to encourage people to vote. Hollenbach won the election.

One of Kentucky's most distinguished governors was the honorable Bert T. Combs, whom I had the privilege of supporting as a candidate and during his years in office. In 1974, having retired from public life, he was kind enough to speak to my class on "Church and Politics." The former governor quickly connected with the students, who eagerly participated in an energized dialogue with him.

William Stansbury ran for Mayor of Louisville in 1976. While I did not actively campaign for him, I did cast my ballot in his favor.

Tom Ward, a former student of mine at the seminary, married a lovely young woman who was an heir to a fortune. Tom became a pastor, then a state senator with an ambition to be governor. He first ran for Lieutenant Governor against Mrs. Thelma Stovall. Both candidates had been speakers in my classes. Tom requested that I rally the African-American vote in his favor, which I attempted to do. But, by the time his call had come to me, it was too late in the electoral process for us to make much headway. He lost the race and was unfortunately saddled with a large debt from campaign expenses.

A committee was formed with the intent to raise funds to retire Tom's campaign debt. A crowd of about 150 persons, including four former governors and several hopeful candidates for various political offices, gathered in the evening at Boone National Armory in Frankfort, Kentucky 16 July 1977. Future governor Martha Layne Collins, and Dr. Harvey Sloane, were also among the crowd. A bluegrass band played until dinner was served. The menu included burgoo, cornbread and iced tea. Governor Julian Carroll arrived and came to the table where Helen and I were seated. Looking at my piece of cornbread, he warned, "Doctor, there is an ant on your cornbread." I replied, "I wouldn't know the difference if I ate it." The governor replied, "Ah, but the ant would."

I shared the platform with the incumbent and three former governors of Kentucky: Happy Chandler, Bert T. Combs, and Wendell Ford. We were also joined by the Lieutenant Governor, Mrs. Thelma Stovall, and Senator John Berry who served as Master of Ceremonies. After I spoke the invocation and turned to sit back down, Senator Berry called on me to make a speech. I was caught off guard, but made some remarks. Anyway, it was a poor performance. The former governors were recognized and each made a speech. "All speeches sounded like sermons. There was a spirit of a revival meeting." Unfortunately not nearly enough money was raised to wipe out Tom Ward's debt, but the amount that was raised helped.

In 1972 Dr. Harvey Sloane ran for mayor against the Louisville Democratic machine's candidate. I accompanied him in canvasses of my neighborhood and at the Seminary, introducing him as "the next mayor of Louisville." He had never run for public office before, but he carried all twelve wards in Louisville! When he spoke to my Christianity and Politics class, the mayor told the students that I had taught him his first political principles. Later, in a losing bid, he ran for governor of Kentucky. He had my full support, which included writing letters and giving speeches on his behalf.

In addition to backing Mayor Sloane, I also lent my support to Creighton Mershon when he ran for membership on the Board of Aldermen of Louisville. Later I supported his sister, Melissa, who ran successfully for the Board of Aldermen from the First Ward.

Of course, as the old saying goes, "to the victor the spoils." I received awards from the Mayor and from the Board of Aldermen. On 31 May 1977 the mayor presented me with the keys to the city and designated me a "distinguished citizen" for my participation in Louisville's civic and political life. On 21 November 1977 Creighton Mershon, by then the president of the Board of Aldermen, presented me with a certificate of merit for similar contributions.

In 1963 I backed Bruce Blythe, that year's Republican candidate from my district for Kentucky State House of Representatives. Bruce won the hearts of his electorate and was re-elected eight times. He was a faithful member of the Sunday School Class I taught for twelve years at Calvin Presbyterian Church in Louisville, Kentucky.

Other political candidates I have supported over the years—some who won and some who did not—included: Fred Cowan, a lawyer and a Harvard graduate, who was elected as a Kentucky State Representative in 1984 and defeated in a bid for Lieutenant Governor.

My letter to the *Courier-Journal* was published 10 May 1991. See below.

Editor
Courier Journal
525 W. Broadway
Louisville, KY 40202
Dear Sir:
I am voting for and actively supporting Fred Cowan for Lieutenant Governor of Kentucky because he is a man of moral integrity, of experience in the practice of law and government. He has a passion for justice and as Attorney General has demonstrated fairness.

He is a person of energetic initiative in tackling tough issues and finding creative ways to solve them. All of these qualities add up to competent and compassionate leadership needed in the role of Lieutenant Governor and for a better quality of life for all the people of the state we love.
Sincerely,
Henlee Barnette

Tom Owen, University of Louisville's Archivist, who ran but lost the race for Mayor of Louisville in 1998. He attended Southern Baptist Seminary 1962 to 1964. He almost won the race against his opponent—Dave Armstrong. I put up a Tom Owen Mayor '98 yard sign and gave some financial aid. As the saying goes, "You can't win them all."

Eleanor Jordan, who ran for US Congress against Republican Ann Northup. My daughter Martha was a tireless volunteer in Jordan's campaign. Since it was Martha's first venture into politics, the loss was especially difficult.

Jerry Abramson had my full support as a candidate, and then the incumbent mayor of Louisville 1985–1998. Jerry was re-elected so many times, he became known as the city's "life-long mayor." He has since become Metro Mayor in the newly reorganized city and county government.

An Especially Satisfying Accomplishment

Tina Ward-Pugh unseated the incumbent alderman of Louisville's Ward One in May 1998. Tina, a graduate of the Southern Baptist Theological Seminary School of Social Work, operated a small repair business. Prior to the election to the Board of Aldermen, she had served as assistant to an alderman and was well-acquainted with the work of that office. My daughter, Martha, and I gave full support to her campaign. On 7 January 1999 it was my honor to offer the following benediction at the installation ceremony that seated her on the Board of Aldermen:

> Gracious God, bless your servants who have assumed aldermanic responsibilities. May they always be aware that they are ministers of God for the common good and the welfare of all the people. Grant to them: Competence to solve tough problems;
> Compassion for people in need; and,
> Courage to do the right thing.
> Anoint them with double portions of your Spirit:
> The spirit of wisdom and understanding;
> The spirit of counsel and strength;
> The spirit of knowledge and the fear of the Lord.

May the power entrusted to all of our public servants be turned to establishing policies that promote justice and peace, so that our earthly city may conform more to that heavenly city.

To these ends let us all "do justice, love mercy and walk humbly with God."

Amen.

Tina insisted on being called "Alderwoman." She led the movement that resulted in the passage of the city's "Fairness Act," ensuring basic rights for gays and lesbians. On Tina's second run for office in 2001 the now fundamentalist administration of the Southern Baptist Theological Seminary attempted to defeat her candidacy by getting seminary students to register to vote. When I showed up to vote at Crescent Hill Baptist Church on Frankfort Avenue, there were two long lines of seminary students waiting to vote. For the first time in memory, a Democrat lost in Ward One's Precinct G150, the seminary's precinct. Tina, despite losing that one precinct, was reelected to the city's Board of Aldermen in a landslide victory.

Presidential Politics

John F. Kennedy ran for President of the United States in 1960. Since he was a Catholic, many Protestants felt that he would be unduly influenced in the political sphere by the Roman Catholic Church. The fear was that the pope would tell the president how to run the country. A great deal of anti-Catholic literature was dug up and played up in print, on radio and television.

Several years before Kennedy became a presidential candidate, I had written a tract titled "Baptists, Roman Catholics and Religious Freedom." I sold it to the Sunday School Board of the Southern Baptist Convention for twenty dollars. They published, I am told, 250,000 copies of the tract. The *New York Times* carried a photo of and a criticism of its content in one of its issues. It was also displayed in the US House of Representatives. The reporter who wrote the story for The *New York Times* did not read the short article, I am sure. He designated it as an anti-Catholic piece. It was actually a comparative study of the religious philosophy of Baptists and Catholics. While all this was going on I was lecturing at Stetson University in Florida, and had predicted that Kennedy would become the next president of the United States.

In 1977 Dr. Glen Dorris, pastor of Louisville's Second Presbyterian Church, visited me at Southern Seminary. He asked that I help elect a Southern Baptist as president. When I asked who the candidate was, he responded, "Jimmy Carter." After hearing more about the governor from Georgia and his political platform, I agreed to work on his campaign. The first thing I did was help organize "Clergy for Carter." We held our meetings in the Second Presbyterian Church during the campaign season. Several ministers in the city participated and gave their support to Governor Carter's presidential aspirations. After he won the election, I was invited to attend President Jimmy Carter's inauguration in Washington D.C.

Democrat Bill Clinton, a former governor of Arkansas, won the presidential election in 1992. His opponent, George Bush, was defeated largely due to the prevailing troubles in national economy at that time. Clinton was re-elected for a second term in 1996. His opponent in that race was Senator Robert Dole from Kansas. Clinton's years were marked by great economic prosperity and large political scandals. Nevertheless, I voted for him in both elections. I continued to provide President Clinton my active support, including what financial assistance I might, through all his troubles.

These are a few politicians who received my support, especially Johnson, Carter, and Clinton. Other politicians at the local, state and national level received my support. I never held a political office, preferring to select and support the persons who possessed the qualifications to get the job done.

21

Vietnam

War is crucifixion.
—H. R. Niebuhr

Old politicians start wars and children do the fighting. Combat personnel largely are composed of youth still in their teens or early twenties. Most are from society's poor and middle classes, with a disproportionate number from various minority population groups. Wars affect every generation for ill, which outweighs the good that comes from them. I have known veterans of five wars whose wounds never healed and whose lives were ruined forever. With a few exceptions, veterans often are treated shabbily by governments and citizens, as was the case of the "Vietnam vets" when they returned home.

Here I want to describe the response of two of my sons, John and Wayne, to the Vietnam War. Their postures reflected the division in America over our participation in that war.

John

My oldest son, John Alexander, was born in Louisville, Kentucky, 5 May 1944. We were living in the Old Haymarket in the Union Gospel Mission house at First and Jefferson Streets. John's birth inspired a poem from his father, written at the Baptist Hospital immediately following the baby's arrival.

The Firstborn

At last the nurse
with bundle small
appeared before me in the hall.
Routinely she remarked:
"You have a baby boy."
I gazed upon that little life
with mingled awe and glee.
And felt that God
had come down
to shake hands with me.

As John grew up, he went to school, was a regular participant in church and Sunday School (and sometimes willingly!), joined the boy scouts, was athletically inclined and loved sports. He was an excellent student and enjoyed an active, positive social life.

Tragedy, however, seemed to stalk John. He saw his mother dying. I do not recall him shedding a tear. But years later a neighbor related how John, then just nine years old, would go to a clump of bushes just outside her window and cry for his mother. We all need a crying place and a laughing place. Growing up, John struggled with the tension between faith and reason. As a teenager he would request prayer from Helen and me, but then declare that he could not believe in God. He could not reconcile the death of his mother, Charlotte, and a God of love.

John played basketball in high school. Unfortunately, he injured one of his ankles and the doctor advised him to give up the game because his foot and ankle would swell each time he played. Upon graduating from high school John enrolled at Wake Forest University, my alma mater.

John transferred to the University of Tennessee at Knoxville at the end of his sophomore year. He graduated Phi Beta Kappa from the College of Liberal Arts as the top student in class of March 1966. He received four scholarship offers to pursue a Ph.D.: University of Tennessee, Ohio State University, University of Florida and University of North Carolina at Chapel Hill. He chose the University of North Carolina. Although pursuing graduate studies, the Selective Service draft board in Louisville ordered him to report for induction at the city's Federal Office Building.

Immediately after learning about the action taken by the Selective Service System, I visited the administrative chief in charge of the Louisville branch. In our conference, I noted that all graduate students were legally exempt from the draft. That did not cut any mustard. So I pressed on. By this time, others in the office had joined the dialogue. They said, "We did not know he could do graduate work." I handed them the front page of *The Knoxville Sentinel* newspaper. On it was a photo of John, featured as a recipient of the Phi Beta Kappa award and first in his class. "Now you know," I said. "Put that in your files."

Even the news article did not cause them to rescind the requirement that John report for induction. So I asked to use the telephone. "What do you want with that?" I was asked. A call to the registrar at the University of North Carolina would prove that John was enrolled. Alas, that strategy didn't work either. Finally, I informed the Selective Service administrators that the following week I would be in Washington DC and would put the matter personally before Bo Callaway—who was influential in the government—and Brooks Hays, special advisor to the President of the United States. I observed that I had served on a Baptist Social Service Commission with the latter gentleman for six years.

As I turned to leave they called after me, saying the matter could be settled right there in Louisville. It was—and John's name was removed from the draft in 1968. Ironically, that same year he left graduate school and enlisted in the US Air Force. He was sent to Lackland Air Force Base for enlisted basic training and then Officer Candidate School.

When John entered officer training, he told me it made a difference. The food was better, facilities better and he didn't have to salute the latrine any more! In Denver-Lower he studied intelligence and photography, then moved on to Westover Air Force Base in Massachusetts. From there he flew to Vietnam's Ton San Nhut Airbase for his first tour of duty. Later, he returned to Westover.

John flew back to Vietnam in 1968 shortly after the Tet (New Year) offensive in January. At the completion of his service he flew back to Beale Air Force Base in California, where he was honorably discharged from the US Air Force with the rank of Captain (O-3). Recognizing the outstanding character of his military service, the Air Force offered to promote him to the rank of major (O-4) if he would remain on active duty. At least four other professors at Southern Seminary had sons serving in Vietnam. These were Professor Bill Cromer's son, Dan; Dr. Eric Rust's son David, an air controller at Ton San Nhut; Dr. Wayne Oates's son, Bill, who served on the Me Kong River; Dr. Frank Stagg's son, Bob, an MP on the docks of Saigon.

When John was in college and the military we kept in contact with him by mail. He wrote numerous letters explaining his experiences; some sad, some glad. His step-mother, Helen, cared deeply for John and his brother, Wayne. She labored and loved without ceasing to bring them through grief and depression following the death of their mother, Charlotte. The two letters that follow reflect something of the spirit and quality of our family communication. We were a closely-knit family, though widely diverse in our views. This made for excitement, intellectual growth and rational action.

> 20 July 1965
> Mr. John Barnette
> Knoxville, Tennessee 37916
> Dear John:
> During the week of July 8-14 I participated in the Training Union Leadership Conference at Ridgecrest Baptist Assembly in North Carolina. My general subject was "Christian Ethics." In three letters prior to my going to Ridgecrest, the secretary of the Training Union Department had stated that he was very anxious that we not enter into controversial areas in our lectures. One letter stated: "My chief request is that they be Bible based, and that we avoid becoming too involved in controversial issues." I showed this statement to Wayne and he almost rolled on the floor. He asked: "How can a message be Bible based without being controversial?"
> My first four messages were well received. The last one had to do with race relations. Here I got some static. I briefly described the philosophy of the protest movement, pointing out that it was based upon love, Ghandi's non-violence, and Thoreau's concept of civil disobedience. Also, during the message I pointed out that each time I attend the Southern Baptist Convention I hear one of our great leaders say that "Baptists are a people of the Book." Then I added that when I observe how Southern Baptists behave in human-relations, I wonder which book they are talking about!
> After the speech a doctor came upon the platform and asked me if I believed in civil disobedience. I asked him if he remembered what Peter and John did after they were released from prison for preaching the Gospel. I related the story of how the mayor of the town informed these two men that

an ordinance was on the books which forbade preaching of the Gospel. I repeatedly asked him what did Peter and John say? Finally he said, "We must obey God rather than man." I said, "Well, you have answered your own question."

Later on, two men from Alabama handed a written statement to the Executive Secretary of the Training Union protesting what I had said. They agreed that the first four messages were really great, but then they felt that the last message on race ruined everything I had said!

During the week I autographed a number of my books. One man from Georgia bought a copy and wrote all over it statements disagreeing with me. There was hardly a blank spot on the chapter dealing with race relations. After he had written all over the book, he handed it back to me. But later he took it back. I could see a gradual change in his attitude toward Christianity and its application to social issues.

I spoke in several cabins and cottages during the evenings after the regular services in the main auditorium. In one cabin there were about fifteen people from Georgia. We started the discussion and inevitably it went from sex to race. A married couple, obviously nouveau-riche and chaperones, became very vocal about race relations. The wife declared that she could not stand "stinkin' niggers" and wound up with a pyrotechnic bang saying that God intended for the races to remain separate. She opined that blackbirds do not mate with bluebirds. I agreed, but pointed out that black cows mate with white ones! "And besides," I said, "We are not birds." I added that I had seen some human beings that were "birds" but that most of us were human beings and that her analogy broke down at this point. I thought I might be thrown out for making such statements, but I survived.

One tragic experience I must relate. A lovely woman about forty years old asked me for a conference. We met in a quiet place in the lobby of Pritchell Hall, and she told me the story of how she had come to Ridgecrest to make a decision. She was the wife of a pastor and had two or three children. Her doctors had informed her that she had MS (Multiple Sclerosis) and that she did not have long to live. Her question was whether or not she should stay with her husband and tell the church about her condition or simply withdraw to a country home which her family owned about sixty miles from where her husband was pastor. She felt that if the church found out that she was sick and could not be of help to her husband in the church that she might be a handicap to her husband. My suggestion was that she stay with her husband, because this would give stability to him and the family. I told her that I thought that the church would be sympathetic and would come with loving arms to comfort her and to a source of strength to her in these final days.

By the way, I received about ten invitations to give lectures on Christian Ethics in churches and assemblies across the country. After the speech on race relations, I think most of those invitations have been cancelled!

Best wishes with reference to your studies.

Affectionately,

Dad

13 November 1969

Lieutenant John A. Barnette

265 F. New Ludlow Road

Apartment 5

Chicopee, Massachusetts 01022

Dear John:

I have just returned from Lexington, Kentucky, where I spoke to the Southern Seminary alumni at the Phoenix Hotel, to the Kentucky Baptist Convention, and then recruited some students for Southern Seminary at the University of Kentucky. Tomorrow I speak at the Sacred Heart Academy on Lexington Road.

We received a letter from Grandmother Ford and she expressed her sorrow about Wayne leaving the country rather than going into the military service. But she agreed that it was his decision to make.

She informed us that your Uncle Ted had a throat operation in which his voice box was removed. He has learned to talk on his hands.

In January, Peggie is getting married. Ruth and Paul live in Starkville, Mississippi, and are very active in the church there.

My dear friend Dr. Clarence Jordan died last week. We are having a memorial service for him the Chapel, November 19. He was in charge of city mission work here in Louisville when I worked in the old Haymarket District. You were born when we lived in the old Haymarket mission.

Let us hear from you.

Love from all of us to you,

Dad

31 August 1970

Capt. John A. Barnette

P.S.C. 2, Box 13317

A.P.O. San Francisco, California 96201

Dear John:

This week we received a letter from Wayne containing several photographs of Jennifer. She is a lovely child and I am sure that Wayne will send you some pictures of her.

Speaking of pictures, please have some photographs made of yourself as you did in Westover Base. Now that you have the rank of captain, your photograph should show two bars.

For two weeks now I have been down with some kind of virus. I must have picked this up in New Mexico when I was lecturing in Glorieta. At Glorieta the doctor put me on Acromicine and some of the brethren accused me of being on "downers." But I managed to make it through the series of lectures with the help of Judge Chrisman and narcotics officer Jay Hand, both of Dallas, Texas.

The Lacyes are on their way to Stockholm to visit Wayne and Ann. Today we sent by airmail a whole box of blankets, baby food, etc. Next Monday, August 31, the whole family starts back to school. This semester I am teaching a course on Christian Ethics and the Ecological Crisis. I have just finished ten chapters of a new book on *The Drug Crisis and the Church*. I just don't have the physical strength to put the finishing touches on it. The publisher is waiting for it. My latest piece from Westminster Press is entitled "Crucial Problems in Christian Perspective."

Your VW is running nicely. I don't drive it very much or very far. Just enough each day to keep it in good shape. A large VW sales and service organization has just opened up in St. Matthew's where O'Keefe operated a Ford place.

Last week I wrote to Purdue University for a copy of their graduate program in business management. As soon as the catalog comes, I will sent it to you. Dr. Wallace Dentom, who is head of the Family relations Department at Purdue, suggested the business school at this university. Wallace always asks about you when I see him. You may not remember Dr. Wallace, but he was a student at Southern Baptist Seminary when you were a young chap coming along.

Write soon.

Love from all of us,

Dad

18 April

Dear John,

Your slides arrived in good shape! We looked at them this evening—some are over-exposed (a little exposure perhaps as you were loading or unloading), but most came out well, including the two handsome ones of you! Several impressive buildings, street scenes, buddies sunbathing, etc. By the way, the one of some "Bar" came out—stay *outa* them joints, buddy!!

It's a crazy mixed up world, isn't it? Since I last wrote we have had the shock of Dr. King's death, riots (not here), etc. What a year to teach

American history!! Henlee was at Duke University at a conference (on "Hope") when all this occurred. Dr. King's brother, A. D. Williams King, pastor of Zion Baptist here, was scheduled to speak in Henlee's ethics class the very week of the funeral! (Cancelled, of course) Was going to outline the strategy of "Poor People's March on Washington" which is scheduled for April 29th. Anyhow, Henlee was in downtown Durham buying tape for a tape-recorder when the state militia cordoned off a whole section of town. Things were tense there and other places, too, but Washington and Baltimore and Kansas City evidently fared the worst. I'm not much of an analyst, but it seems the Negro, in his despairing hopelessness, is fighting back at the *symbols* of white discrimination, i.e., the *property* of the white man as opposed to the *life* of the "honkie." And the white man doesn't seem yet to comprehend that desperate frustration and explosion of long-controlled hatred—and keeps hitting back at symptoms rather than basic causes.

I was distressed to hear expressed by my school children the distorted, racist-type views—parroting their parents, of course. But even worse was what some of the teachers expressed! One said, "They are right to give the reward money to the man who did it!" And another was furious about the "flag flying at half-mast for a man who urged sedition!!!", etc.

The funeral was covered by T.V. almost as extensively as the Kennedy one. Interesting to see Nixon, Humphrey, Bobby and Ethel Kennedy, Edward Kennedy, Mrs. JFK, Eugene McCarthy, Romney, Rocky and Happy, etc. all in a cluster in the Ebenezer Baptist Church!

[A page to this letter is missing.] …. Thirty-two more teaching days till vacation! I'm *so* relieved we will be right here! We plan to buy the kiddos a tent for the backyard (where the pool used to be)—Henlee looked at Sears and found ol' *Jesse* in charge of that department. Ron wants to see these slides soon, he says.

Last we heard from Wayne he was headed toward East Berlin. Hard telling where he is now!

Hope you're not working too hard—looked like you had a real tan in those slides! Saw a T.V. special by Charles Collingwood Tuesday evening on "Hanoi"—rather perceptively done, I think. According to CBS, he's the first T.V. commentator from our country invited—or granted permission—to film over there.

Take care of yourself, John. We devour your letters again and again—and think of you <u>so</u> often! Write when you can!

Love,
Mom

Wednesday, 27 April 1967
Louisville, Kentucky
Dear John,

It was good to hear from you. Sorry I've been so terribly negligent about writing. Henlee's clipped every item on the housing ruckus 'cause he's been quite involved. Went to a couple of demonstrations, but not after the court injunction against same. It's difficult to see the end to all this, especially with the lack of leadership from Schmied. Several of our students have been arrested for "demonstrating"—etc., etc. – most of the action has been around the south end, though they *did* drive through Cherokee Park the other evening, leading reporters and police on a wild goose chase!

Claypool was on a television "special" on The Moral Side of the News the other night—really laid it on the line! And lots of the staid Crescent Hill Members are *seething*!!! "Why doesn't he stick to the *Simple Gospel*??!!" It's really rough!

Henlee's new book was written up in the *Courier*—about six lines! It's due out May 8th—hope it sells well. Incidentally, the tuition has gone up at U of L. In fact, I will probably go to summer school, then teach in the fall. I have a possibility of a job at Barret, and that's just too good to pass up!—esp. since I'll have to get at least one more year of "classroom experience" before being certified as a "guidance gal."

Saw *Jesse* at drugstore tonight. Said Ron is still "waiting it out." Learned at church that Bob Stagg (soph at LSU) was classified 1-A—parents went down to draft board, they didn't have *any record* of his being in college. Boy, what a fun place *that* is!!—the draft board place, that is! Newton is still hobbling around with a cane, etc. Think he's returned to his base in Ohio, though.

"Our priest" came for my S.S. class this past Sunday. He was "new" to us, teaches philosophy at Bellarmine, was fresh out of Ohio State with his Ph.D. The girls all thought he was a livin' doll, and he really was articulate—He didn't convert any of us!

Kentucky Southern is really in financial straits, and in danger of losing accreditation—or rather, not *achieving* it! The college asked Kentucky Baptist Convention to "turn it loose" <u>with</u> a stipend of several thousand dollars—which it did, reluctantly. The school wanted to take federal grants, but still is ineligible due to lack of accreditation...—vicious cycle. Burhans is pretty despairing at this point.

Wayne was home recently, but only briefly—for a concert. Things seem to be working out well for his year at Munich. And he still has his 2-S classification.

Haven't picked my horse in the Derby yet—probably Damascus, but I'll have to consult the forms next week—or consult my bookie! (Just joking.)

The Hull's fence (remember it?) has been "vandalized"—two gates and some supportive pipe removed in the dead of night!!!! Of course, I've accused the Bennetts of lifting 'em, but they stoutly deny any part of it! It obviously was a "spite" act because if someone simply needed two gates, they coulda lifted ours right beside the Hull's—instead they removed one from front and one from back.

We're really looking forward to your coming home at the end of next month. Too bad you can't be here for Music Night at Emmet Field May 9—Martha will do a violin duet (screech!) with another gal (She's better on piano, believe me!) Jimmy continues to mature (I think)—he found an old Cub Scout Scarf and hat and this has become his official "costume" for the past week! He *is* learning to read a bit.

The New Orleans trip was grand for Martha Ann. But now "how ya' gonna keep 'em down on the farm"...? You and Jim were the only ones she wrote while there.

Take care and let us hear from you. How long a leave will you get?? Jimmy is literally crossing off the days!

Much love,
Mom

After a semester of graduate study at the University of Kentucky following his tour of duty in the Air Force, John began work with the Veterans' Administration as a claims adjuster, a position he held until retirement. Here he helped many veterans improve their quality of life.

In Louisville, he met and married Janice Karman, a lovely and gracious woman. St. Edwards Catholic Church, where it was my joy to officiate. They were blessed by a son, John Andrew (Drew), now a graduate student at Dayton University (Ohio). When first returning from Vietnam, John had joined Louisville's Christ Church Cathedral (Episcopal). After marriage, he joined the Roman Catholic Church and has been a devoted member of a local parish for many years.

Wayne

Wayne was born 18 May 1947 in Birmingham, Alabama. We lived in a two room home. John slept in the kitchen. Wayne had been given the wrong "baby formula" at the hospital and he cried for a week because that nutrition caused him gastric discomfort. After he got the right formula he was a happy lad ...and the rest of his family was happier, too.

Wayne attended the same elementary schools that John did, the same church, Sunday School, same Boy Scouts, had the same parents and yet they were different in personality and philosophy. Wayne was more Gandhian and John more Niebuhrian. Both were athletic and loved sports, their schools, and church. Both excelled in academics and in social activities. Both were deeply hurt at the death of their mother.

Wayne, like his brother John, thought deeply about life. At age three, Wayne asked me a serious theological question: "If God made everything, who made God?" I was dumbfounded and told him to ask his mother! Charlotte gave our three year old theologian an answer that satisfied at that time in his life. To this day he wrestles with the question.

When as a four-year old he sat on a fire-ant hole and was bitten, he asked me: "Did God make those ants?" My answer was in the affirmative. He then declared: "I hate God."

He was an excellent student and a lover of classical music, especially Mozart. After high school classes, he would come home, drop his books and make for the Southern Seminary music library where he would listen to Mozart and read. He was selected as a part of the National Honor Society of Secondary Schools (1964), Phi Sigma Tau National honor society in philosophy (1967), Kentucky Junior Academy of Science (1963–64), National Merit Scholarship, National Science Foundation Scholarship at Centre College Kentucky (1964).

Wayne especially enjoyed basketball and soccer. He played on a church team in Louisville. Much was learned about sports from foreign students attending the Baptist seminary. He regularly would join students playing various sports on the Josephus Bowl, a grassy section of the Seminary campus.

Wayne excelled in German and science at Atherton High School. A Swedish family, the Backa Birger Ericssons, lived in campus housing. Mr. Yurli Ericsson was a student in Religious Education. His wife and Helen became close friends. The Ericsson children, Hans and Karin, also struck up a close friendship with Wayne. They taught him to speak Swedish.

Always a sensitive person, Wayne early became aware of the race issue. As a member of Louisville's Crescent Hill Baptist Church in the sixties, he invited several young blacks from nearby Beargrass Baptist Church to attend his church which had no blacks in the congregation. He led them right down to near the front pews and sat with them in worship. Earlier as a child, he saw a bulletin board in front of a church declaring: "Welcome Everyone." He turned to me and asked: "Do they really mean that?"

At the prestigious small Centre College in Kentucky, Wayne excelled in science and math. He continued to wrestle with the philosophical question: "Why is there something rather than nothing?" This was the title of his philosophical essay presented to his class in philosophy about 1967. He also began to study the role of the Christian and war.

During his freshman year, Wayne worked in the summer at a European Bottling Plant in Germany stacking up Coca-Cola bottle racks. It was tough work. After six weeks he quit and hitchhiked to Austria, returning to Germany to study German at the University of Vienna. His brother John sent him the money for the cost of the course. Following that experience, Wayne returned to Centre College for his second semester.

When his junior year came, Wayne attended the University of Munich in Germany. Here he studied under Max Müller, the distinguished social philosopher, and majored in German. He returned to the USA in September 1968.

On week-ends and holidays Wayne came home from college and sometimes brought a couple of friends. They seemed to enjoy being in our home. A letter from one guest reads in part: "I want to thank you for your hospitality ... I only wish I could have stayed longer as there seems to be so much to learn right there in your home. I was particularly interested in your discussion of the separation of church and state."

On 30 May 1969 Wayne married his classmate, Ann Marie Lacey, daughter of Dr. and Mrs. Forrest Lacey of Knoxville, Tennessee.. The couple graduated from Centre College 1 June 1969. On 15 July 1969 Wayne was ordered to report for induction into the Armed Forces of the United States.

Wayne and his young bride, however, had airline tickets for Canada—and from there to Sweden. I drove them to the airport in Louisville. On the way I attempted some talk about "pioneer spirit" and facing the unknown. Then I asked "Are you sure you don't want to reconsider?" His hand covered hers and he declared "No." As I saw their aircraft disappear into the distance, I was struck with the thought that I might never see them again on American soil. But then, in the words of

Luther's great hymn *A Mighty Fortress Is Our God*, a time may come to each of us when we are called to follow our convictions and let "goods and kindred go"—perhaps forever.

On 10 September 1969, the Associated Press called at my home announcing that my son Wayne Barnette had been granted residence in Sweden along with twelve other American "defectors." The Swedish Emigration Service had made the announcement. Now the Associated Press wanted a story. I gave them a few comments concerning Wayne and added that I had another son who was a Vietnam veteran. The Associated Press thought that made a great story, and the message went out to all their newspaper clients.

On 11 September, our telephone at home rang. The caller was Jean Howerton, a reporter from the *Courier-Journal*. I made it clear to her that both Mrs. Barnette and I wholly approved of both of our sons' decisions with respect to military service at that time.

On September 12, the *Courier-Journal* carried the news about Wayne as a front-page story. My pastor, Dr. John Claypool, called and said, "I am sure that you are going to catch all hell and I just wanted you to know that I am supporting you."

The Bennetts, who live just behind us, called shortly afterward and expressed their support. (Rev. Bennett was chaplain at the mental hospital in Anchorage, Kentucky.) The telephone kept ringing, and I finally left the house for the seminary just to get away from it. Some nasty calls came to the seminary, but they never reached me.

In the evening, the *Louisville Times* called, and I offered some corrections to the story that appeared in the morning *Courier-Journal*. One glaring error was that Wayne was "frantically" opposed to the war in Vietnam. The word should more appropriately have been "radically."

That same evening, the Metro-Broadcasting Company of New York called and requested an interview. Then, at about 7:30 P.M., a reporter from the *Birmingham News* called. He said that he had been a former student at Samford College in Birmingham and that he had read one of my books. The Associated Press called several times over the next few days asking for pictures of the family. We steadfastly refused.

We were approached by more than just the local and national press. The World News Feature Syndicate did a story for *Match* (the *Life Magazine* of France) and *Der Spiegel* (*Time Magazine* of Germany).

We received a number of beautiful letters from people. The vice president of Bellarmine College was one of the first to correspond. Some very prominent people in the city of Louisville wrote us very supportive and encouraging letters. Many of the students at Southern Seminary expressed their sincere concern for my son and our family, as did some of the faculty. We also received a lovely letter from Sister Mary Catherine, a Catholic nun and Ph.D. student in theology at the seminary.

To be sure, letters also came branding Wayne a traitor and coward. Some so-called ardent patriots did not have the courage to sign their names to the messages of condemnation they felt compelled to send us.

A 16 September 1969 editorial in *Cento*, the Centre College newspaper, carried an *In Memoriam* to Wayne:

> Last spring students mourned the death of a Centre graduate killed in Vietnam. Memorial services were held and the courage of the young man who had given his life in the service of his country was praised in a declaration delivered by the President of the College. This week papers contained reports of the so-called "defection" of Centre graduate Wayne Barnette. No memorial services have been planned and no declaration will be forthcoming; the event, however, is no less worthy of commemoration, for Wayne has cut himself off from our society in a way paralleled only by death.
>
> The deliberate and considered acts of conscionable men involving great sacrifice are always deserving of praise even when they might challenge our personal and arbitrary conception of duty. By avoiding prosecution for draft resistance Wayne has made a sacrifice most of us would consider unthinkable. Though we may be reluctant or incapable of judging the correctness of the decision we none the less can commend the dedication to conscience the deed requires.

In Sweden Wayne helped to organize and became a co-director of the Center in Stockholm. It opened the first week of June 1970. A letter from Wayne and Ann describes the nature and function of The Center:

Dear friends—

We opened this office the first week of June. It is run by deserters and is concerned with helping American deserters and resisters adjust to life in Sweden. We provide information to the new deserters about the Swedish bureaucracy, jobs and housing, how to meet girls, etc. We also contact counselors—priest, sociologists, psychologists, lawyers, etc.—for deserters and resisters who have need of this service.

The Center is dedicated to social service for the deserter-resister community here. Those of us who work here represent no one point of view. We are here to be used, to be of use to all sections of the community.

We are anxious that guys thinking about coming to Sweden know that we are here at their disposal. We will answer inquiries about conditions here, and will help new guys get settled.

We are anxious that your organization feel free to ask us for information—we will reply.

The Center needs money. It also needs old cameras, guitars, radios, English books, winter coats, records, etc. We welcome all contributions, and will see that they get distributed. We'll use the money to build a budget for the Center.

In determination—Wayne and Ann[1]

In the spring of 1970 Wayne enrolled in the University of Stockholm and later in the University of Lund, founded in the twelfth century. Here he had a brilliant record in Russian and German and received the *Filosofie Kandidat*. I am told this degree would be equivalent to a doctorate in some American universities.

Wayne would not return to the United States under the pardons of President Nixon, Ford, or Carter arguing that he had committed no crime. So he continued his studies. In the summers he went to eastern satellite countries of The Soviet Union and learned their languages. He, of course, could not visit NATO countries without being arrested.

The Swedish Broadcasting Corporation sent Örjan Öberg and his assistant to our home 8 October 1970 to interview us about Wayne. They were interviewing seven families of seven defectors to Sweden. Our interview occurred in our back yard with Helen, Martha, Jim and me. Director Öberg said to me, "You have one son who is gung ho, the other one

---

[1] The story of deserters and defectors in Sweden is told by Thomas L. Hays in *American Deserters in Sweden* New York Association Press, 1971. Wayne's situation is described in the book.

is a CO [conscientious objector]. Now what are you?" Response: "I am an SCO" "What is that?" he asked. "I am a selective conscientious objector. As a Christian, I select the wars I will support." He got the distinction and understood my position.

Almost five years after his departure from the USA, Wayne received a letter from the U.S. Attorney General declaring that charges against him had been dropped, that he would not be arrested if he came home. Dr. Forrest Lacey, Professor of Law at the University of Tennessee and Wayne's father-in-law, secured the services of a lawyer from California to handle Wayne's case. Wayne had registered as a CO, but had not received papers to appeal a first legal rejection of that status. Hence, the case against him was ultimately dropped. The Attorney General further invited Wayne to visit in his offices. On 10 March 1974 Wayne and his family returned home from their stay in Sweden.

The story about John and Wayne, according to the press, was important because it reflected the divide in the nation over the Vietnam War. On one side were the Pentagon, politicians, corporations, my country "right or wrong" superpatriots, and on the other side the peace movements, CO's, protestors and pacifists. The latter felt vindicated by the publication of Robert McNamara's memoirs, *In Retrospect: The Tragedy and Lessons of Vietnam.* McNamara was Defense Secretary during the Vietnam War and a chief architect of the war. In his book he declared: "We were wrong, terribly wrong."

Despite our differences of opinion on issues, our family was close knit in the bond of love. There were never any nasty arguments about critical issues. We agreed to disagree and to respect each others' views. When we discovered we were wrong, we quickly confessed our mistakes.

To our surprise we had a flood of calls, letters and cards from friends and people we never knew supported us as parents and a family. Pastor John Claypool of Crescent Hill Baptist Church and members had always openly stood by us. We also had strong support from the Catholic Community. One of the most beautiful and poignant letters came from a nun. She wrote:

Dear friend in Christ—
Sometimes—without warning—life brings us to a communion service that church knows nothing of. I felt that yesterday—as I shared your coffee

and suddenly realized I likewise shared the poignancy of your son's presence.

Once—in my innocence—I thought that celibates made to God the ultimate sacrifice of childlessness for the sake of the Church. How greater is the father's loss who must keep adjusting as his boys grow into separate sons.

I bless and thank you.

Wayne taught Russian at Vanderbilt University where he earned a Ph.D. in that language. He also played on Vanderbilt's soccer team. Today (2004) he is in business for himself as translator of Slavic and Germanic languages for multinational corporations.

22

War, Amnesty, Peace and Patriotism

War is hell.
—General William Tecumseh Sherman

I have always had a strong sense of patriotism, tempered by a strong commitment to peace. My uncle was a soldier during World War I. Once, when my cousin and I were playing as marching soldiers, my uncle told me that my cousin would make the better soldier. I was hurt and never forgot that unkind remark. As a teenager, I sought to enlist in the US Marine Corps. In line with other enlistees, I approached the old recruiting sergeant. He directed acceptable candidates to various stations to continue the process. Those who were not heavy enough were told to go around the corner, eat all the bananas they could and come back. When I stepped up the sergeant took one look at me and barked "Go around the corner, eat an anvil and come back!" That public rejection devastated me and still lingers in my memory.

My life has spanned six major wars: World War I, II, the wars in Korea and Vietnam, the Gulf War, the Afghanistan War, and the Iraq War. As a lad, I did not question American's involvement in World War I even though I was not aware of its causes. My father presented me with a ten dollar Liberty Bond, issued to finance the battle against "Kaiser Bill" of Germany. Also I learned the popular war songs of the times, such as, "Over there, Over there" and "It is a Long, Long Way to Tipperary, But My Heart's Right There."

Likewise, World War II received my full support. It was a just war against an unjust regime. Two of my brothers served in the US Navy during that global conflict. It was a just war because Hitler invaded defenseless nations like Belgium, Austria and Poland. The world was under genuine threat by the military power and aggressive ambitions of fascist Nazi Germany.

The Korean War

The Korean War (1950-1953) was fought by the forces of the United Nations (primarily by US and South Korean forces) to prevent North Korean Communists from taking over South Korea. It was a terrible war as the media and historians are beginning to reveal. My friend of more than eighty years, Major General Turner C. Rogers, was a hero of the Korean War. A pilot, he flew the legendary P-51 Mustang long-range fighter airplane. A highly decorated service member, his awards included the Distinguished Flying Cross for Heroism. About three and a half million casualties were suffered, two million by North Korea and one and a half million by the United Nations forces. A peace treaty has never been signed and Korea remains divided. The Korean War was one of the most destructive of the twentieth century. Perhaps as many as 4 million Koreans died throughout the peninsula, two-thirds of them civilians. (*The New American Desk Encyclopedia,* Concord Reference Book, 1984, p. 6.)

US participation in the Korean War was justified in the sense it was entered on proper authority. (President Truman ordered it; the intention was to contain communism). On the negative side, thousands of civilians were killed; atrocities were committed on both sides; there was no victory and the goal of peace was never formally achieved.

Vietnam

Measured by the criteria of the "just war" theory, America's participation in the Vietnam conflict was overwhelmingly unjust and unwise.

According to the *justum bellum* theory:

1) a just war must be just in *intention*. (The original intention was not merely to save South Vietnam, but to support French Colonialism and to contain Red China.)

2) A just war must be just in its *cause*. (The United States intervened in a civil war and not a defensive one.)

3) A just war must be conducted under *lawful authority*. (This war was never approved formally in accordance with the Constitution.)

4) A just war must be just in *conduct*. (The use of napalm, area bombing, vast ecological destruction, the burning of villages "to save them," killing of civilians, and the condoning of the use of torture make it difficult to believe that just means were used.)

5) a just war is *proportional*, one in which the evil of war must not be more than the evil to be corrected. (What good was accomplished could not possibly be greater than or equal to the vast destruction and killing of millions of people for a dubious "peace with honor.")

6) All means for peace must be exhausted before initiating a war. (No serious efforts were made to enlist the United Nations in a peacekeeping role. It was the intention of the US to keep Vietnam divided North and South.)

7) Finally, before a war can be considered just, there must be a reasonable hope for victory. (Given our government's strategy in Vietnam, some early observed that the war could not be won even by our vast superiority in the air and on land; General MacArthur, the legendary World War II commander who later gained additional notoriety in the Truman administration, warned that any nation that engaged in a land war in Southeast Asia must have a hole in its head.)

US Secretary of Defense Robert S. McNamara and President Lyndon Johnson finally confessed that American intervention in the Vietnamese conflict was a terrible mistake. (See *In Retrospect: The Tragedy and Lessons of Vietnam.*) Tapes of Johnson's comments about the stupidity of our participation in the conflict are now available. He refused to end the war because he did not want to be the first American president to lose a war. The war was finally brought to an end during the Nixon administration

Seminary students were divided on America's participation in Vietnam. A few could not rationally discuss the issue. In the 1990s a secretary at Southern Baptist Seminary discovered a report on a student (We will call him "Y") dated 1968. It read in part: "Larry Franklin in to report Y. conduct in cafeteria involving H. Hollis, H. Barnette. Y became angry threw chair at table hit Larry in knees."

Here is the rest of the story. As a professor I regularly ate lunch with a group of students in the cafeteria and dialogued with them. Students asked about my stand on the Vietnam War, then in process. They knew but just wanted to start a conversation. I described how the French withdrew when the Japanese invaded Vietnam leaving the Vietnamese to fight the Japanese. Ho Chi Minh, I noted, unified the first movement against the Japanese with American support. When I declared that Ho had become the George Washington of the Vietnamese people, Y became very angry, picked up a chair and threw it at my end of the table. It struck students Larry Franklin and Harry Hollis. So far as I know no punishment other than reprimand was received by student Y. When the above occurred five faculty members had sons serving in Vietnam.

Through articles and lectures I protested the American participation in the Vietnam War. Among these were "Vietnam: Some Proposals for an American Exodus" *Western Recorder*, 15 August 1968 and elsewhere. Also I published articles on modern warfare and the Christian conscience: "New Dimensions of Warfare," Chapter 5 in *The New Theology and Morality: Thinking about the Unthinkable.* Philadelphia: The Westminster Press, 1967; "War and the Christian Conscience;" *Review and Expositor*: 66 Supplement (May 1969).

The Gulf War

In 1991 the US military engaged in The Gulf War. This war was just in terms of authority. It was waged by The President, Congress and allies. The intention was to free Kuwait from Iraqi captors under the Dictator Saddam Hussein. American soldiers defeated the Iraqi army and freed Kuwait. Here again civilians were killed. It was a just war and an unjust war.

US participation in the Bosnia-Kosovo conflict was aimed at peace in the Balkans. It was authorized by the President. This is a just war principle. Again civilians were killed. "Ethnic cleansing" was practiced, that is, the effort to eliminate a whole ethnic group until the NATO-based military force intervened.

War on Terrorism

After terrorists attacked the World Trade Center and The Pentagon (9-11-01), President Bush declared war on terrorism. Countries harboring terrorists would be held accountable. The President specifically named North Korea, Iran and Iraq as nations that posed a great danger to the United States.

In the development of the President's foreign policy the war on terrorists became a war against dangerous regimes. So the attack on Afghanistan and Iraq. Saudi Arabia was not condemned by our government, yet most of the terrorists of 9-11-01 were from there.

We are discovering that the war on terrorism is not just another war. It is a war led by Islamic extremists who hate America and the Western life-style. It is a clash of ideologies, cultures and civilizations. This war will be long and costly in terms of lives and resources. Al Qaida is a network of terrorists located in places all around the world, including the United States. Osama bin Laden is the leader and chief financier of Al Qaida.

Extremist Islamic terrorists are totally committed to destroying the western way of life by every means possible. Suicide bombers kill and maim innocent people in the name of God, Allah, believing they will go straight to paradise.

Unfortunately the war on terrorism got diverted to Iraq before Afghanistan was stabilized.

The War in Iraq

Some evangelical and Baptist religious leaders firmly hold the war in Iraq to be a just war. By no stretch of the imagination can this present war be a just one. It is just only in the sense that it was authorized by the President and Congress. On the negative side: It was not a defensive war but a pre-emptive one against a sovereign nation; its intention is highly questionable. Was it personal vengeance of President Bush? Could it be thirst for Iraqi oil? There was poor intelligence; there was poor planning for reconstruction and stability; there was the use of deception to urge us into war. it was claimed that there was an immediate threat from Iraq's use of weapons of mass destruction. No weapons of mass destruction have been found and no hard knowledge of any linkage of Iraq to Al Qaida. Our soldiers have not been adequately equipped against enemy fire. Moreover some soldiers' stay in Iraq has been extended beyond the time promised. A just war must be proportional which means the evil of war must not inflict more damage than the evil to be corrected. War in Iraq has caused thousands of deaths and much destruction. True, some schools have been opened, electrical power turned on, and other improvements. All means for peace must be exhausted before beginning a war. The United Nations requested more time to search for weapons of mass destruction. Our government lost patience and unilaterally entered the war minus the support of the United Nations. Now our administration is pleading for its aid. Hundreds of extremist Muslims from neighboring countries have invaded Iraq, joined forces with opponents of America's presence in that country. Every day they attack American soldiers and citizens. Already there is talk about another Vietnam.

Now with the disclosure of the terrible treatment of Iraqi prisoners in prisons operated by the American military the US will find it more difficult to win over the hearts and minds of the Iraqis.

The classical just war theory which has guided the church for centuries is no longer possible in modern warfare. Civilians die with soldiers. Pre-emptive wars will likely continue. The US has set a precedent for other nations to practice pre-emptive wars. Weapons of warfare will become more accurate and destructive. Future wars will be fought by advanced technology and by remote control by instruments in the sky. Whole cities may be destroyed by weapons of mass destruction.

Amnesty

After the withdrawal of American troops from Vietnam, I turned my attention to support the cause of amnesty for those Americans who resisted military conscription during the conduct of the war. By amnesty, I meant universal and unconditional amnesty for those who resisted the draft. My own son, Wayne—a resister who found sanctuary in Sweden after having been illegally drafted—refused to return under pardons offered by presidents Nixon, Ford and Carter. Wayne believed the term "pardon" implied a crime, and he firmly held that he was guilty of no such thing.

In dealing with moral and political issues related to amnesty, I was fortunate to be invited to participate in programs on a national scope. I invited students in my Christian Ethics class to go with me to an Interfaith Consultation at Peabody College in Nashville, Tennessee, on 24 October 1973. Two students joined me and we drove to Nashville. To my surprise, one of the students had just completed his tour of duty in the US Marine

Corps. The other one had been a US Army Green Beret. Both had seen combat in the Vietnam War and neither one supported amnesty for draft resisters. By the time they returned to Louisville both men had become supportive of universal amnesty.

The main address at the Interfaith Consultation was given by Henry Schwartzschild, Director of Project on Amnesty for the American Civil Liberties Union. My topic was "Theological and Ethical Bases for Amnesty." I grounded amnesty in the theology of resistance, reconciliation and reformation. It was carried widely in the religious press.

I always desired to say and do at home what I did and said in other places. So I participated in the 26 April 1974 "Interfaith Conference on Amnesty—Veterans Issues" at the Louisville Presbyterian Seminary. In the conference I served as moderator of the "Parents' Panel," where the parents of draft resisters met. In this panel we discussed a number of dimensions of amnesty from an academic point of view and then as an experiential issue. There were sixteen men in our area who had been resisting the draft. My son was in Sweden. Others were in Canada and England.

The parents each made comments about how they viewed their son's situation, expressing the sense of loss endured and hope that their sons would return soon. I reported that my son was fortunate in that he spoke Swedish, Russian and German, and had been in Sweden previously. He had enrolled at the Universities of Stockholm and Lund and served as the Co-director of The Center, an organization that welcomed military deserters and draft resisters, providing various forms of aid and assistance in adjusting to the Swedish culture.

We closed our session by pledging to engage in action supporting universal and unconditional amnesty, to support one another, our sons and all other draft resisters. I wrote several articles on amnesty. Among these are "Agony and Amnesty," in *The Christian Century*, 29 September 1971, "We have pardoned others…" *The Louisville Times*, 9 December 1975, A-23. I received letters of both praise and condemnation for efforts. These and others will be sent to the Wake Forest University Archives in Winston-Salem, North Carolina.

In addition I pled to our Baptist denominational leaders to provide support for these men. An example follows:

28 December 1971
Arthur Rutledge
Executive Secretary-Treasurer
Home Mission Board
Southern Baptist Convention
Atlanta, Georgia
Dear Arthur:

For some time I have been thinking that one of our Southern Baptist agencies should perform a ministry to our young men who confront the military draft. It appears to me that we need a chaplain to develop a program to meet the needs of our exiles, those in prison and deserters from the military. Also this program would minister to the thousands of men returning from Vietnam who are depressed, disillusioned and often rejected by their fellow Americans. Families of GI's also need help.

All of these young men need help and counseling from their church leaders. The situation on our college and seminary campuses calls for leadership in ministering to men confronted with the draft and who are having problems of re-entry into our culture. There is the drug problem among our GIs and on and on.

Surely these Baptist men deserve some sort of spiritual ministry from their denomination. A few years ago some of us (myself and a couple of students) made ourselves available to counsel with young men in the seminary and those in the community who were facing the draft. On almost every Baptist college campus the draft counselors are students who do their work on a voluntary basis. So far as I know they have no help from any of our Southern Baptist agencies.

These are just thoughts that have come to me and I would like to see some program beamed in the direction of the thousands of Baptist young people who are troubled about the military.

Best wishes for a happy New Year.

Yours for the Kingdom,
Henlee Barnette

I am not aware of any specific action taken by the denomination in response to my request for aid to draft resisters. These men were taught at home, in Sunday School and church that it is wrong to kill. When they put the teaching into practice, they were not only deserted by their churches, but in many cases also suffered their condemnation.

Responses to Amnesty Actions

Responses of readers to my articles and actions on amnesty were filled with praise and condemnation. Laity, pastors, editors, and service men wrote expressing strong feelings and convictions about unconditional universal amnesty. The following is a sample of the negative responses received:

> Professor H. H. Barnette:
> I am thoroughly *against* amnesty for any hippie or any scum. If the dog gone cowards are afraid to defend our country then let them stay in Canada, Sweden and under no circumstances allowed to return to the USA. Perhaps that should include Gerald Ford who proposed the scheme to protect some and the likes of you that wear the clerical garb.
>
> Also, let the Vietnam refugees go back where they formerly resided as they want to do, but we provide them with jobs and there are Americans more suitable and willing to work then what I have seen on TV or read in the liberal papers. We are a country that tries to help and then get kicked in the puss as many countries have done for years and are still doing today. Buying friendship never solved a thing.
>
> Why don't you stick to your work or get the hell out as you certainly are not teaching the right thing. A grave diggers job or garbage collector is more your style!
> A concerned citizen
> (*He didn't have courage to sign his name.*)

Some respondents personalized the debate by mentioning my draft-resisting son. The following letter represents the attitude of many Southern Baptist pastors at the time:

> Dear Dr. Barnette
> Let me be one Southern Baptist who is willing to speak out on the amnesty question.
>
> Your son rejected this nation. He wasn't forced to leave. I'm sorry he felt as he did, but since he doesn't like our type of government I'm happy for him in his new residence.
>
> I object to many of our laws. I "lose" in most elections. We made a number of bad choices in Vietnam. Nevertheless I'm going to stay and make it a better land.
>
> When our children go wrong or take a course that cannot be justified, we would do well to admit that wrong is wrong. Your attitude is one that reveals a standard of "what my child does is right." If he had not have been a perfect

child in your sight, you would have a better system of ethics and morals today.

Sincerely,

the pastor did sign his name.

My reply to the pastor was as follows:

November 20, 1973

Dear Sir:

It was thoughtful of you to write me a letter objecting to my view of amnesty. The tone of your letter indicates that you are absolutely right in your position on amnesty and that no one else has any right to disagree—a thoroughly unBaptistic view.

You have the fallacious notion that I speak for amnesty just because my son is a war resister. He went to Europe as a teenager and had no intention of returning to the US to live. Moreover, I wrote articles against our intervention in a civil war in Vietnam. This was during the sixties and I stood for amnesty then. I do not feel that my son "went wrong," but went right. He refused to kill in an unjust, immoral and illegal war. He felt that it was his patriotic duty to refuse to do so. Senator Carl Schurz said on the Senate floor: "Our country, right or wrong. When right, keep it right; when wrong, put it right." Thousands of young war resisters tried to "put it right." For this they were branded as criminals. Millions of American agreed with them but they, because of age and sex, were not forced to make the agonizing decision as to whether to disobey, flee or go to prison. Again it was partly the courage of the self-imposed exile that awakened the rest of America to the fact that our policy in Vietnam was wrong. Now the majority of Americans know that it was wrong.

You say that I would have "a better system of ethics and morals" if I had not seen my son as a perfect child. What kind of ethics does a church have that teaches a child: "Thou shalt not kill," "Do unto others as you would have them do unto you," "Love your enemies," and "Obey God rather than man" and then rejects him when he puts these teachings into practice?

When young men like my son had the courage to put these teachings into practice, their own churches rejected them. No wonder some churches have a credibility gap.

What kind of ethics is it that sanctions an unjust, non-defensive war in which millions are killed? The war in Indo-China can never be squared with the *justum bellum*, just war, theory which has guided the churches through the centuries with reference to Christian participation in war.

What kind of ethics is it that demands punishment for young men who have the courage to resist war cooked up by power hungry presidents and politicians, greedy businessmen and Pentagon people who lied to us about the war? We have amnestized these people, but not those whose only "crime" was not to have any part in an unjust war. Not only was it an unjust war, but it was an illegal one (never approved by Congress which the Constitution requires). The fact that Congress recently put curbs on the President's power to make war on his own says something to us about the abuse of that power in relation to the tragic Indonesian War.

What kind of ethics is it that demands punishment for those who on grounds of conscience refuse to participate in the military and lets thousands of Americans escape the draft by college deferments and clever lawyers who found ways for their clients to avoid participation in the military?

What kind of ethics is it that forgives the rich, the powerful and crooked politicians (Agnew was put on probation for a felony) and will not forgive those who stand for righteousness?

Yours for peace,
Henlee Barnette

Some, including many Roman Catholics, responded warmly to my position on amnesty, as the following letter demonstrates:

World Justice and Peace Office
Province of St. Joseph of the Capuchin-Franciscan Order
1000 West Center Street
Milwaukee, Wisconsin 53206
November 9, 1971
Dear Dr. Barnette:
Your recent article in the *Christian Century* has prompted this office to embark upon the enclosed project for amnesty. [Several articles were enclosed.]

The enclosures explain who we are and what our strategy will be. We invite criticism as to how we can be more effective. In particular I wonder if you could share with us some of your information concerning historical precedents (especially the role of church groups) and what groups are in the forefront of the movement today.

I must admit that my own research concerning the amnesties after the First and Second World War have generally shown them to be shams. However because of the uniqueness of this war in this century, I have not at all been discouraged. Thank you in advance.

Sincerely,
James R. McCarville
Assistant Director

Peacemaking

Peacemaking has not been a priority in much Christian theology of the nineteenth and twentieth centuries. Nor has the church been very concerned about social peace in the world. Rather, emphasis has been on buildings, budgets and membership numbers. I attempted to ground peacemaking in the Holy Scripture to give peace a higher priority in theological discourse and the church.

Granted, my writing was terribly inadequate as reflected in articles I published and lectures I presented. Among these were "Seek Peace and Pursue it", the *California Southern Baptist*, 12 August 1970. Also I wrote a "Resolution on Peace" for Dr. Duke K. McCall to present at the Tokyo Baptist World Alliance Meeting (1970). Earlier I published "Paths to Peace" in the *Florida Baptist Witness*, 28 December 1950.

I belonged to several "peace movement" organizations. Among these were the Baptist World Peace Committee. When in the Soviet Union, I observed the word *mir* (peace) on everything from billboards to match boxes, from badges to huge signs stretched across streets calling for world peace. I wrote Congressman Brooks Hays and informed him that the Soviets were in an all-out propaganda program for peace. I noted that Dr. Charles F. Boss, director of the Methodist Peace Program—traveling in the U.S.S.R. with the American delegation—had a budget of $135,000 undergirding his organization's efforts. I urged Congressman Hays to work for a Southern Baptist program for world peace. A Southern Baptist World Peace Committee was formed, to which I was elected. With Professor Frank Stagg, I participated in peacemaking promotion activities on Southern Seminary's campus. I also taught courses dealing with war and peace, placing an emphasis on the theology of peacemaking and its role as the basic calling of the church.

For several years I held membership in the Baptist Peace Fellowship of North America. That organization's central goal was to seek *shalom*—the special Hebrew word for thoroughgoing peace—for the individual and the world.

Numerous wars go on even in so-called "times of peace." These conflicts—limited to regional civil wars and hostilities between small countries—are popularly called "brushfire wars." Our task as Christians, regardless the level of conflict, is to be peace*makers* not merely peace talkers, hopers and wishers. Peace is made to happen. Let us "seek peace and pursue it" (Ps 34:14; 1 Pet 3:11).

Patriotism

Patriotism is one of the most perverted words in the English language. For some it means "My country, right or wrong." This smacks of blind obedience to government regardless of its policies. It is a narrow kind of patriotism in which pride in the nation tends to become ultimate and idolatrous.

In contrast to the "cult of patriotism" or the "super patriots," there is an authentic patriotism that takes seriously the statement of Senator Schurz: "My country, right or wrong. When right to keep it right and when wrong to put her right."

Phony patriotism is described by Samuel Johnson as "the last refuge of a scoundrel." He was speaking of those who wrap themselves in the country's flag and, in the name of love for country, commit all sorts of evil which under any other disguise would be grounds for criminal charges. Among these scoundrels are those politicians who cynically manipulate gullible people, steal from the taxpayer, send our youth into illegal wars, deny the people's rights enshrined in the Bill of Rights, support policies that result in the pollution our air and water, appeal to the basest motives to enhance their own egos and to gain and secure power, and lie to the citizenry when caught in the wrong to save their political hides.

Authentic patriotism has many dimensions and expresses itself in numerous ways. It includes love for one's country and concern for the welfare of other countries; it is a feeling of kinship with one's own people, and loyalty to the basic values of freedom and justice that make the nation great; it places morality above the material interests; and is associated with symbols and rites in terms of songs, the flag and the pledge of allegiance.

Jesus' patriotism was not provincial but extended to all humanity. He rejected the extremes represented by the Sadducees, who were blind to injustice, and that of the Zealots, who believed that injustice could be overcome by violence. Instead, he taught the way of love with justice.

A Pilgrimage of Faith

National Anthem

This brings us to our national anthem. For many years I have been unhappy with it. I published one small article in the *Christian Century* on the subject. The pathetic phenomena of our way of life is the halfhearted and fuzzy manner in which we sing our national anthem. Recall how it is sung at the opening of athletic games, political rallies and in some of the schools of our land. Few even know the words of the first stanza, much less the other three. Few appear to be caught up in the spirit of the song and inspired by it.

There is evidence that the music of the "Star Spangled Banner" came from an English drinking song used in taverns and that the words were written by a Baptist. The music is difficult to play and the lyrics are a challenge to the majority of Americans. Hence, our present national anthem should be put in mothballs and a new one written that would inspire love for our country, true patriotism and selfless sacrifice on the part of Americans. As a matter of fact, we have largely substituted "God Bless America" and "America the Beautiful" for our national anthem.

The new national anthem should catch the true spirit of our American heritage and the principle of democracy in the context of the changes in our historical situation. It should clearly articulate our sense of vocation and destiny as a nation in a pluralistic society and in a world greatly inter-connected by geo-politics. Today (2004) the national anthem is enjoying a resurgence of popularity due to a revival of patriotism after 9-11-2001. But few know the words and even professional singers are reluctant to sing it in public.

23

International Relations

Globalization calls for a global ethic.

In the 1960s I prepared a course on the role of the church in foreign relations. With the approval of President Duke McCall, I invited Congressman Brooks Hays to the seminary to serve as professor of International Relations.

He visited the campus and we talked about the Christian Ethics Department and his role in relation to the course. He would be free to develop that area in which he had considerable expertise. He had served the Congress from the state of Arkansas. During his tenure our government had dealt with numerous problems relating to foreign affairs. He also had served as a special advisor to President Kennedy.

Unfortunately we did not succeed in securing Mr. Hays, and the International Relations Department never developed at the seminary. Despite our early disappointment, work in that area continued with my successor, Dr. Glen Stassen.

In a previous chapter reference is made to a conference with Nikita Khrushchev that initiated a cultural exchange program between the United States and the Soviet Union. That was during 1957, as the Cold War was really heating up. It is my belief that this conference with Khrushchev was the catalyst which resulted in the resumption of student and cultural exchanges between the Soviets and the US It is not too much to say that the seeds were sown in that exchange for the eventual beginning of the end to the Cold War.

International relations have to do with the politics of diplomatic, economic, military and socio-cultural relations between countries. We increasingly talk about "global politics" or "geo-politics," for we are more aware of global thinking in our day-to-day lives. For example, the US military often works in cooperation with the United Nations and NATO for the purposes of peace and order around the world. Diplomacy is the path of international bridge-building through which countries may settle differences. Globalization, the expansion beyond parochialism of any one nation's pursuits in relation to other countries, is increasingly prevalent in the political life of the world. This developing global perspective is also evident in the worldwide religious sphere.

Victor Karpov

A Nuclear War Institute was held by Loyola University's West Baden College in West Baden Springs, Indiana, on 8–10 November 1963. Jesuit priest James C. Fleck, a student, founded the institute out of concern over the devastation that would be caused by a nuclear conflict. Fifteen authorities in science, education, government and religion participated in the program. Among these were Victor Karpov, First Secretary of the Washington Embassy of the USSR.;[1] Alain Enthoven, an Oxford University graduate with a doctorate from Massachusetts Institute of Technology; Dr. Paul Ramsey, Chairman of the Department of Religion at Princeton, who addressed justice and war. The USA and the Soviet Union had just entered into a nuclear "test ban" treaty. It was the center of much of our discussion.

I served as a commentator on Karpov's speech that was titled, "To Live or Survive?" He spoke of the significance of the nuclear test ban treaty between the USSR. and the USA. Both nations so stockpiled nuclear weapons that each had "overkill capacity." From a moral point of view, Karpov declared, nuclear war cannot be justified. He asserted that nuclear war could be prevented by "peaceful coexistence" in our relationship with other countries. Further, he argued that efforts must be made to disarm nations and destroy nuclear weapons arsenals. The immediacy of the devastation wrought by nuclear conflict demanded that we act now to prevent such a war from ever taking place. Karpov concluded that nuclear war was not inevitable if we "want peace, work for disarmament and peaceful coexistence of all nations."

---

[1] Karpov later became Chief Negotiator for the USSR in efforts to reduce nuclear weapons arsenals of the USSR and the USA.

Following is my response to Mr. Karpov's message. I agreed with many of his ideas, but did not trust the Soviet Union to keep its part of the envisioned treaty.

Peace is one of the major topics of discussion in the Soviet Union. From Khrushchev in the Kremlin to the poor peasant on the Kolkhoz, one can hear the message of peace. "Peace to the world," and "For peace and friendship" are slogans which appear on everything from huge placards stretched across city streets to the lowly matchbox.

At a conference in the Kremlin, Mr. Khrushchev said to a delegation of which I was a member: "No sane person wants war; there are no more staunch supporters for peace than in our country." In that same conference, Khrushchev said that the way to bring about peace is the establishment of confidence and that the most practical way to do this is to remove all trade barriers.

Americans, I believe, sincerely desire peace and would agree that the first step in this direction would be the establishment of mutual confidence and trust. But we find it difficult to trust the leaders of the USS.R. for several basic reasons.

1. We have no mutual ultimate moral ground upon which to stand. In *The Great Soviet Encyclopedia* communist morality is defined as, "the principles and norms of conduct of the fighters for communism, of the builders of communism." And Mr. Shiskin in his book, *The Basis of Communist Morality*, says that: "back of the principles and norms of communist morality stands the force of the whole people which has created these norms." Lenin put it very simply when he said that communist ethics is derived from "the interest of the class struggle of the proletariat." Therefore, the communist ethic is classcentric. Hence, that conduct is right which furthers the Communist Revolution—wrong, which hinders it. Therefore, "the end justifies the means" and it is legitimate to resort to "zigzag" policies, brutality, murder and slavery to achieve communist goals. Up to now Soviet leaders have not even accepted the rules of international law. We have, therefore, no common code of moral law as a basis for understanding, confidence and peace.

2. Mr. Karpov, we would like to have confidence in the promises made by the heads of the Soviet Union. In speaking of bourgeois morality, Lenin described the capitalists as living by the principle: "Promises are like piecrusts—they are made to be broken." This statement is often taken out of context and made to appear that Lenin is describing communist morality. Nevertheless, the actions of Soviet leaders are in keeping with this principle, for they have broken many promises and treaties since 1917. Even before the

revolution started, Lenin promised "peace, land and bread." In the Soviet Union the people may have peace and bread, but they certainly do not have any land. Land was immediately confiscated by the government and people forced to work for the State. We hope that the [promises made in the] test ban treaty will not [similarly] be broken.

3. We would like to believe that by the term "peace," Soviet leaders mean "peace on earth good will toward men." But we have the feeling that they do not think of peace in this sense. Mr. Karpov cites a German military expert who once said that war is a continuation of politics by other means. Did not Stalin declare that peace is war "other than by military means"? (*International Press Conference* 8/84, 28 November 1928, 1590). When the Soviets placed missiles in Cuba, most Americans lost all confidence that they might have had in the Soviet's announcements about peace. The tensions created recently on the German autobahn by halting our military convoys increases our distrust in Soviet leaders.

4. Mr. Karpov states that the best way to avert war and to exclude it completely from society is to achieve general and complete disarmament. He further indicates that the Soviets were working hard for this goal. But we find it difficult to have confidence in such claims. For example, in today's newspaper the Center for Strategic Studies at Georgetown University reports that the Soviets are beginning the production of "a new family of bombs." Among them is the gigaton bomb, which must be the granddaddy in the family for it will have the potential of 1000 megatons.

5. The communists do have a "just war" theory. "Just" wars are fought by communists; "unjust" wars are those fought by capitalists. Khrushchev is clearly on record that he will continue to support "wars of liberation," and "brush fire wars" to drive out the "imperialists" and those who impose colonialism upon weaker nations. Apparently, the imposition of communism on the satellite countries of Europe is viewed as liberation rather than colonialism.

6. The people of the USSR. want peace as well as the people of the US Once when I was in Odessa, I went to the beach on the Black Sea and a woman came out from the crowd and said to me: "We must never have another war. I lost my home, my husband and my three sons in the last war." The people in the Soviet Union know something of the devastation of war and therefore they want peace. Twenty-five million families lost their homes in World War II.

But the Soviet leaders do not appear to want peace. Before we can have confidence in them, they must demonstrate a desire for peace in concrete terms. Then we can sit down at a conference table and negotiate in good faith. When the Soviet leaders show by their deeds they really want peace, I think that our leaders will meet them halfway on all issues.

Mr. Karpov, no doubt, feels that I have made a lot of unfounded statements. If I have, and he can show where I have erred, I shall gladly repent and accept the truth.

When I concluded this speech, the attending audience rose to offer an ovation for my comments. Most vocal in plaudits were Roman Catholic nuns, members of theology faculties and students.

United Nations

On 7 June 1954 members of a subcommittee of the Senate Foreign Relations Committee, chaired by Senator Alexander Wiley, Wisconsin, heard the pros and cons of revising the United Nations Charter. The discussion occurred in the science building of the University of Louisville. Senators listened with interest and responded with dignity, though some speakers were emotionally critical of the United Nations.

I came to the defense of the UN after a critical statement by Mrs. Bennett F. Hughes, Kentucky State Chairman of Correct Use of the Flag. She appeared to be ready to sack the UN in the name of God. My extended comments and some dialogue with the subcommittee are reported below:

Mr. Chairman and Members of the subcommittee:

As I understand it, this subcommittee is not concerned with whether the witness likes or dislikes the United Nations. Rather it wants to discover what changes, if any, "could be made in the Charter in order that it may most effectively promote the security and well-being of this country and best contribute to general world peace."

Amendment to the Charter is difficult, if not almost impossible. Any permanent member of the Security Council can prevent the adoption of any proposal for reform of the Charter. In the light of the present situation, the Soviet Union is not likely to approve any revision of the Charter which will make for the security and well-being of this country or promote the peace of the world.

Nevertheless, assuming that the Charter can be changed, at what points should it be revised?

General Revision

A Pilgrimage of Faith

There should be a general revision of the Charter. It is involved, repetitious and loaded with ambiguous provisions. No doubt this is due in part to the fact that it was conceived for the pre-atomic era. It should be made more simple, direct and relevant to the needs of this solemn hour.

Veto Power

More specifically the veto power should be eliminated as it applies to membership and constructive measures which the majority of the nations would approve. Under the present arrangement any permanent member of the Security Council can black-ball the admission of a new member.

Regional Arrangements

Revise the Charter so that regional security arrangements will be more intimately integrated into the UN system of collective security. This would preclude the possibility of a regional agency undercutting and weakening the UN collective security and avoid the polarization of power into two major opposing camps. Negotiations would then be on a multilateral rather than a bilateral basis.

Charter Change by Interpretation

These proposed changes in the Charter would strengthen it. But even if the Charter is not changed as to text, it is *de facto* changed in content by interpretation, non-application and supplementary agreements whereby members extend or restrict their obligations under the Charter. So we need not greatly despair at present if the Charter is not revised.

Despite Weaknesses and Failures, UN an Effective Medium

Finally, we must beware of falling into Utopian quicksand by thinking that plans for Charter revision, universal disarmament and the elimination of the veto are nostrums which can quickly cure the radical ills of our time. Certainly we must keep these goals before us, but at the same time be willing to take the next practical steps in their direction. The UN, despite its weaknesses and failures, is still the most effective medium by which international ethics and a relative world peace can be achieved.

I am not giving uncritical and blind worship to the UN. If I wanted to give it a theological sanction, I could do that, because there are 111 articles in the United Nations Charter, there are 111 verses in the Sermon on the Mount, and we are meeting in room 111.

In response to that remark, laughter broke out among the subcommittee members and others in attendance. The chairman then interrupted my commentary and a dialogue ensued, the record of which follows:

Chairman: Just a moment. Is it your opinion that if the UN were to go out the window, so to speak, be abolished, the nations of the earth would have to have a substitute if they wanted to try to formulate some plan for peace?

Mr. Barnette: Yes, sir. I think there would have to be some sort of alternative; and the critics of the UN have not come up with a realistic alternative.

The Chairman: Well, is it not also true that if in an organization—I care not what the organization be—the members of the organization are not morally straight, then the organization is not at fault; it is the membership that is at fault?

Mr. Barnette: Yes, sir.

Chairman: Would you apply the same rule to the UN? Assuming that the Kremlin and its stooges would play the game according to the rules that we think should be applied in international procedures, do you not think that we could get along lots better?

Mr. Barnette: Yes, sir.

Chairman: Any questions, Senator Gillette?

Senator Gillette: No questions, Mr. Chairman, but I want to compliment this gentleman on his closing statement that the UN, despite its weaknesses and failures, is still the most effective medium by which international ethics and a relative world peace can be achieved.

There are many of us who feel that it does mark the high point in attempts to achieve international cooperation.

We also recognize at the same time the thing that you have recognized; that it has weaknesses and has failures; but your suggestion that, instead of abandoning it, we continue the efforts to try to make it as effective as we can, is very helpful.

Thank you.

Chairman: Senator Cooper?

Senator Cooper: I, too, would like to say that I think his statement was a very moderate and sensible statement. I think he would agree that the troubles in the UN reflect the troubles in the world. Things cannot be any better inside the UN than the things that are happening in the world.

What would you consider would be the result if the UN should disintegrate, if we should withdraw, which I think would mean disintegration? What avenues would you see that many countries throughout the world would then have as to any consultation upon peaceful measures?

.... What avenue would a small country have, such as a country in southeast Asia, to consult with us, or how could we reach them effectively?

Mr. Barnette: All of the lines of communications would be closed to the smaller nations. They would have no recourse to an organization whereby they could bring their grievances and their hopes and their desires as a nation.

Senator Cooper: Do you think that, in all likelihood, the struggle between the great powers would then be intensified?

Mr. Barnette. Yes, sir, because there are moral forces which are brought to bear upon the situation through the UN that could not possibly be brought to bear otherwise.

Shortly thereafter the hearings were adjourned. That evening, the *Louisville Times* carried a brief report of the meetings in which Mrs. Hughes and I, with opposing points of view regarding the utility of the United Nations, were quoted.

An Ambassadorship

President Bill Clinton in 1993 was seeking someone to be ambassador to Austria, a much sought after post. By way of a registered letter, I recommended Swanee Hunt. She had attended, with her husband, the Southern Baptist Theological Seminary. She was not identified as a student in the directory for security reasons. Her father was H. L. Hunt, the Texas billionaire. Swanee and my wife Helen had struck up a friendship. She would occasionally come to our house where Helen and the children enjoyed her company.

I wrote the president as follows:

25 August 1993
President Clinton
Office of the President of the United States
Capitol Building
Washington, DC 20500
Dear Mr. President:
Let me recommend Swanee Hunt of Denver, Colorado, for Ambassador to Austria. I have known her for many years and found her to be a person of integrity with unusual commitment to democratic ideals and competency in

implementing them in terms of business, relationship to others and the political process.

Swanee is a person of sincere compassion for those in need and who struggle to survive as her Hunt Alternatives Fund reveals in a very practical way. She is sensitive to the needs of others and can work with those at the highest cultural level.

In my judgment, Swanee Hunt will be more than a run-of-the-mill ambassador by engendering respect of the Austrians, promoting our interests as a nation and restoring a sense of our own pride in American Foreign Affairs.

Respectfully yours,
Henlee Hulix Barnette, PhD
Senior Research Professor
University of Louisville, Medical School

A few days after I sent the letter, I received a call from the U. S. Secret Service who requested my evaluation of Swanee. I noted that she was ideally qualified to fill the role as ambassador to Austria. She was fluent in German, an accomplished musician (her husband in a second marriage was Director of the Denver Symphony), and she raised one million dollars for the Clinton Presidential Campaign. She received the appointment and I received an invitation to her swearing-in ceremony in Washington D.C.

24

Connecting

Love is the connecting rod between speaker and audience.

An electrician spent a whole day trying to get the door chimes to function at my daughter's house. He gave up. Since I had done some simple electrical work around my own house, I took a look at the problem. I traced the wire leading from the chimes to the outlet and discovered that it was not adequately connected.

Connecting with Students

Connecting with audiences on college campuses, especially at some Christian schools where required religion courses are felt by many students to be an imposition, seemed especially challenging during the difficult years of the sixties and seventies. I discovered just how real was the existence of skepticism and an attitude of rebellion among many students. The positive side to that outlook of suspicion and rejection of the *status quo* was the students' readiness to protest war, racism, politicians, big corporations and religious oppression.

In the 1960s I was invited to give lectures at William Jewell College in Missouri. Students were required to attend chapel and they were a rebellious bunch: inattentive, often reading newspapers, talking to each other, tossing objects about. Dr. Gordon Kingsley (later to be president), chairman of the lectureship committee, forewarned me that anything could happen. Indeed, the distinguished preacher, Dr. John Killinger of Vanderbilt University had been "hooted" during the last chapel session.

The day I spoke to the people in the chapel it was filled. Dr. Kingsley had chastised the students for their behavior. I had just gotten my speech underway when a student in the balcony held a bunch of papers over the edge, waited a moment and then dropped them on the congregation below. It looked like giant sized snowflakes were falling from the balcony.

Of course, everyone looked at me to see how I would handle the situation. Ignoring the incident, I proceeded to say, "A certain man had two sons. One graduated as the top student in the class with Phi Beta Kappa honors. He was offered large scholarships for his Ph.D. program in four major universities. Rather than pursue such a program, he enlisted in the US Air Force, spent two tours of duty in Vietnam and rose to the rank of Captain. The other son when drafted, said "Hell no, I won't go" and left for Sweden where he became chairman of The Center which received draft resisters from the United States.

By this time I had the students' full attention and added that the young men in the story were my sons. I said that I approved of both of their actions because they both made courageous decisions. Their decisions were made in the light of three criteria:

> 1) They examined what they believed to be the facts about our
>   intervention in Vietnam.
> 2) They formed their own convictions.
> 3) They had guts enough to act on their convictions.

I concluded that to be a mature authentic person and not an "other-directed person" in decision-making, you have to gather the facts, form your convictions and have courage enough to act upon them.

I closed by relating how I had recently been lecturing on another college campus. The chairperson of the lectureship committee inquired if I wanted to know what the students were asking about me. Of course I did. She replied that they were asking: "Is he for real?" In other words, is he authentic or just a phony. At the next lecture I discovered on the blackboard behind me the following question in large letters: "If you were arrested for being a Christian, would there be enough evidence to convict you?"

I concluded that we are only as real as we have the convictions and courage to live by them. I then sat down. That "unruly bunch" responded with an enthusiastic ovation. I had connected.

Also in the 1960s, I gave a lecture at Georgetown College, a Baptist school in Kentucky. Some students on the front row of the chapel were reading comics; some were in amorous action and some chitchatting. This went on while the chairperson was trying to introduce me. I walked to the podium and just stood there observing the situation. After a while the students began to glance up to see why I was not saying anything. Finally, when I had their attention, I said, "Now when you pull my string I will do my thing." After some laughter, I made my speech, which was well accepted.

On 4 March 1977 Philip Berrigan, brother of Dan, Catholic priests who protested against war and the nuclear arms race, spoke to a Christian Ethics class at Southern Seminary. He was originally scheduled to speak at Louisville Presbyterian Seminary. I invited him to come over to Southern Baptist Seminary and speak to the ethics class there, as well. Before Philip could get here he was jailed. Later, a judge released him to give the lectures at both seminaries. Professor Glen Stassen served as host at Southern Seminary. The largest lecture hall at Southern was filled to capacity when Philip Berrigan spoke. There appeared to have been some anxiety about the event among the seminary's administrators.

Philip and Dan were "theologians of resistance." If some students were disappointed because Philip did not explain the exact nature of the "theology of resistance" nor provide a specific strategy on how to apply it, more were intrigued by the challenge he laid down. He left it for the students to figure out and apply the stance from their own experience and learning. He did not spoon-feed his audience. He had connected.

Connecting in the Church

In the early 1940s I was preaching in Louisville's old Union Gospel Mission, located in one of the nation's worst slums. Little children were the routine victims of malnutrition. Some stood on the streets begging, selling pencils and seeking to enlist passersby to "come up and see my mama." As pastor of the mission I accepted such invitations much to the embarrassment of the mothers when they discovered I was a minister. They were invited to the Mission. I found little children in vermin and rat-infested rooms, some who were locked in while parents worked or spent time in bars.

All of these children had one thing in common: they were hungry. Some times they came to the services at the mission. In one worship service

I referred to a martyr and declared that he was burned at the stake. A little fellow on the front pew jumped to his feet and exclaimed: "A steak!" He had the image of a delicious steak for dinner. I had connected, not with a religious urge but with one of his gnawing physical needs.

In the 1950s I was invited to speak in a fashionable black Methodist church in Louisville. I prepared a rather erudite sermon. After being graciously introduced to the congregation, I proceeded to preach in a pedantic, unemotional and unexciting manner. Once I made a rather warm and relevant remark and a black man on the front seat called out, "Well." This encouraged me to "rev up" the homiletical rhetoric. Response from several was encouraging: "Yes," "Lord, help us," "Uh-huh." Then I forgot myself and got in what Dr. John Sampey, a former president of the Southern Baptist Theological Seminary, used to call "high G." The distinguished looking black man on the front seat jumped up and cried: "Now you are free. Go!" I did, for I was truly free.

It was my joy to preach in many African-American churches throughout my years in Louisville. Among these was Zion Baptist Church, the largest in the city. For some reason I was able to connect with the pastors. I suspect it was due to the fact that I talked about justice in race relations and the value of every individual before God for whom Christ died. Then, too, I was a professor in a well-known seminary. My gracious hosts trusted me and felt we had kindred minds and spirits.

In those days, prominent black churches had "going away" sermons preached by guest ministers upon the departure of a well-loved pastor to another field. Dr. D. E. King was the distinguished pastor of Zion Baptist Church. He accepted a call to the Friendship Baptist Church in New York City in 1964. On the basis of our friendship, he invited me to do the "going away" sermon. The church was filled and notable black leaders, including Frank Stanley, Sr., editor of the city's black newspaper, *The Louisville Defender*. Stanley was chairman of the evening's program. The sermon I preached is recorded here in abbreviated form.

A Prophet and His Community

Dr. and Mrs. King and family, chairman Frank Stanley, Sr., my fellow Christians. I deem it a high privilege to be in this historic church and to participate in this significant service honoring Dr. King.

As a theologian of a sort I thought you would expect me to speak in theological terminology. Recently, I was told that a theologian is one who reduces the *obvious* to the *obscure*. But I shall speak clearly and I hope relevantly.

Biblical nomenclature or symbols describing the role of the minister are varied: prophet, pastor, teacher, evangelist. Dr. King is all of these, but I tend to think of him under the rubric of "prophet."

A prophet is called of God to be "for speaker." He is primarily a "forth-teller" rather than a "fore-teller" of apocalyptic events.

A prophet is concerned about the moral and spiritual character of his community, local, national and world.

As a prophet of the living God, Dr. King has made an immeasurable and constructive impact upon the city of Louisville in the areas of religion, morality, civic righteousness and education.

As a prophet, he has had a concern for the religious climate of our community. He has served Zion Baptist Church for eighteen years as pastor. He has served as Moderator of the Central District Baptist Association. His ecumenical spirit has found expression in his service as a member of the Executive Board of the Louisville Area Council of Churches.

Dr. King's ministry has been extended abroad in thirty-three countries, including the Soviet Union where he has preached in churches in three Republics.

As a prophet, Dr. King has been concerned with the moral character of the community. A true prophet has a strong passion for justice in society. He seeks justice and righteousness in human affairs.

He has taken seriously and demonstrated in his own life Micah 6:8: "He has showed you, O Man, what is good—to practice justice, love mercy and walk humbly with God."

To practice justice appears to be a comforting idea. But try it some time! "Blessed are those who hunger and thirst after righteousness" (Justice). (Matt 5:6). We have spiritualized this text so as to make it meaningless. Righteousness in this beatitude is more than a conventional standard of respectability. That man is truly righteous who is engaged in the struggle of right against wrong. To be righteous is to participate in the cause of righteousness or justice in human relations.

To implement his passion for righteousness, Dr. King has served as a member of the Louisville Human Relations Commission, as a member of the Board of Directors of the Southern Christian Leadership Conference and he is a life member of the NAACP. Basic changes in the political and social structure for a more just city government has been shaped by his ministry.

Dramatic expression of this modern prophet's social concern was seen in his participation in the March on Washington and the March on Frankfort where he led us in singing "We Shall Overcome Some Day."

A prophet is concerned about the intellectual character of the community, Dr. King began his ministry as a teacher of Social Science in Alabama at State A & M College. He understands the mind and heart of students and is in constant demand to lecture and to preach on college and seminary campuses. He has served as chairman of the Board of Trustees of the National Trade and Professional School, Washington D.C.

Southern Baptist Theological Seminary has been enriched by Dr. King's ministry, for he has given himself unreservedly to that institution. Faculty, students and staff of Southern have come to think of him as "the preacher of the year." Recently two students were heard in conversation on our campus. They had just heard Dr. King speak in our chapel. One remarked: "Why don't we take Dr. King from Zion Church and put him on our faculty." The other one replied: "Yeah, and we'll be willing to trade two for one."

All of the sermons Dr. King has preached through many years at Southern have been superb, but among those that are most memorable are "Don't Die on Third," "Were You There When They Crucified My Lord?," "The Inestimable Worth of a Baptist Preacher's Head," and "A Man Who Walked With God."

As you go from us to serve in another great church, here is a text to hearten you: "As thy days, so shall thy strength be." (Deut 33:25)

In 1958 I had the pleasure of delivering the address at the inauguration of Willie Lawnsie Holmes as president of Simmons University. Founded in 1879, it offered courses in the arts, science and even medicine for black students. (Today it is a Bible college.)

Holmes was from Stafford, Alabama, and received his B.A. in 1950, the B.D. at the Southern Baptist Seminary in 1954 and entered the graduate program for the Th.M. (Master of Theology) that same year. He was, I believe, the second black to graduate with the Th.M. During his academic program, he also served as pastor of Eminence Baptist Church in Eminence, Kentucky. I got to know him as a student in classes at the seminary.

Among others, I made the following remarks in the inaugural address:

The goal of Christian education is the development of persons with religious devotion as well as critical intelligence. In the Great Commandment, Jesus linked religion and intelligence. He commanded us to love God with our minds and hearts. Saintliness and scholarship, then, are the goals of theological education.

In order to achieve the above goals, President Holmes, I challenge you:

To build a college which will have academic respectability and will become an intellectual center for your denomination.

To provide intellectual and spiritual leadership for your faculty and students.

To develop and maintain a fellowship of faith and learning in this institution.

To provide the kind of education for students of this institution that will evoke consecration as well as intellectual achievements.

To lead this institution to develop the leadership characterized by religious devotion and critical intelligence.

To develop intelligent and consecrated leadership for both the church and the community.

As you face these challenges and seek to implement them, may you have the wisdom of Solomon, the courage of Amos, the statesmanship of Isaiah and the gentleness of Jesus.

This was a time of increasing racial tensions in our community. Despite the divide, my remarks were received with warm enthusiasm. It was an honor to lecture at Simmons University and to preach in the church where President Holmes was pastor.

25

Innovations

*The dogmas of the quiet past are inadequate
for the stormy present.*
—Abraham Lincoln

For a century the curriculum of the Southern Baptist Theological Seminary changed very little. When I arrived at the Seminary, focus was on basic courses. Only two electives were in the curriculum, and those only by virtue of the power of the personalities teaching them: Dr. John R. Sampey, the seminary's president; and Dr. William Owen Carver, the much beloved professor of missions. For an elective Dr. Sampey taught his favorite Old Testament book—Isaiah. Dr. Carver taught Christianity and Current Thought. As former GIs entered seminary following World War II demand grew for an updated course of studies. I was appointed to a committee to revise the curriculum. Dr. Wayne Oates became chairman of a pastoral care program, a needed course for returning military personnel. Less emphasis was placed on Greek and Hebrew. Instead of two years of Hebrew only one was required and, while two years of Greek were required, the student no longer had to read all the New Testament and some of the supplementary materials in Greek.

During my twenty-six years on the faculty, I introduced several new courses and organizations to the academic community at Southern Seminary. Among the courses were: Biblical Ethics; The Church in the World; Classics of Christian Ethics; Ministerial Ethics; The Black Church and Social Justice; The Problem of Addiction: Gambling, Alcoholism and Drug Abuse; Christian Ethics and the Ecological Crisis; Bioethics; Baptist Social Ethics; The Church and Politics; Christian Ethics and Foreign Policy; War and Peace; Church-State Relations; Christianity and Communism;

Christianity and Revolution; Student Travel in Russia; The Drug Crisis and the Church; The New Morality. It was my privilege to be instrumental in building the Christian Ethics Department at Southern Seminary in those days. The department's teaching staff grew from just one, me, to three full-time teaching professors.

When I first arrived for studies at the Southern Baptist Theological Seminary in 1940, student clubs mostly were related to the past. Some of these were "Everyman's Club," "Dodeca Club," "Shakespeare Club," "Browning Club," and others. Few had anything to do with the community at large. Over the years, several new organizations were launched at the seminary with my participation. All of these endeavored to look beyond merely the interests of immediate community to a broader perspective.

William Wallace: Offering for Medical Missions. After the 10 February 1951 death of Dr. William Wallace in Wuchow, China, at the hands of the Communists, I proposed in sermons, lectures and speeches that we Southern Baptists honor Dr. Wallace as a Baptist martyr. In March of 1962, I wrote an article, published in several Baptist state papers, suggesting that we establish "The William Wallace Week" at Southern Seminary. Mr. Greg Wolcott, co-star in the TV series "Eighty-seventh Precinct" and many other films, read the article and flew out to Kentucky to talk with me about Dr. Wallace. I suggested that he propose to the Baptist Brotherhood of the Southern Baptist Convention that we set up a yearly William Wallace Offering similar to the Lottie Moon offering. Southern Baptists had a female saint in Lottie Moon, whose memory was the cause of much inspiration to the Woman's Missionary Union. I believed Southern Baptists needed a male saint for the Brotherhood Commission.

When we first came upon the offering idea, I did not know that Wolcott was planning to make a movie about the life of William Wallace. The movie was made, but the memory of the martyred doctor was never embraced by the Brotherhood Commission as I had hoped.

On the other hand, Southern Seminary did establish the William Wallace Week and for several years we honored this great doctor's missionary service and memory. One of our speakers for the yearly observances was Dr. Robert Hingson, inventor of the varidose jet injector. With this instrument, he could immunize whole towns and cities in a very short time. Received from the legendarily poor seminary students and the school's equally challenged faculty that year was a remarkably generous $1,200. The money went to purchase three portable intramuscular vaccination guns for hospitals in South Korea, Indonesia and Nigeria. The guns made it possible for tens of thousands of people in those countries to be immunized against dreaded diseases.

Additionally, I recall that after Doctor Hingson spoke in the seminary chapel, one trustee approached him and said "I will purchase a gun for Kenya, Africa." It was indeed unfortunate that this program lasted only a few years. I was under the impression, and on occasion was so told, that some in leadership believed the seminary emphasis week was unwelcomed competition with the more established and denomination-wide annual Lottie Moon Offering for Foreign Missions.

I have a large folder in my filing cabinet with materials describing the story of the origin and development of the William Wallace Week. Also there are three or four research papers done by students in classes dealing with this subject.

A recent letter I sent to Dr. Daniel Vestal (October 2000), Coordinator of the Cooperative Baptist Fellowship (Atlanta, Georgia), proposing a Wallace project for that organization brought a promise of taking "your request seriously." Time will tell.

Clarence Jordan Institute of Christian Ethical Concerns. At a memorial service for Clarence Jordan held in the chapel at Southern Seminary 19 November 1969, twenty-one days after his death, I proposed the establishment of the Clarence Jordan Institute. Also, I had stationed persons at the various entrances of the chapel to receive an offering for this institute. This is the first time an offering like this had ever been taken in chapel and I might say the last one.

I had talked with my good friend Dr. Frank Stagg about the project, and he gave me much encouragement to proceed with the project. Indeed, he was the first Vice-Chairman of the project and remained a faithful supporter of the institute. On 2–3 May 1974, the first lecture series associated with the Clarence Jordan Institute of Christian Ethical Concerns was held at Southern Seminary. Dr. Robert Bratcher, translator of the Good News Bible (New Testament section), was one of the speakers. He lectured on "Communicating the Bible to Modern Man." Mrs. Clarence Jordan spoke about the Koinonia Farm, which she and Clarence founded in 1942 near Americus, Georgia.

The Clarence Jordan Institute was re-named The Clarence Jordan Center. Dr. Paul Simmons became Chairman of the Center upon my retirement. As noted above, when Southern Baptist fundamentalists took control of the seminary Dr. Simmons was forced to vacate his faculty position. Current seminary president Albert Mohler told me the center was still in existence but had no funds. Upon further inquiry, I was informed that the center's funds already had been exhausted by the time Paul Simmons left the seminary. Dr. Simmons denies that report and has indicated that there was a considerable amount of money left in the treasury upon his departure from the school. I can only imagine that the funds were swallowed up by the seminary's general fund.

The Ethics Luncheon. In the fall of 1976, I announced to my seminary classes that we would have an Ethics Luncheon on campus in Mullins Hall. Those who wished to join me and share dialogue about current ethical and social issues were welcome to attend. Two students came: David Lynn Hughes, a student from Texas, and a lovely woman named Ellen Grace Fleming, who was from Franklin, Kentucky. The group began to grow and David wanted the group to be officially organized and approved by the seminary faculty. I was reluctant to pursue official recognition of the meetings as a seminary organization because of my concern about the likely controlling requirements that would be imposed by the school's administration. But David insisted and the group was officially approved by the administration and faculty. The group met on Wednesdays with an attendance that averaged between twenty-five to fifty students. As of April 2001 this organization was called the Ethics Club. As is presently the case with all programs at the recently reorganized seminary, the club promotes solely an agenda of fundamentalist theology and ethics.

There is nevertheless a wonderful postscript to this story. The two students who came to that first meeting in 1976 eventually married. David went on to law school and is practicing law in Corpus Christi, Texas. Ellen is a chaplain in one of the large hospitals in that city. David is an active churchman. He helped to establish the church to which the couple now belong. Along with the pastor, they carefully drew up the constitution and by-laws so as to ensure freedom of worship and all manner of Christian service.

Ecoclub. I have described above the founding of this project. There was a feeling among some that this group did not have much to do with "real" theology. The club encouraged students to collect papers, discarded beverage cans and other articles to be recycled. It turned out to be a positive and worthwhile project in awakening the social consciences of the seminary community. Theology gets no more "real" than this; providing an avenue to find practical application for what works for the head to work as well through hands, feet and hearts (Jas 1:22; 2:17–18).

Bioethics

In the early 1970s I became seriously interested in the emerging discipline called Bioethics and offered a course on the subject.. The first description of the course for the catalogue was entitled "Ethical Frontiers" because I knew I could not get a course entitled "Bioethics" past the curriculum committee. Paul Simmons, now Dr. Paul Simmons, former professor of Christian Ethics at Southern Seminary, and Earl Shelp took the course. Simmons has written numerous books and articles on the subject and presently teaches ethics at the University of Louisville School of Medicine. Earl Shelp wrote his doctoral dissertation on bioethics. He became a teacher of medical ethics at Baylor University School of Medicine and one of the founders of the Center for Ethics, Medicine and Public Issues. This organization is affiliated with Baylor's School of Medicine and the Institute of Religion at Rice University in Houston, Texas. Shelp has written extensively in the area of bioethics and has edited a number of books on the subject.

During September and October of 1975, I gave four lectures on bioethics at Louisville's Calvin Presbyterian Church in the adult Sunday School class. The gist of these lectures was published in both the religious and secular presses.

In May of 1977, after I had become a recognized academic contributor to the field of bioethics, the Board of Trustees of the University of Louisville elected me to the post of Clinical Professor of Psychiatry and Behavioral Sciences. One of my projects was to develop a book on medical ethics. The book, *Exploring Medical Ethics*, was published by Mercer

University Press in 1982. I also gave the Christian Theological lectures at Stetson University that were subsequently published by that school's press as *Biblical Perspectives on Bioethical Problems* in 1981.

Exploring Medical Ethics won high praise from some members of the University of Louisville's medical faculty within the Department of Psychiatry. I used it as a basis for discussion in Grand Rounds, a monthly meeting of the medical staff. One particular psychiatrist, however, was strongly critical of the book and especially of its final chapter dealing with humor as a tool for therapy. The chairman of the department praised it and declared, "I am looking for the second edition." A rabbi on the staff (Dr. Waller) reported that the only thing he disliked about it was the title. It should have been just "medical ethics." He concluded: "My people can accept almost everything in the book." The psychiatrist eventually re-read the last chapter and began himself to use humor as a diagnostic method with patients. The chapter, titled "Humor as a Therapeutic Tool in the Healing Process," inspired him to become—in addition to his medical practice—a performing "stand-up" comedian. He verified this in a personal letter to me. Also, he uses humor as a diagnostic tool in his practice of medicine.

Book Review Editor

The year 2004 marks the ninety-ninth year of continuous publication of the *Review and Expositor*, founded and originally published by students and then the faculty of the Southern Baptist Theological Seminary. With the takeover of the seminary by the fundamentalists the faculty withdrew the journal, and it is now published by a consortium of sponsoring Baptist institutions and patrons.

From 1957 to 1966 I served as book review editor. I believe at that time only Dr. William Owen Carver had served longer in this role. My first task was to develop a new format and then issue a guideline for reviewing books. Category one was reviews of books by the faculty; two, Biblical Studies; three, Historical-Theological Studies; four, Pastoral-Practical Studies; then Books Received and Books Reviewed. After more than half a century the format in general is still used.

It was my privilege to write several articles for the *Review and Expositor* on war and peace, ecology, politics, race relations, the Sermon on the Mount and others. Also I reviewed many books—too many. In this role my hunger for knowledge was fed.

Speaking of books, Dr. Kevin Cosby, pastor of St. Stephens Baptist Church in the predominantly African-American West End of Louisville, wrote a book titled *Get Off Your But*. At an autograph party in the Hawley-Cooke Bookstore the crowd was composed almost entirely of Blacks. While Kevin was talking about the book, I slipped in and took a back seat. When he recognized me he declared: "My distinguished professor. What an honor." As he was about to continue his lecture I remarked: "Remember I taught your grandfather who graduated among the first African-Americans from Southern Baptist Seminary and who founded St. Stephen Baptist Church." At that time, 2001, it was the largest African-American church in Louisville and possibly in Kentucky.

Festschrifts

I have been honored with two festschrifts by former students and friends. The first is by Professor Paul Simmons, editor and contributor to *Issues in Christian Ethics*, Broadman Press, 1980. It consists of thirteen essays and a bibliography of my writings and publications (1942–1979).

Festschrift two, *Perspectives on Christian Ethics*, was published in 1991 by Mercer University, Macon, Georgia. Dr. Rollin Armour, Department of Religion at Mercer, served as editor and wrote the volume's introduction. Seven essays follow, five of them by my former students. Dr. Paul Debusman, the former reference librarian whose longstanding employment at Southern Seminary was recently so unjustly terminated by the fundamentalists who now control the school, provides a bibliography of my writings: books, reviews of my books, encyclopedia and dictionary articles, journal articles and audio-visual materials through 1990.

26

First Retirement—A Retreading

Old professors of Christian Ethics never retire;
they just retread for the rest of the journey.

After twenty-six years of service, I retired as Professor of Christian Ethics at the Southern Baptist Theological Seminary in 1977. Normally a full professor who retired was retained by the seminary as a Senior Professor, given part-time teaching responsibilities, but did not vote in faculty meetings. This continuing relationship with the seminary was denied me. Appeals on my behalf from the school's Historical-Theological Division, some faculty members and others—such as Dr. Paul Simmons, Dr. Glenn Hinson, staff members and students—were of no avail.

Three leaders of the student body organized a protest movement which would involve the *Courier-Journal*, a television station and the seminary community. As the time approached for a planned demonstration, three students came to my home to report on the progress of the movement. Though I surely appreciated their intentions, I was able to dissuade them. I had received and revealed to them a significant bit of correspondence from the Dean and Board of Trustees of the University of Louisville School of Medicine.

Dear Doctor Barnette,
The Board of Trustees of the University of Louisville, at their meeting held on 18 April 1977, confirmed your appointment as Clinical Professor in Psychiatry to become effective 1 May 1977.

We are delighted to have you as a member of our volunteer faculty[1] in the Department of Psychiatry and look forward to having you work with us in our teaching program.

With warmest personal regards, I remain,

Sincerely yours,

Arthur H. Keeney, M.D., D.Sc.

Dean, School of Medicine and Professor of Ophthalmology

The students reluctantly refrained from the demonstration but kept on protesting. Students organized a Henlee Fan Club with logos on T-shirts. One came to my last class wearing a T-shirt proclaiming, "Give Them Hell Henlee."

Comments also came from the last class. Those were voluntary statements by students in my last class in Christian Ethics, 20 May 1977. Over sixty students wrote statements of appreciation and affection and presented them to me at my last class in Christian ethics on 20 May 1977. The various sentiments are reflected in a few of those notes, here following:

Thank you, Dr. Barnette, very much for one of my most stimulating courses during my seminary career, with regard to the widespread needs for Christian action today. Best wishes in the years ahead as you continue to make a Christian impact on our society.

Dr. Barnette, I've enjoyed your class very much and have been impressed with you and your manner of teaching. I also appreciate the outside resource persons used in lectures. May the Lord continue to use you.

You are one of the finest professors I have ever had. Thanks for being the caring, ethical teacher you are. It was a privilege to sit under you.

Dr. Barnette, you have bothered my conscience and made me see the responsibility of discipleship. Thank you for helping me mature.

Staff and faculty also spoke and wrote appreciatively. I view the comments as great compliments. Among these were:

---

[1] Voluntary faculty at the University of Louisville's School of Medicine were ordinarily provided no salary. I was paid a modest salary from a grant for twelve years.

Dr. Barnette fears no man because he loves every man. (Page Kelley, faculty member)

There is only one thing wrong with Dr. Barnette. He is ten years ahead of us when it comes to critical social issues. (Welby Collins, seminary security guard)

A recognition service in my honor was held in the seminary chapel. A resolution signed by the faculty was presented to me. It was written by Professor Peter Jones for the faculty committee:

The Faculty of the Seminary wishes to record a spontaneous expression of gratitude to Professor Henlee Hulix Barnette, friend, colleague, scholar. For thirty-one years he has served Southern Seminary as student and teacher, and it has mattered that he was here. The Faculty regards him as a colleague of academic substance and holds him in real affection.

As a scholar he has published prolifically, and his volumes have enjoyed widespread use. His books on calling and vocation have put thousands of young people in his debt, and his volumes on ethical issues have been of sufficient substance to serve as college and seminary textbooks. His colleagues note with appreciation his long tenure as Book Review Editor for the faculty journal and his exacting literary standards. A distinguished student of Niebuhrian Christian realism, he remained nevertheless a lover of Rauschenbusch, and like him, never diminished the importance of personal conversion and the necessity of repentance. Professor Barnette, previously a millhand and Hay Market pastor, functioned as a constant seminary conscience.

As a colleague Henlee has been a highly distinctive person. He terrified his classes with the proclamation that he was "a barbarian with a thin veneer of Christian culture," but his colleagues suspected that the self-designation should be turned on its head. Henlee apparently considered it impolite to enter or leave a room without imparting a humorous epigram or sage aphorism. He courageously sponsored the controversial but historic seminary visit of Martin Luther King, Jr. Acting Dean Barnette served admirably in the late fifties "to replenish the faculty." He maintained an abiding interest in his students far beyond graduation and basked in their reflected glory like a father.

Henlee Barnette has incarnated and symbolized the essence of Christian ethics at the seminary for more than a quarter of a century. The faculty will follow his continuing ministry with its interest and prayers and with the joyful anticipation of continued fellowship with him.

On behalf of the student senate, John Hewitt made a presentation explaining that students desired to place some significant books in the library in my honor. Hewitt read the following:

> For thirty-one years Henlee Barnette has been a compassionate and committed teacher but also and perhaps more importantly a friend of students. He has helped to make our passage here a little more familiar, a little warmer. He has helped to tear down some of the partition that makes us strangers. When it came time for us to do something this spring to honor Dr. Barnette we approached him about the possibility of purchasing some significant volumes in the field of Christian Ethics to present to the library in his honor. He called me one Saturday afternoon and said, "John the library has every book that we have recommended. Let me try out an alternative idea on you. Why not spend the money and do something for our handicapped students?" So the student senate has voted and the project is underway to construct ramps at the library and at the entrance to the chapel. That will help to break down the partition on this campus which separates some of us from each other. That those on our campus who are bound to wheel chairs or crutches, that are unable to get around as freely as you and I, might be able to enter the library for study and chapel for worship with ease. We have voted on this. There is a possibility that we might come to you and ask for your support. But we think it is an indication and will be an example to all who will come here in years to come--of what Henlee Barnette stood for, tearing down barriers, crossing borders, helping to make things a little more open, a little freer. To Dr. Barnette we present this in your honor and to your dedication.

Likewise the Board of Trustees of the seminary passed a resolution:

Resolution

Whereas, Henlee H. Barnette has served the Southern Baptist Theological Seminary for thirty-one years as student and teacher, as moral conscience and prophetic witness, as scholarly and popular author;

Whereas, he has served beyond the seminary community through the many students he has trained—who have become leaders in churches, denominational agencies and elsewhere; through his sensitive involvement in Louisville's civic and political affairs—which has been much appreciated by the politically prominent and by just plain people; and through the many articles and books he has written—which have been translated into several languages and continue to be read widely:

Whereas, he has served the seminary faithfully and loyally through times of crisis, has led the faculty as Acting Dean, and has made valuable contributions to rebuilding the faculty;

Whereas, he has stimulated creative thought, leading students to see more than two sides of important issues, has led in ethical issues concerning politics, peace, ecology and medicine, has exemplified openness to students and been their advocate through the years, has championed the cause of the victims of injustice, oppression and prejudice, and has brightened the day of colleagues, fellows, students, janitors and especially secretaries;

Whereas, he has done all this with courage that knew where silence might be more yellow than golden, with spirit that can be irenic without avoiding controversy unduly, with serious humility that does not always take self overly seriously, and with frequent humor in the midst of adversity and where it might not be expected;

Therefore, be it resolved, that we give thanks to our Creator, who must have a sense of love, of justice, and of humor, for giving us such a man, and that the Board of Trustees by this resolution express to Dr. Barnette appreciation and best wishes.

Adopted by the Board of Trustees, Southern Baptist Theological Seminary, 20 April 1977.

In addition, the Trustees awarded me the status of Emeritus Professor of Christian Ethics with certain rights and privileges: secretarial help, post office box, parking and use of the library. I am sure that this honor was wholly the work of the trustees. Dr. H. H. Hobbs, distinguished preacher, pastor (Oklahoma City First Baptist) and author was a member of the seminary's Board of Trustees. To kid me a bit he wrote to me a letter explaining that *emeritus* was a Latin word—"e" means out and "meritus" means deserves: thus, "deserves to be out." About ten years later Dr. Hobbs retired and I wrote him a letter. He retired as emeritus pastor. I carefully explained to him the meaning of the word *emeritus.* He wrote back immediately saying that my letter went into a file of treasured items.

Retirement Dinner

Faculty, staff and students worked hard to make my retirement dinner an event to remember. Dr. Paul Simmons, on sabbatical at Princeton

University, returned from there and served as emcee at the dinner. Dr. Glenn Stassen served locally.

Dr. Wayne Oates presented "anecdotes" at my retirement dinner held at Executive West Inn 31 May 1977. Here he noted our long friendship, along with me being his confidante and counselor in two of the major decisions of his life: his decision to marry Pauline Rhodes and his decision to go into the field of religion and medicine. He also showed slides and made comments.

Mayor Harvey Sloane and his wife were present. He presented me with a Key to the City of Louisville. Also he presented me with a letter. Here is one paragraph:

> I am very grateful for the associations we've had in the past few years. I am pleased I had the opportunity to participate in your Christian Ethics classes. You are one of those special people who sees a need to integrate ethics into every aspect of life. I was honored to have you as an active campaigner for me when I ran for mayor. I have appreciated that same active support during my term. To have a person of such high integrity working for me has been a gratifying experience. I want to express my thanks to you for these opportunities to establish a meaningful relationship with a person I deeply respect. You have been an inspiration to me.

Among other speakers were Foy Valentine, Executive Secretary of the Christian Life Commission; Harry Hollis, also with the Commission; Glenn Hinson, Professor of Church History; Clyde Francisco, Professor of Old Testament; Marvin Tate, Professor of Old Testament.

The last speaker was the Reverend J. V. Bottoms, pastor of Louisville's downtown Green Street Baptist Church. He was the first African-American to graduate from Southern Seminary after the Day Law was modified to allow blacks to attend graduate schools with whites if they could not get their needed training in black schools. He concluded his moving message by saying, "Don't give up until you go up." Speaking at Rev. Bottoms' retirement as pastor of Green Street Baptist Church I concluded my comments with the same words: "Don't give up until you go up."

Final Seminary Graduation

The Southern Baptist Theological Seminary's Class of 1977 requested that I be the guest speaker at their graduation banquet. This was quite an honor for me. Robert Crouch, president of the class, introduced me. The theme of my message for them was simple: "Christ's call for courage—courage for the living of these days." I wished for the graduates the courage to be, to see, to know, to care, as well as the courage of humor and the courage of "the path less traveled by."

Thanking Out Loud

Dr. Duke McCall's presidential notes in alumni magazine, *The Tie*, were titled "Thinking Out Loud." Hence, the title of my farewell talk, "Thanking Out Loud," to the seminary community—attempting to thank everyone for the wonderful exodus I was given:

> So many persons have participated in and contributed to my retirement celebration that I find it impossible to personally thank each one. Therefore, the following statement is one effort to express my gratitude in writing to those groups which have helped to make my departure from the seminary a joyful and meaningful event.
>
> To the members of the faculty, who have refrained from grinding corn for the Philistines, steered clear of the wasteland of mere intellectualism, and manifested a sensitivity to the needs of colleagues and the community, I give thanks. Especial thanks are due to those faculty members who planned and executed the banquet in my honor and produced the resolution read in chapel.
>
> To members of the student body, I give thanks. Ours has always been an I-Thou relationship. Our affection has been mutual and expressed in terms of recognition, regard, and respect for one another as fellow-students created in the *imago Dei*. So many of you worked diligently to make my last class in Christian ethics a festival of fun, and I am deeply grateful.
>
> To members of the administration and staff, I give thanks. You are the life support system of the seminary community. Some of you have gone the second mile to make my egress a pleasant and painless experience. Special thanks are due to the secretarial staff who voted me "Boss of the Month" and typed my messy manuscripts.
>
> To the trustees, I give thanks. You serve gratis and for God's glory. For the meaningful resolution, the status of Professor Emeritus of Christian Ethics, and other actions, I am grateful.
>
> To friends everywhere whose hearts have never turned dark against me in spite of my faults and failures, who know me so well and still undergird me with prayer and affection, I give thanks

For those who have disagreed with me, I give thanks. You have made me rethink many of my convictions on moral and social issues. As a result, my beliefs have been clarified and deepened concerning the relevance of the gospel of Christ for the Christian in the totality of his or her personal and social relationships.

After a quarter of a century as a teacher at Mother Seminary, I take leave. She has been good to me and for me. "The lines have fallen to me in pleasant places."

Colleagues and comrades in the cause of Christ, I will always thank my God upon every remembrance of you.

Hail and Farewell!

Henlee Barnette

27

The Medical School

The doctor helps, but God heals.

Each year I write a poem or saying in the flyleaf of my date book. For 1977, I wrote the following, which became prophetic:

> Two roads diverged in a wood, and I –
> I took the one less traveled by,
> And that has made all the difference.
> (Robert Frost, "The Road Not Taken")

Spring semester of 1977 was my last one at the Southern Baptist Theological Seminary. Having attained sixty-five years of age, I was no longer permitted faculty status. A Senior Professorship had been denied me. Dr. Wayne Oates had departed the seminary in 1974 to assume a full professorship in the Department of Psychiatry, University of Louisville School of Medicine. Upon hearing of my own imminent departure from the seminary, he secured for me a clinical professorship in the Department of Psychiatry. Wayne was not only a brilliant professor, but also served as an unofficial pastor—marrying, burying and counseling the professors and staff of the medical school. My dear friend also secured a significant fund out of which to pay me a salary for teaching in the medical school for years to come.

Two roads confronted me: serve as an occasional lecturer in colleges and interim pastor of churches or, at my age, take a demanding position in the medical school. I chose the latter and it made all the difference. Wayne introduced me to Dr. John Schwab, Chairman of the Department of Psychiatry. He was a gracious man and offered me a warm welcome on board. A bit to my surprise, the faculty and staff of the department welcomed me with sincere appreciation and we bonded in friendship and work.

I served in the Norton Psychiatric Clinic for mentally ill patients. My role was theological and ethics consultant. Also I served on the psychiatric consultation team that was made up of a psychiatrist, a resident (in training) psychiatrist, a psychiatric nurse, a psychiatric social worker and an artist trained in mental and emotional disorders. We sought to meet patients' needs from a holistic approach to health care. I helped plan and participated in didactic seminars relating to faith and health. The topics touched included guilt, suicide ideation, death with dignity, pastor/physician relations, patient/physician relations, genetic engineering, biomedical reproduction, euthanasia and others.

I also had a role to play in medical education. This involved supervising second year medical students on psychiatric rotation as they conducted their first interviews with hospital patients. After introducing the medical student to the patient, I would observe their interactions. Then in a private conversation, I would suggest ways to better relate to patients. A grade for the student and a written report was sent to the Director of Medical Education in Psychiatry.

Another task that fell to me was the supervision of resident physicians, especially foreigners who had difficulty with English or were experiencing trouble with cultural adjustment. Grand Rounds was a program designed to provide continuing medical education to doctors, nurses and other healthcare professionals. Faculty members took turns lecturing. One of my lectures on loneliness as an ethical issue in medical practice was so well received that a day was set aside for lectures on the subject by the faculty.

It was a joy to serve as the unofficial chaplain to the children of Norton Hospital Academy who had mental and emotional difficulties. It was also a tremendous source of satisfaction to me that colleagues came for counseling in times of both crises and calm. In addition, I occasionally lectured in other hospitals and in churches, colleges and universities on medical ethics.

A part of my teaching contract at the University of Louisville's School of Medicine was that I would write a book on medical ethics. Despite the cardiac health issues I was negotiating at the time, *Exploring Medical Ethics* was published in 1982 by Mercer University Press. It received favorable reviews in the press, medical journals and in theological journals. Nancy Flowers, M.D., Professor and Chief of Cardiology, University of Louisville School of Medicine wrote: "This thorough and pertinent treatment of an often neglected aspect in the education of a physician should be mandatory reading for the medical student twice—once as a freshman, once as a senior."

E. Clinton Gardner of Emory University declared: "This volume provides an overview of ethical issues in contemporary medicine---is simply written, clinically informed and holistic in its approach."

Dr. James D. McNeely, Medical Director Norton Psychiatric Clinic, wrote to me saying: "I believe that it will be very useful to our medical students and to our psychiatry residents in training. I am very much looking forward to a more leisurely and thorough exploration of its depth. As you know, the one chapter that I reviewed for you on guilt I found to be a very thorough treatment of the subject and it was certainly very helpful to me in distilling my own thinking on the topic."

In the *Journal of the Kentucky Medical Association*, Stephen L. Smith observed: "Recognizing the author's background and the design of the book, the physicians may well take note of another point of view."

Theological Consult

Doctors began to call on me for consultations about patients with religious problems. One of the first theological consult requests came from a Jewish psychiatrist. His patient was criticizing the doctor for not praying for him. We visited the patient's room in the clinic. Immediately the patient, an elderly gentleman, said to the doctor, "You won't pray for me." The patient then turned to me and commented, "He will not pray for me." The doctor requested that I pray. The patient and I went down on our knees right there on the floor and I prayed. At the next meeting of the consultation team the psychiatrist reported that his patient's mental health began to improve following our prayer. The doctor confessed, "God, he almost converted me!"

Not long after that, a staff member at Norton Hospital wrote me a letter, part of which appears below.

5 January 1978

Dr. Barnette—Something happened at Norton's hospital just prior to Christmas that I wished to share with you—and have waited until the sanity of post-holidays returned to tell you. Apparently you were assisting with the readmission of a former patient diagnosed with senile dementia whom you may recall as John S. I was not present at the time, but Dr. Sheldon Chase was. He came into the nursing station on Six West, rather shaken. He said that you were with John S.'s family, and that they had requested that you pray for John. Sheldon said that he left after a few moments because he knew if he stayed he might be converted. That God, if there is a God and whoever he might be, was present because he said there was a power in that room he could sense. Sheldon had the usual sparkle in his eyes and his ever-present grin as he lit up his damnable cigar—but his reporting back of what he had witnessed was no joke to him nor to us.

A woman was brought into the clinic who prayed "without ceasing" (as Paul the Apostle commanded). No one could get her history or communicate with her. A young psychiatrist on duty that day was called in on the case. He ordered us to take her to room number twelve and he would solve the problem. We did and a voice (the psychiatrist's) came over audio saying "I am the Lord your God and I have heard your prayers and you don't need to pray any more." Whereupon the patient exclaimed, "Lord, somebody is imitating you!" She went right back to praying. Later, after she had for a while paused from her prayers, I visited and cared for her until she was well enough to go home.

One woman became so frightened she was hospitalized. Some preacher had told her that Jesus was coming on a certain date that was fast approaching. Responding to a theological consult request, I visited the woman and heard her story. At our next meeting I listened to her story again. "Do you believe the Bible?" I asked. Her answer was affirmative. "Let me read from the Bible," I said. "Heaven and earth will pass away, but my words will not pass away. But about that day and hour no one knows, neither the angels of heaven, nor the Son, but only the Father." (Matt 24:35–36)

I explained that in this passage Jesus has in mind the second coming, the event she was worried about. Only the Father in heaven knows when heaven and earth will pass away. She became calm and began to heal in the days ahead.

At the medical school I found an environment in which one could freely pursue the truth with professionals whose minds were generally open and who insisted on intellectual honesty. It was highly gratifying to have colleagues who respected, supported and accepted me as a professional in my field of service. Among these, I remember best Dr. Spafford Ackerly, founder of the Department of Psychiatry at the University of Louisville School of Medicine; Drs. John Schwab, Chairman of the Department; Wayne E. Oates, Herbert Wagemaker, Clifford Kuhn, Jess Wright, William Bradnan, Gisela Kolb, David McNeely, Sheldon Chase; and staff members Gene Hedden, George Dunn, Jean Sloan and others.

In the wider medical school my very dear friends were Drs. Leo Horan, Chairman of the Department of Medicine; Nancy Flowers, Professor and Chief of Cardiology of the University of Louisville School of Medicine; and pathologist Ryland Byrd.

Medical problems continued to plague me in 1978. Among them was a coronary dysfunction that required a double bypass. Dr. Laman Gray, Jr., on the staff at Norton where I served, did the surgery. Several skin cancers were removed by Dr. Charles Gaba. Diabetes became an increasing problem for me. Colon polyps were removed and there were the annual virus attacks. In spite of all this, I managed to do my work at the medical school, at church and on the lecture circuit.

In an ethics class a medical student inquired, "Why is Christianity superior to other religions?" In a state-controlled hospital or school, you have to be careful about imposing your religious convictions on others. So I gave a general answer: (1) The incarnation. Jesus came to us as a person and we can look into his face and see what God is like. Contrast that to the gods of the Greeks, Romans and others. (2) Jesus is the authentic human being and in our finiteness we fall short of what it really means to be human. (3) Christianity is the most materialistic of all the major religions, relating to this world as well as to the next. Eternal life begins here and now. (4) Christianity takes history seriously. (5) Christianity has inspired scientific progress, social reform and democracy. These points, I suggested, convince me of Christianity's superior character.

Grand Rounds

Each professor on the medical faculty had an opportunity to lecture in Grand Rounds. One of my turns came on 29 April 1987. I decided to introduce my book on medical ethics, *Exploring Medical Ethics*. A panel had been chosen to review the book: Drs. John Schwab and Cliff Kuhn, a psychiatrist, and Rabbi Waller, a clinical professor and head of a nearby Jewish temple. My abbreviated remarks follow:

Someone has observed that publishing a book is analogous to having a baby. After delivering *Exploring Medical Ethics*, published two months ago by the Mercer University Press, I began to experience postpartum blues. I found myself wishing that I had made use of prenatal diagnosis. For the fetus had some flaws: a few typos and terms that I would not now use. Prenatal therapy would have corrected these defects. (Some readers may feel that I should have opted for selective abortion.)

I felt even worse when I woke up and discovered that I had consented to talk about *my* book in Grand Rounds! How presumptuous can one get? But I told myself that it would be something different despite the appearance of being an egotistical exercise. It helped also when I learned that three distinguished scholars would respond to the contents of the volume. I felt that after their devastating critical evaluations my sense of guilt for writing the book would be desensitized, if not dissolved. I thought that a vigorous verbal ear beating would meet my masochistic needs.

Some more concrete things happened that aided me in climbing out of my pit of depression: 1) forthcoming favorable comments and reviews; 2) the book was chosen by a committee to be published by a respectable press; 3) a dean of a school of medicine was on the committee; 4) at least one university professor has adopted it as a text for the fall semester.

My task is to present a brief "biopsy" of the book. Drs. Kuhn, Waller and Schwab will respond in that order. A basic purpose of this volume is to present a work on medical ethics from an ethico-theological perspective. Numerous volumes have been written from an anthropocentric and secular humanistic posture. Only a few have been published from the Judeo-Christian stance.

Methodologically an inter-disciplinary approach is used involving *inter alia* philosophy, sciences, social science, psychology, ethics and theology. In addition the case method is utilized wherever feasible.

After a brief overview of medical ethics in historical perspective, there is a chapter on ethical alternatives in moral decision-making: legalism, antinomianism, utilitarianism, situationism, consequentialism—all of which may be subsumed under the rubrics of deontological and teleological ethics.

My own ethical posture is that of contextual principled-agapism. *Agape,* to will and to work for the well-being of all of God's creatures and creation, finds universal formulation in the so-called Golden Rule (actually, it is a principle). This ethical motif is found, *mutatus mutandis*, in most major religions, philosophies and in the psychiatric and psychological theories of many distinguished scholars: Allport, Frankl, Sullivan, Frieda Fromm-Reichmann, Carl Rogers, Erik Fromm and Erik Erickson, to mention a few. Erickson's George W. Gay lecture at Harvard Medical School and Delhi Medical School in India dealt with the Golden Rule in the practice of medicine.

In the remainder of the book this agapaistic principle is related to physician-patient relations, loneliness, guilt, homosexuality, *in vitro* fertilization, surrogate motherhood, genetic engineering, communicating with patients in extremis, death and dying, and humor as a therapeutic tool in psychotherapy.

In addition there is a bibliography for further reading and an appendices of medical codes. Despite what Dr. Robert Veach says in his magnum opus, *Theory of Medical Ethics*, medical codes are important for both physician and patient. The Doonesbury cartoon that ran in our local papers on 13 March 1982 is a classic example of the powerful impact of the Hippocratic Oath.

The *Sitz im Leben* is this:

Dr. Henry Kissinger, former Secretary of State under Richard Nixon, is lying in a hospital bed recovering from bypass surgery while his surgeon reads the patient's chart. Someone pauses at the room's door and calls out, "Get well soon, Doc! All your enemies miss you." Kissenger's surgeon speaks: "Some people just won't let old wounds heal, eh, Dr. Kissinger? Well, I can sympathize with their feelings. When I helped crack your chest last month, I myself started to thinking about my days in Anti-War Movement. It was an amazing moment. As we finished up the third bypass, it suddenly dawned on me that I was holding the heart of the man whose policies had once condemned thousands to death! Then I thought of my Hippocratic Oath."

Said Kissinger, "Good Oath, that."

Following my remarks, the panel got to work. Dr. Clifford Kuhn gave the sharpest criticisms in his evaluation of my book. Later he became a standup comedian and appeared in numerous write-ups in magazines and papers. He also wrote articles on healing and humor. He founded Laugh

Doctor Enterprises. He offers workshops and entertaining presentations on health and humor. In my class in Christian Ethics at Southern Baptist Seminary, where he had been a guest lecturer, Dr. Kuhn emphasized the need of a sense of humor, especially for ministers.

Recently I read a statement about him in the *University of Louisville Journal*. I cut it out and sent it to Dr. Kuhn. In the right hand corner I inscribed: Remember the last chapter in *Exploring Medical Ethics*, titled "Humor as a Therapeutic Tool in The Healing Process?" The letter below contains his response:

> 27 April 27 1998
> Henlee—
> It was great hearing from you. Thanks for your note.
> I hope you remember Chapter Twelve in *Exploring Medical Ethics* is where it all started for me. I will always be grateful to you. I hope you are well. I think of you often. A picture of the two of us at Wayne and Pauline's Fiftieth Anniversary Bash hangs above my desk.
> Regards,
> CCK

Dr. Kuhn uses humor with success as a therapeutic tool in the healing process. He is a deeply caring person. At my ninetieth birthday party he sat with me at the Barnette family table. My son Jim, who also was present, had studied under Dr. Kuhn's supervision as part of the requirements for completing his Ph.D. through the seminary.

I left the Medical School in 1992 to give my full time to my wife who was dying of cancer. A decade after my departure, I was told that my name was still on my old office door. I longed to return but never made it. In the meantime I have destroyed more than one hundred case studies of patients I have worked with to avoid having them falling into the hands of others. I have not lost complete contact with the medical school personnel for I see them at gatherings on occasion and have lunch with my successor once per week.

28

The Healing Power of Humor

A merry heart does good like a medicine.
—Proverbs 17:22

A chapter in my book, *Exploring Medical Ethics*, deals with humor as a therapeutic tool in the healing process. I discuss humor and health in historical perspective, including some of what the Bible teaches: "A cheerful heart is a good medicine, but a downcast spirit dries up the bones" (Prov 17:22, NRSV).

Hollywood movie producers long ago discovered the value of humor and how to exploit the basic need of people to laugh. Norman Cousins, distinguished editor of *Saturday Review of Literature*, experienced the healing effect of humor during a serious illness. Today there is a growing awareness among medical professionals of the healing power of humor. Hospitals increasingly have recognized humor as an important component in any given regime of therapy. Psychiatrists have of late embraced a greater appreciation for the therapeutic value of humor in addressing mental illness. Across the years I have seen the value of humor in interpersonal relations, politics, education, religion and even at funerals.

Cheaper by the Hymn

In the early 1930s I was invited to "hold a revival meeting" at a church in a North Carolina cotton mill town. The church was a simple frame building and most of the people in attendance were cotton mill workers. The choir sang old gospel hymns and special selections from a Stamps-Baxter quartet hymnbook. Use of the songs from this collection became the focus of conflict. Some in the church were ready for "new music." Others decidedly were not. The church almost split, and the choir director resigned because he loved the old foot patting, emotional and heaven-oriented hymns.

During the last service at the close of the revival, the pastor instructed the choir director to choose an appropriate hymn for the love offering to be taken by ushers for the evangelist. The hymn he chose was "Jesus Paid It All." The offering was a little over seven dollars. Perhaps all of those hastily thrown together sermons were worth no more. Or did the congregation take the song literally—Jesus paid it all, so we need not pay the evangelist much.

Fielding Questions

For many years, Dr. W. W. Stout served as a missionary in China. Of course, he had to come back to the States after the communist takeover of that great country. Before his retirement, Dr. Stout taught at Georgetown College in Kentucky. He became passionately concerned about the problem of alcoholism in this nation. For years he worked on a project related to this serious problem. He greatly desired to tell others about it.

When he was in his eighties, I invited him to speak in my Christian Social Ethics class at Southern Seminary. He lectured with great enthusiasm. He overdid it, fainted and fell to the floor. A nurse was called and we tried to revive him. He finally came to and, while still on his back on the floor, said "I am now ready for questions from the students."[1]

Seminary Smiles

As a professor at the Southern Baptist Theological Seminary, I received numerous invitations to preach in rural churches. Few ever requested my *curriculum vitae*. But on one occasion a deacon called and invited me to preach in a country church in Kentucky. He told me a bit about the church, how to get there, time of worship, and about how many would be present. Then he gave me his address and said, "Please send me your *biological* data."

---

[1] Later, Dr. Stout came to my office at the seminary and announced that he would never be able to complete his project because he was going blind. He wanted me to work on it. We secured students to read to him and he went on with his work.

As each of my seminary classes began I would ask if any student had criticism of me or of the course, that they please talk with me before talking about it to other people. After one class had been in progress for about three weeks, a student came to my office and said, "Well, you asked that we come by to see you if we had any criticisms." I replied, "Certainly! Sit down and tell me all about it." He said, "Well, I don't think you're taking the lectures very serious [incidentally we always had fun in my classes and there was some laughter] and furthermore, the lectures are boring." I said, "Well, if *you* think the lectures are boring, how about my situation? I have to give them!" There was no smile on his face and I knew he had a real problem. I suggested that unless he developed a sense of humor, he was going to end up in a mental institution. Sure enough, he ended up spending several weeks in a local psychiatric ward. He took another of my classes when he came back to school and was a superb student. He had learned to laugh at himself. After he graduated he took a position with a university on the East Coast.

Seminary professors would often call on students to offer a prayer before the lecture. In one of my classes in Christian Ethics a student had fallen sound asleep. Another student seated by the snoozing learner awakened him and whispered urgently, "Dr. Barnette just called on you to pray." Sleeping Beauty immediately stood to his unsteady feet and began to pray aloud—in the middle of my lecture.

More Holy Hilarity

When student A. Moncrief Jordan (Southern Seminary class of 1959) was asked for a memorable classroom experience, his response: "Clarence Jordan's visit to Dr. Barnette's ethics class. One student tried to counter Clarence's inclusive spirit (racial) by pointing out that blue birds and red birds did not associate. He was reminded that those same creatures did not attend seminary either."

Evangelist Billy Graham, the governor of Tennessee, and other notables were in attendance at a Laymen's Conference in October 1956. I presided at the chapel service. Speakers were allotted only a certain number of minutes due to a very tight schedule. A chaplain spoke and went over his time. He was describing how the natives of some country were yelling "Go home Yanks." I stepped up to the pulpit and placed a note where he could see it. He read it and meekly reported, "It says, 'Yankee go home.'" He sat down to the audience's gentle laughter and audible sighs of relief. This was an application of "instructive" humor.

In 1974 Professor Bryant Hicks prayed at a student-faculty prayer meeting to kick off the Summer Missions Week. His prayer was as follows: "Lord, we pray you would send the Word of your Spirit to turn this campus up-side down." The following afternoon a tornado destroyed one hundred large trees around the seminary neighborhood, blew cupolas off Mullins Hall, the roof off Foster Hall and wrecked several automobiles. Behind Mullins Hall I discovered a small red sports car that had been crushed by the twister. The bumper sticker on the hulk read, "Smile, God loves you." Wayne E. Oates, Professor of Pastoral Care and Psychology of Religion, looked over the campus destruction after the tornado had hit and commented, "Mercy, it looks like the seminary curriculum!"

Vodka and Vision

In the summer of 1957 I traveled with an American delegation for about a month in the USSR. On one occasion we visited a collective farm near Kiev in the Ukraine. The communist boss insisted that we toast our two great nations. On the table before us was a small glass of what I thought was water. I was told that it was a very mild wine. Our communist guide insisted that we drink it lest we offend our host. After the spoken toast to peace and friendship between the great USA and the great USSR, we drank the contents of the glass. It was like a blowtorch hitting my esophagus. I could not breathe for a moment. It was pure Russian Vodka! This frightened me and then I felt angry. An American farm journalist next to me stood and announced that some of us did not drink alcoholic beverages. So, our host had us offer another toast with water! The water, however, seemed only to exacerbate the first beverage's effect.

Shortly following those convivial moments, we started toward a dairy barn to see the cows. By that time I was so dizzy, I could hardly tell a tractor from a cow. I crawled up into our bus until my dizziness passed and my vision cleared. I rejoined the group at the dairy. In one section the cows were milked by machines and in another by a team of women. We asked the communist boss why he didn't use more milking machines instead of all those women. He replied, "Because those cows prefer the personal touch!"

Healthy humor is a sign of a healthy mind. It is what the Bible teaches; it is healing to the body and soul. So find yourself a laughing place and stay healthy.

29

The Best is Yet to Be

Old age brings on theological thoughts.

Robert Browning, the poet of optimism, has a great line about the compensations and gifts of growing old. At age fifty-eight (old age in his day) he wrote:

> Grow old along with me!
> The best is yet to be,
> The last of life, for which the first was made:
> Our times are in His hand
> Who saith "A whole I planned,
> Youth shows but half; trust God: see all, nor be afraid!"
> —from *Rabbi Ben Ezra*, by Robert Browning

After observing sick and suffering old people at home, in institutions and the world we begin to think that poem was a victim of shallow optimism. At age ninety-two, I have discovered that Browning touched on a truth: the best is yet to be for many of us.

There is the blessing of a growing self-identity or self-understanding. As we advance in age we tend to look within. Often we discover things we are totally unaware of or have forgotten. Rembrandt painted more than sixty portraits of himself to discover the spiritual channel to his innermost self. Here he had a clearer vision of what was in himself and in others. To see oneself eye to eye takes courage, but it brings, as Henri Nouwen declared, healing to the innermost self.[1]

---

[1] See *Aging*, Garden City, NY Doubleday Press, 1974, 141.

With advancing age we can grow a wholesome sense of solitude. It is so important to transform our loneliness into solitude. Jesus is a spiritual model for achieving authentic solitude. He often withdrew from the crowd to a lonely place to pray (Luke 5:16).

Prayer is a channel to solitude. There are many others: reading good books, listening to inspiring music, enjoying art and meditation are all enablers to spiritual solitude. So find yourself a "lonely place", a *shalom* zone, where the door of solitude will open to you.

There is the blessing of service the elderly can perform. So many channels of service confront us daily. Recently a man called me and said he had an appointment to see his doctor and had no way to get there. He is one of the thousands who need help that the functionally elderly can serve. One church has an Oasis Club (Older Adults Still in Service) to aid the needy in the congregation, from plumbing to purchasing groceries for the homebound. This sort of service has to it a rich theological basis: Jesus taught us to feed the hungry and thirsty, clothe the naked, visit the prisoner and the sick, welcome the stranger (Matt 25:31–46).

As we "older folk" enjoy ministering to the needs of others, we begin to meditate on last things: death, judgment, heaven, hell, all last things. Old age brings on theological and philosophical thoughts.

An old song declares "Life's evening sun is sinking low; a few more days and I must go." We must all go and walk through the "valley of death." But by faith we do not walk alone. By faith in the risen Christ we will never walk alone in this world and the world to come.

Author Studs Terkel has written a book with the title taken from an old hymn: "Will the Circle be Unbroken?" Here he writes about death. He claims not to be a religious person, but a spiritual one. He desires a death with dignity. His is the liberal attitude toward life and death. Terkel believes that hell is here on earth.

Will the circle be unbroken and will we know each other in heaven? When this question comes up, I remember what Dr. John R. Sampey said when he was asked the question by a seminary student. He remarked, "Do you think we will be bigger fools up there?" The Apostle Paul hints that we will know more than we do now on earth. In this life "we see through a glass, darkly; but then face to face: now I know in part; but then shall I know even as also I am known" (1 Cor 13:12).

The Sadducees of Jesus' day did not believe in the resurrection. They asked the Lord a question about the resurrection they did not think he could answer (Matt 22:23–46). They knew that Moses' law called for Levirate marriage (Deut 25:5). That is, if a brother dies and his widow has no children, the surviving brother or oldest male relative must take her and produce children. The scenario the Sadducees set before Jesus was that of a woman marrying each of seven brothers as one after another of the men died. They asked to which brother would the woman be married in the resurrection?

Jesus noted that the Sadducees were ignorant of the Scriptures. First of all, in heaven people will neither "marry nor be given in marriage," but will be "like the angels." Angels are spiritual beings and messengers of God and they are sexually neutral. Unlike in the afterlife as described by the *Koran*, Jesus described a heaven in which there would be neither a sex drive nor any need for it. All emotional expression will be in praise and service of God.

Why do we have this longing for heaven? I once read a sermon by a pastor of a mega-church. In it he gave nine reasons why he wanted to go to heaven. Listed first among these was delicious food. Nothing was said about continuous learning or the thrill of increased knowledge. Heaven will be a boring place if all we do is praise God in earthlike worship services and run meaningless errands for Him. I want to take an advanced course in grace to learn why God loved us so much that He gave his only Son for our redemption.

As we approach the end of life, we begin to think about our last day: What will I be doing? What will be my last act? Have I made things right with others? So I bring my last day into today and strive to live in the light of it. I hope my death will be in dignity. I do not wish to live to be a helpless and useless old person. I recoil at the idea of artificial means being applied to keep me alive after I am really dead. I wish to die without tubes running like tentacles from my body. Hence, I have made several copies of my Living Will available to those likely to be involved in my final days. I want to go like my ancestors all the way back to Adam. My father and grandfathers died at home. I vividly remember my grandfather being hauled to the graveyard in a pine box on a wagon drawn by two mules. He bypassed the morticians and was buried in dignity. Likewise my father discovered that he was terminally ill while in a hospital, called for his clothes and went home to die. All of his children, grandchildren and friends came by to see him and to say goodbye before he died. I call his death Kalosthanasia. *Kalos* is the Greek word for "morally good" and "esthetically acceptable." *Thanasia* is the Greek word for death. Hence, the term identifies a death that is morally right, dignified and does not shock one's esthetic sense.

This does not mean that I want to "go gentle into that good night." I will "rage against the dying light."[2] It means that if I am terminally ill and can no longer rage and fight, I want no "heroic" medical interventions or "extraordinary means" to keep me alive. When my son Jim was a small boy, he was aware that I was an old man and he asked, "Will you live to be seventy?" Reply: "I don't know." He commented, "I think death should be a celebration for a Christian." When my Great Transition occurs, let my death be a celebration of:

> Any burden I have shared to lighten the load of others;
> Any speech I have made that has inspired in others the love of learning;
> Any counsel I have given to guide others to a richer life;
> Any book I have written that has made the reader more knowledgeable;
> Any deed I have done that has ministered to human need and glorified God.

I have worked hard all my life: chores at home, as a water boy on a road gang, as a cotton mill hand, as a pastor of churches and missions and as a professor in two universities, a seminary and a medical school. So let me die working.

Let me die thinking. I have always had a hunger to know more. Here we see things "through a glass darkly." No one has all the truth. This, Nietzsche declares, would kill one like a bolt of lightning. When I think of Truth, I recite an ancient Hebrew prayer:

---

[2] Dylan Thomas, "Do Not Go Gentle into That Good Night" (1952).

From the cowardice that shrinks from new truths,
From the laziness that is content with half-truths,
And from the arrogance that thinks it knows all truth,
O God of Truth, deliver us.

I long to penetrate beyond the surface of things, beyond "the glass darkly" to the inner core of reality. My college professor of philosophy urged us "to pursue the truth wherever the manifestations of truth may be found." These manifestations are all around us. But no one can "tell the whole truth, nothing but the truth" in court or in science because they do not know the whole truth. Ultimate truth is in a person, Jesus the Christ.

Jesus
He is the Way;
Walk in it;
He is the Truth;
Seek it;
He is the Life;
Live it. (John 14:6)

Let me die sharing the burdens of others. Everyone is carrying a burden, whether seen or unseen. So I must be kind to everyone and empathize and share their burden. "We share our mutual woes, our mutual burdens bear." So goes the old hymn. "Bear one another's burdens and in this way you will fulfill the law of Christ" (Gal 6:2, NRSV). I must identify Christ in those who are hungry, thirsty, naked, imprisoned. Ministry to those who suffer these afflictions is ministry to Christ incognito. A seminarian informed me that he could not participate in such a ministry. Then I gently told him he was in the wrong vocation.

Walt Whitman, had a great capacity to empathize with those hurting. He said, "I do not ask the wounded how he feels; I become the wounded person" (*Song of Myself*). Let me die empathizing with the suffering, the wounded, the depressed, the lonely.

What if the Sadducees, atheists, and unbelievers are right when they declare there is no resurrection, no after-life and no fellowship with those who have died in the faith? Have I lived a false faith? Are there no loved ones waiting just beyond the river, beyond this life? I summon one of my favorite writers, Pascal and his wager:

> Let us weigh the gain and the loss in wagering that God is.
> Let us estimate these two chances.
> If you gain, you gain *all*;
> if you lose, you lose nothing. (*Pensees* 233)

So may I go in hope into that good night like the dawn of a thistle carried by a gentle breeze.

Selected Reference Sources

Adams, Laura. "Henlee Hulix Barnette: The Fight for Human Rights and Social Justice; One Man's Role in the Civil Rights Movement." Unpublished paper for HN 300–05, Butler University, 12/02/80, personal file

Armour, Rollin S., editor. *Perspectives on Christian Ethics*: *Essays in Honor Of Henlee Hulix Barnette.* Macon GA: Mercer University Press, 1991.

Barnette, Henlee. "My Pilgrimage as a Professor." Unpublished paper, personal file

Debusman, Paul. "A Bibliography of the Writings of Henlee Barnette." In *Perspectives on Christian Ethics*: *Essays in Honor Of Henlee Hulix Barnette.* Edited by Rollin S. Armour. Macon GA: Mercer University Press, 1991.

Lature, Dale. "Henlee Hulix Barnette: Moral Conscience for Southern Baptists." Research paper presented to Dr. Walter Shurden and Dr. Frank Tupper, Southern Baptist Theological Seminary, 4/30/77 personal file.

Marsalis, Charles. "Henlee Hulix Barnette: Moral Conscience of Southern Baptist Theological Seminary." Unpublished paper, 11/15/77 personal file

Munro, Clarice Susan. "Bishop of the Haymarket," *Courier-Journal Magazine* (23 March 1952): 6–7.

Sherouse, Craig Alan. "Groundwork to the Ethics of Henlee Barnette." Unpublished paper. 11/29/77 personal file

Sisk, Ronald D. "The Ethics of Henlee Barnette: A Study in Method." Ph.D. dissertation, Southern Baptist Theological Seminary, 1982).

————. "Henlee Barnette and Race: A Case Study in Biblical Ethics." Unpublished seminar paper for Church History Department, Southern Baptist Theological Seminary, 4 December 1979.

Christian Ethics Today. "Henlee Hulix Barnette: A Special Salute." 3/4 (September 1977): 15–22.

Light. "An Interview with Henlee Barnette." Nashville: Christian Life Commission of the Southern Baptist Convention, 1984.

Towers (weekly campus news magazine)and *The Tie* (alumni magazine) published by the Southern Baptist Theological Seminary, Louisville, KY.

The Whitsitt Journal. "Barnette to Receive Baptist Courage Award." Spring 1997: 1–5

Appendix 1

Relations with the Russians[1]

On 24 July 1957 a group of Americans, of which I was one, had a two-hour conference with Nikita Khrushchev, Premier of the USSR. We met around a long table in his office within the walls of the Kremlin. The top boss of the Communist Party had just decentralized industry, demoted the old Bolsheviks Molotov, Kaganovich, Shepilov and Malenkov. Too, the communists were celebrating their fortieth anniversary, and young people from all over the world were beginning to pour into Moscow for the "Youth Festival." It was a strategic moment to talk with the most powerful person in the communist world.

When we arrived that afternoon at his office, Khrushchev was in a rare mood. He was optimistic, humorous, cocksure. The questions we were to ask during our conference had been given to the premier in advance.

This is the record of Khrushchev's remarks:

Question 1: Do you think it would be helpful to have more exchanges of interviews on the radio and television between American and Soviet leaders?

Khrushchev: I think it would be very useful indeed and would aid in every possible way, but to make it fruitful we should not indulge in propaganda. We should emphasize those things which unite us and not divide us. This is not because we fear propaganda, for we have been able to use it and meet it more effectively than America.

Question 2: Do you feel hopeful about the achievement of international peace despite the things which divide us?

[1] Reprinted with permission. Henlee Barnette, "Relations with the Russians," *Review and Expositor* Vol. LVI, 3(July 1959): 250–258.

Khrushchev: This is a very important question. If we lose hope in the question, the future will be dark indeed. But I and my colleagues have hope and feel sure that common sense and wisdom will triumph and win the minds of the people.

Question 3: What in your opinion are the principal obstacles to working out a program of disarmament and an end to the cold war?

Khrushchev: I do not know exactly what to advise on this question, but the main thing is confidence. When US statesmen say, "Give us proof and then [we shall have] confidence," I say that you cannot have proof without confidence. For to try to secure it without confidence is self-defeating and going around in a vicious circle. The principal thing is that we must live on one and the same planet. The question is war or peace. If it is to be war there can be no confidence. But we want peace and peace presumes confidence and trust. When you came in here (office) nobody asked you to turn your pockets inside out because we trust you. We have confidence in you. If you take two opposing armies and one raises the white flag of surrender, there comes a time of confidence when negotiations are carried on peacefully. Sometimes this backfires as it did for us in Budapest in World War II. Our Ambassador was shot, but this is a risk we have to take. We must still have hope. We must have confidence not control. The more rigid control, the less there is of confidence.

Question 4: Would you be willing to end the Atom Bomb tests permanently?

Khrushchev: We would sign an agreement to tomorrow. Today, if you like!

Question 5: What effective means of inspection and control of the Atom Bomb would you propose?

Khrushchev: We have proposed such a system. We have a vast territory and we hear that small tests are made in the US which go undetected. Therefore there would have to be control posts on our territory to detect even the smallest tests. We have agreed to US inspectors on our territory at certain points so that even the smallest test would be detected. So far all our proposals put forth in London have received no answer.

Question 6: Would the Soviet Union be willing to participate in a mammoth program for the development of the under-developed areas of the world under the United Nations?

Khrushchev: We have expressed readiness to do this if there is first disarmament as this would release our funds to develop such countries and also would benefit the whole of humanity. A concrete proposal to this effect was put forth by Foure of France and we supported it. The trouble is that as soon as we accept a proposal that the West has put forth, the West denounces it. Many of our proposals were put forth earlier by the West and we were not willing to accept them then, but later when we proposed them they would not accept them.

Question 7: Wouldn't it have been better if you had accepted them at the beginning?

Khrushchev: No, because the Western powers counted on refusing them and when we did accept them they rejected them.

Question 8: What is your decentralization program?

Khrushchev: I want to say a bit more about why the US would not accept our proposals at first. All your public pronouncements against the Soviet Union are unfounded. I am full of esteem for your president and there were very good relations between us when he was [the Allied Forces] Supreme Commander. He was an honest soldier, but the president cannot alone pursue a policy. I don't know who pressures him. Monopolists have a vast influence on the government and only profit from the cold war as they furnish munitions and render aid in armaments. This is absurd and divides us and leads to hate. But the monopolists must make huge profits from it. This makes possible a very high taxation of the people by frightening them about war. There are only a handful of monopolists and every one of your democracy has one vote, but with dollars the monopolists can get lots of votes. You know better than I how this is done. You probably know the name Hewlitt Johnson. When we were in England and his name came up, he was called the "Red Dean". Why? Only because he is a consistent advocate of peace. He is not a communist. It makes us all the more proud when an honest man who is against war is called "Red." We greet them even though they are not Reds. Johnson is far from it. We differ philosophically, but we agree on one thing—peace.

I can now answer your question about the reorganization of industry. The essence is that before reorganization, management was vertical. There were ministries in Moscow with branches in all towns. Under that system all the administration was from one center. In one city there would be representatives from twenty to thirty ministries. When there was a question all twenty representatives might have to go to Moscow to settle it and then go back. The result is a vast correspondence and a huge bureaucracy. No one is infallible, not even a minister no matter how clever he may be. His mistakes under that system would become the mistakes of the Soviet Union. Criticism of a minister or ministry from below would never reach Moscow and thus he would be immune to the criticism of workers or the industry. Now there are regional or local economic councils and the administration of industry rests with them and criticism is addressed to them. Whereas an administration used to be run from one center, now there are 105 centers or economic councils. Each economic center has specialized departments and the head of each department has broad power to answer questions arising under him. This has lessened bureaucratic tendencies and brought the administration closer to the factories and made possible greater constructive criticism. We have freed tens of thousands of people from empty paper work, made it possible for them to enter into the productive aspects of the economy. Not only are they free, but the hundreds of thousands of people who read these papers are free from this mad house too. We have been reorganizing now for several months and have paralyzed the entire bureaucratic apparatus but industry is working marvelously. The results you have perhaps seen in our papers. This reorganization brings billions of rubles for the economy. That is the economic side. On the political side there is more democracy. The initiative of engineers, scientists and workers is greater much greater and they have an opportunity to express their views.

Question 9: What things do you think the US can do more effectively to bring about peace?

Khrushchev: The most important thing is to liquidate the vast trade barriers. Not because we need to sell to you or you need to buy from us. The quantity is not important, but trade brings confidence. In the old days traders were robbed and killed, but they still came and they brought confidence. To think that in this day and age we are not trading is fantastic. We are interested in your trade and you in ours. If you don't want strategic things to be sold this is all right, but a ban on trade can only exist if people are contemplating war. Even Soviet cooks are not allowed in the US, probably because the US is afraid they will shake the foundation of its way of life! I met a farmer by the name of Gasston who is a specialist on hybridization of corn. He was very nice and wanted to invite a group of agronomists to the US. They were refused entry by your government and when he went to champion their entry he had no luck. How can we improve prospects for peace, we cannot even discuss corn!

Question 10: We had an exchange of farmers recently, didn't we?

Khrushchev: Yes, but only once then it stopped. We would like to maintain the exchange. We favor an exchange of engineers, as we have ideas of engineering even as you do. Mankind has always exchanged ideas. Regarding the concern that our delegations may find out military secrets in your country, we need no exchanges of military personnel. But our airplanes and bombers are no worse than yours and our rocket airplanes are better than yours. We do not need to exchange military goods. We had the hydrogen bomb before you did. So your security regulations do not hold water. Even in the war our tanks, though fewer than yours, were as good as the US or German tanks.

The idea of not letting people into our respective countries is stupid and foolish. I don't know if such words are polite and I don't want to insult, but I think so anyway. When people respect or accept a certain idea or system, that depends on their will; but you can't ignore the fact that Bulgaria, Romania, Albania, China, one third of Germany and North Vietnam exist. When we set up our system, we didn't ask Dulles. You hate communism and we capitalism, but that's not important. We have done wonders in our country and you envy us because we are the second greatest power in the world and will, through communism, soon be first. We must subdue passion and subordinate it to common sense. Some politicians are blinded by hate and, like a bull seeing red, they charge forth blindly. Let us exchange scientific information and cooperate with each other.

Question 11: What would you suggest for our group to tell others when we return to the US to promote peace?

Khrushchev: Tell the truth about what you have seen in the Soviet Union. Tell of our ideas and beliefs of peace and brotherhood. Your method is up to you; the main thing is peace in the world, friendship between peoples. We must bring peace and ban the hydrogen and atomic weapons. These are the ideas that move all honest people.

Question 12: Would an exchange of students between the US and Russia be helpful?

Khrushchev: Such an exchange existed formerly between our countries. Several of my friends went to the US and studied there. One, Semiyan, is Deputy Prime Minister of the Ukraine. Deputy Foreign Minister Kuzmitsoff is another. After the war this exchange unfortunately stopped. We remember the great American Roosevelt—a wise and intelligent person—who correctly understood the historical process. Unfortunately, with his death cooperation stopped. If we resume cooperation, this will help the whole world as we are the two most powerful countries. If two small countries fight this is sad, but if two big countries fight this is a catastrophe.

In the days gone by you were absolutely superior over us, but this is no longer true. We still have a lot to learn from you but you have much to learn from us, and we should learn from each other on an exchange basis. Last year your specialist, the engineer Morgoss, met with us and we gave him the Order of the Red Banner for his work on the Metro. I esteem him, but he told one untruth. He said he was formerly in civil engineering in Italy and is now working on housing in Turkey. But I know he was a concrete engineer in America and is now probably doing the same thing in Turkey. He thought he fooled me, but he only fooled himself because I believe he is working on American air bases.

Question 13: Under what conditions would you be willing to participate in an exchange of students and how many do you think you could take, perhaps 5000?

Khrushchev: No, that would be too many as we would have to pay for their stay in the US and that would be too expensive.

Question 14: But you are a rich country?

Khrushchev: Yes, but we have no US dollars.

Question 15: Then we will pay for your students and you can pay for ours?

Khrushchev: All right, please. Some think we fear such exchanges and that our students will turn to capitalism. Perhaps some may, but this would be no tragedy and would not shake our country even if some decided to stay in your country. The same thing could happen with your students here, even though I am sure you would pick the staunchest supporters of capitalism to send. This in no way stops our desire for these exchanges.

Question 16: Do you want all kinds of exchanges?

Khrushchev: Yes, certainly. We'll eventually—when we get a bit richer—all be able to go abroad from here and if some people decide to stay abroad, we wish them success. But perhaps people will go to the US and be happy there at first and then cry to come back. There are such people in the US. Let them come here.

Question 17: We have heard in America that Jews are not permitted to go freely to Israel. Is this true?

Khrushchev: It is true to some extent and to some extent not true. We don't allow just anyone to leave the Soviet Union. We issue passports to those whose visits are expedient. We recently, though, allowed a great number of Jews to go to Poland and we knew that many of them would go to Israel from there. I am sure the time will come when all Jews—and Russians, for that matter—who want to go to Israel will be able to do so. I know there are many Jews who have gone to Israel who want to come back here as life is not very sweet for them there.

Question 18: Is it possible for Jews who have relatives in Israel to go there?

Khrushchev: Yes, I think this is possible. Recently the prime minister of Denmark asked us to grant permission for three Jews to leave the Soviet Union and we granted his request.

Of course, we think that Israel has been engaged in aggressive warfare. They recently attacked Egypt and they often make raids against them. The intelligence units of the US often use Jews who have fled for their purposes and this is not good for our security. We do not want an honest man who goes to visit his relatives to be turned into a traitor to his country. But these are only temporary difficulties which will be removed with the improvement of relations.

Question 19: But Egypt refuses to permit Israel's boats to pass through the Suez Canal and the Gulf of Aqaba and often raids Israel's territory. Is there not blame on both sides?

Khrushchev: Yes, it is a complicated question. You must understand the situation of the Arabs. They lived on their own land and were forced out of Israel. They are suffering and can't have good feeling towards Israel. Also there was the UN decision on the boundaries of Israel, but she violated these boundaries and grabbed territory. There needs to be cooperation on both sides to solve the problem.

Question 20: Can any minority group such as the Jews open a theater anywhere in Russia? Would you encourage this?

Khrushchev: This is a very old question. There used to be many Yiddish theaters in many cities, Moscow, Odessa, Kiev, Luav. During the war we lost many Jews. It was a tragedy. In western Ukraine, for example, which came over from Poland, large numbers of Jews paid money to Nazis to escape and fell into the hands of the executioners. They were executed when they got to Poland. You have seen in your travels the culture and customs of many different republics—Georgia, Kazakhstan, Uzbekistan and Tajakistan. But the Jews are dispersed throughout the USS.R. We wanted to unite them and established Birobidzhan for this purpose. All that is left now in Birobidzhan are signs in Yiddish at the RR stations, but there are no Jews there. There are many Jews in the government and even in the Central Command of the Party. They are assimilated into the Russian culture and language. If we had seven-year schools for Jews in the Jewish language, where could the graduates go? We would have to establish ten-year schools, special universities, for them. Other Republics have their own territory and their own language and we encourage this, but the Jews are dispersed and engulfed in the culture where they live. They enjoy all the benefits of the Republics where they live and complete equality in economic and political respects. What other freedoms can there be? They can live and work freely and there can be no greater freedom. Our position is that it all depends upon the will of the Jews. If they want to create a state within our borders like Birobidzhan nobody is against this and it exists to this day, but the initiative must come from the Jews.

Question 21: Under what conditions would you be willing to see Germany reunited?

Khrushchev: We have set forth our policy very clearly. We have only one condition for the reunification of Germany. We hold that the Germans themselves should find a solution to the problem. West Germany is operating on a capitalistic basis, East Germany a socialistic basis. We believe that both have grounds to exist and to develop. Thus the Germans themselves must bring about the reunification without interference.

Question 22: Under what conditions would you be willing to withdraw all troops from foreign countries?

Khrushchev: If the United States and other Western powers agree to withdraw troops, we will do it together. We are ready to do it now. This would make way for disarmament.

Question 23: Are artists freer in the Soviet Union than in democratic countries?

Khrushchev: It all depends upon what you mean by freedom. Our government encourages artists to contribute to the welfare and culture of the people. In a capitalist country the artist is not free to do this, because his work is done for profit. In the Soviet Union we have highly developed our art in the theater and the ballet, but you don't have your national opera because capitalists must make profit. I am not going to say more about this because some will think that I am giving out anti-capitalist propaganda!

Question 24: Would you care to comment upon the recent shake-up in government?

Khrushchev: Our press has set forth enough light on the subject. Members of the anti-party [Molotov, Kaganovich, Malenkov and Shepilov] estranged themselves from the life of the people and held to old concepts. But conditions have changed. Previously we were alone in socialism, but now there are many socialist nations. The anti-party group did not meet the changing situation. The Twentieth Congress and the Central Committee will not tolerate people of this position. However, they are still members of the Party.

After the formal conference, we lingered for a quarter of an hour more taking pictures and talking informally. We emphasized the fact that we desired peace and friendship among all nations. Khrushchev declared: "No sane person wants war. There are no more staunch supporters for peace than in our country."

He does not appear to be insane, and the people of the USSR. profess to want peace. But we should not be lulled into complacency by these impressions. It is the ultimate aim of the communists to take the world, to sovietize all nations. If we are to survive as a nation of free people, it is imperative that we strengthen our spiritual, moral, economic, political and military forces. At the same time, we must seek to break through the Iron Curtain and establish more effective lines of communication with the citizens of Sovietland. We must try to convince them that we are not "warmongers," but that we sincerely seek a just and lasting peace for the world. It must also be made crystal clear that we do not want peace at any price and that we are ready to lay down our lives to preserve and to promote our faith and freedom.

Postal Rate Commission
Washington DC 20268–0001
John W. Crutcher
Commissioner

March 2, 1990

Dr. Henlee H. Barnette
The Southern Baptist Theological Seminary
2825 Lexington Road
Louisville, KY 40205
Dear Henlee:
You are absolutely correct. The cultural exchange program between the Soviet Union and America was initiated by our visit with Nikita Khrushchev in July of 1957.

I remember the occasion well. We had very little advance notice that our group would have the an opportunity to interview Khrushchev, whose emissaries had told us that our questions must be submitted in writing in advance. Jerome Davis knew it would be impossible for us all to agree on the list of questions, so he huddled with a select few to help him draft the list of questions. I remember well that I suggested we propose a gigantic student exchange with the Soviet Union involving 5,000 students on each side. Jerome looked at me with astonishment and said, "Why, they would never agree to that number." I replied, "Of course they wouldn't, but our purpose is to challenge him with the concept." We then discussed other cultural programs which might profitably be exchanged and agreed on questions relating thereto.

Khrushchev's response was exactly as Reuters reported in that article in the *New York Times*. When we first hit him with the 5,000-student figure he protested that they couldn't do it, but when we followed on to find out why they would not exchange the students he said that they didn't have the dollars to subsist that number of students in the United States. We replied, "You don't need dollars. We will take care of your kids with dollars and you, in turn, will take care of our students with rubles." Khrushchev clapped his hands together and said "All right, let's do it." He then got a shrewd look in those beady little eyes and said, "I know what you are thinking. You think when our young people get to America, they will see how rich you are and they will all want to become capitalists." He said, "Some of them may, but you have to understand that you will have 5,000 students in the Soviet Union and some of them might want to become communists." Then he laughed and said, "Personally, I think that might be good for each country."

I have no idea how Reuters' correspondent got hold of Elmer McLain and his wife as sources for their article, but I do remember that Jerome asked me to help him to write an article to sell to the press when we arrived in Paris. We did write such an article and sold it for $200 to United Press International when we arrived in Paris.

Our article also appeared in the *New York Times* and a long list of US papers and, of course, it was big news in the State Department, even before we got back upon American soil.

To the everlasting credit of the State Department, they immediately challenged the Soviet Union to put up or shut up on the subject of student and cultural exchanges. Whereupon a series of meetings occurred at an Ambassadorial level between the United States, represented by Ambassador Lacey, and the Soviet Union. In January 1958 they announced their agreement on the first cultural exchange. When they got down to hard negotiation, the 5,000 students we had suggested had dwindled down to 20 and those 20, when they arrived in America turned out to be hardened, cold-eyed members of the Communist Party who were presumed to be "safe for solo."

It is a long and fascinating story and I am grateful you are interested in the historical facts of the matter.

Edie and I remain in good health but terribly busy. I have just returned from a long trip to New Zealand where I mixed business with a lot of pleasure.

My love and best wishes to you and Helen and all the Barnette clan.

Sincerely,

John Crutcher

21 August 1957

Mr. Nikita Khrushchev
First Secretary
Communist Party of the USS.R.
Moscow, Russia
Dear Mr. Khrushchev:

This is to thank you again for the conference you granted to the American Seminar on 24 July. All of us were impressed with your rare sense of humor, your frank and clear answers to our questions, and your concern for the cause of world peace.

Personally, I came to deeply appreciate the Russian people. I have never met in any country a people more friendly, polite and generous. I recall that you urged us to go back home and "tell the truth about what you saw." A close reading of the enclosed report in the *Louisville Times* (one of our leading evening papers in America) indicates that I am trying to give the positive side of the picture as well as the negative.

I am a Baptist among 12,000,000 others in America. Naturally, I visited Baptist churches in the USS.R. I discovered that Baptists are devoted Christians. They deeply love their country and are loyal to their government. They do not have a seminary in which to train their pastors. The Baptist Seminary, I am told, was closed in 1928. I do not know why, but in America we get the story that the government closed it. Anyway, I feel that Baptists, being the largest evangelical group in Russia, should be allowed to have a seminary. The Greek Orthodox Church has a great seminary at Zagorsk. I was informed that Russian Jews were permitted to open a seminary last year. I, along with millions of other Baptists in this country, would be happy to learn that Baptists in Russia have a seminary in which to train their pastors.

Thanking you again for your kindness, I remain
Sincerely yours,
Henlee H. Barnette

Appendix 2

Race Matters

April 26, 1961
Dr. Martin Luther King, Jr.
Ebenezer Baptist Church
407 Auburn Avenue, N.E.
Atlanta, Georgia
Dear Dr. King:

This is to express my sincere appreciation for your chapel message and lecture to my class in Christian Ethics when you were on our campus. The excellent way in which you handled the questions in the class has been commented upon by many of the students. All that you said was insightful and inspiring to our hearts. I made the observation in one of my classes that your presence here was the best morale booster that we have had this year. As you will recall, you received a standing ovation at the conclusion of your statements to the class in chapel. This was the first time that I recall anyone getting a standing ovation in chapel.

By this time you have become aware of the fact that we have received some criticism from the "Alabama Baptist Layman's Group" because you were invited to speak at our school. I do not know anything about this group, but it appears to me to be a fundamentalist and rabid segregationalist group. I do not think that it reflects the attitude, as it claims, of our Southern Baptist leadership.

You will be interested to know that Reverend W. J. Hodge, head of the NAACP here in Louisville, will be speaking to the Alabama group this week and that Dr. George Kelsey of Drew University will be giving the Gheens Lectures for next year in Ethics.

Be assured of my continuing interest in your prophetic ministry.

Gratefully yours,

Henlee Barnette

Martin Luther King, Jr.
Ebenezer Baptist Church
407 Auburn Avenue, N.E.
Atlanta, Georgia

May 3, 1961

Dr. Henlee Barnette
The Southern Baptist Theological Seminary
2825 Lexington Road
Louisville, Kentucky
Dear Dr. Barnette:

This is just a note to acknowledge receipt of your very kind letter of recent date and again to express my appreciation to you, the faculty and students of the Southern Baptist Theological Seminary for making my recent visit there such a meaningful one. I don't know when I have had a more rewarding experience. The great expressions of moral support that I received from Southern Baptist Theological Seminary will be of inestimable value for the continuance of my humble efforts. Please extend my warm best wishes to the many friends that I met on the campus, and I hope that we will be able to renew the fellowship in the not too distant future.

I was very glad to have your clarification on the Alabama Layman's group that made the critical statement concerning my visit. When I first saw this reported in the press, I wondered if this group represented the attitude of the Southern Baptist leadership.

Best wishes to you in your work, and may the days ahead bring us closer to the ideal of the brotherhood of man.

Sincerely yours,
Martin Luther King, Jr.

Memorial Service for Dr. King

Scripture: Psalm 55
"In Time of Trouble: Martin Luther King in Retrospect"
Dr. Henlee H. Barnette
Professor of Christian Ethics
The Southern Baptist Theological Seminary

Here is a man in trouble and in a troublesome city. Fear, crime, looting, rioting, fraud, graft and corruption characterize the urban community in which he lives.

All of this sounds familiar to the contemporary American citizen. At home there are the problems of crime, riots, looting, poverty and assassination. Abroad our nation is engaged in a tragic war in Vietnam. Our Western allies are pulling away from us. Russia is in the Mediterranean seeking to dominate the situation there.

How does one respond to trouble? This is important for the individual since his response to crises is a revelation of his character.

It is a significant question for a nation. Arnold Toynbee notes that the destiny of nations is determined by the principle of challenge and response. Unless a nation responds creatively to moral and social issues it will die. Toynbee lists twenty-one civilizations which have been cast upon the rubbish heap of history because they did not respond creatively to crises.

Three basic responses to trouble are articulated in Psalm 55.

First, there is the impulse to escape. "Oh that I had wings like a dove! I would fly away and be at rest." (Ps 55:6). Have we not all wished for wings to escape from our problems? A popular song of a generation back gives clear expression to the wish to escape: "Let's take a boat to Bermuda; let's get away from it all." But the wings of a dove are not strong enough to lift a man's soul out of the midst of a troubled existence. As Uncle Remus declares: "You can't get away from trouble for there ain't no place that far away." The Psalmist discovered this fact.

There is a second response to trouble. We can call upon God to fight out battles for us. "Destroy their plans, O Lord, confuse their tongues; for I see violence and strife in the city." (Ps 55:9) We can implore God to destroy evil. This introduces the problem of theodicy. Why does God permit evil in the first place?

Recently a little dialogue went on between a mother and her ten-year old daughter. After the child had witnessed via T.V. the first 10 days of violence in April, she asked her mother a probing question.

Daughter: "If there really is a God, why does he allow so much violence?"

Mother: "Free will; we are not puppets on a string." (Obviously this issue had been debated before.)

Daughter: "But, then why doesn't God do something?"

Mother: "God did do something. He came to earth to show us how to live."

Daughter: "Well, he had better do it again; the first time didn't take."

But God doesn't settle all the evil problems for us.

Life is a battle. Paul urges every Christian to put on the whole armor of God, for we wrestle not against flesh and blood, but against "principalities and powers." When the mythological and eschatological garments are stripped from the "principalities and powers," they turn out to be the evil traditions of men and the demonic power structures. These are the real enemies against which the Christian must do battle. God will equip us for the struggle, but he will not take us out of it.

There is, in the third place, a positive way of dealing with trouble. "Cast your burden on the Lord, and he will sustain you; he will never permit the righteous to be moved." (Ps 55:22) You say, "But this is escapism." Hardly, for casting burdens upon the Lord is related to righteousness. We have been misled by the popular hymn; "Take your burden to the Lord and leave it there." God will not permit us to shift our burden to him, but he will share it when we are engaged in a righteous cause. This is what the Beatitude means: "Blessed are those who hunger and thirst for righteousness, for they shall be satisfied." Here righteousness means a righteous cause.

On 4 April 1968, an assassin's bullet removed from the land of the living a prophet with a righteous cause. He had an intense hunger and thirst for a righteous cause and found his satisfaction in prophetic action. He was persecuted for righteousness's sake. His name will go down in history and our children's children will read about him.

Yet not many Southern Baptists from the Convention level to that of a local church identified with him or his cause. This in spite of the fact that he was one of us, a Baptist. Few of us marched with him and supported his cause for social justice. The faculty and administration of Southern Baptist Seminary neither held a special memorial service in his honor nor sent a message of condolence to their bereaved Baptist kin. We are grateful that some students of the seminary did have a brief memorial and did send a message of sympathy. With these exceptions, we left it to the Catholics, the Jews, the government and the labor unions to do him honor in his death.

Perhaps we felt that it would be hypocritical to do him honor in death, since we did not support him in life.

Oh, we salved our consciences by permitting our departed brother, Martin Luther King, Jr., to speak from the pulpit in the chapel and to lecture in a Christian ethics class.

After his chapel address, we gave Brother Martin a standing ovation, the only one ever accorded to a speaker in the seminary chapel. Yet we did not translate our praise into practice. We did not identify with him and his cause.

Now is the time for all of us to assume the burden of righteousness. This means that the shape of our ministry will be prophetic. Our seminaries must become more involved in the crushing issues of the larger community. The church must become prophetic and cease piddling with petty programs of self-enhancement. Some churches spend more time debating about what kind of carpet should grace the sanctuary floor than they do about the problems of war, poverty and social justice. They remain uninvolved in this

> ...stupid world where
> Gadgets are gods and we go on talking
> Many about much, but remain alone,
> Alive but alone, belonging ... where?
> Unattached as a tumbleweed.
> (W. H. Auden, *The Age of Anxiety*)

This nation has produced only three major Baptist prophets: Abraham Lincoln, Walter Rauschenbusch, and Martin Luther King, Jr.

Lincoln was brought up a Baptist; Rauschenbusch was a Baptist church historian and the most brilliant interpreter of social Christianity; King was a Baptist preacher and a charismatic leader of the Civil Rights Movement

All were crucified by their contemporaries. They felt the agony of the cross. The same ecclesiastics who participated in the stoning of these prophets and insisted on an orthodox view of the cross never felt the pain of it. Now we praise these dead prophets, but we can't endure living ones. We cannonade the living prophets and canonize them when they are safely removed by death.

A prophetic ministry involves a cross and a cause. "Must Jesus bear the cross alone . . .?" In the closing scene of Marc Connely's *Green Pastures*, a voice is heard in the distance: "Oh, look at him! Oh, look, dey goin' to make him carry it up dat high hill! Dey goin' to nail him to it! Oh, dat's a terrible burden for one man to carry!"

Church Leader Calls for Racial, Political Equality
Winter Haven Daily News-Chief Volume 33, No.59 page 1.
Winter Haven, Florida
Wednesday, 5 April 1950

Speaking to 1,206 delegates to the Florida Baptist Woman's Missionary Union today at Nora Mayo Hall, Dr. H. H. Barnette, Department of Religion at Stetson University, called for racial equality in education and political affairs, but said the races should be kept distinct.

"We must move from a level of passion to the level of Christian teaching in our dealing with the racial problems," he told the group.

"It is a fallacy that God ordained the Negro to be the servant of the white man, and a casual reading of Genesis, from which this idea is supposed to come, will reveal that God in no way curses any race," he said.

"It is also a fallacy to think that the Negro is inherently inferior, for science has shown that no group or race is inferior. Nor is it dangerous to educate any one group or race," he added.

He said that a segment of society which lags behind others intellectually in our culture is open to "isms"—especially to communism.

"We must guard against instilling prejudice in the minds of children and we must go from a desire to improve racial relations to deeds."

He called for Baptist clergymen to set examples of religious tolerance, telling of work that had been done in Birmingham toward bringing about closer harmony and cited examples that have been done by Baptist organizations in the South to alleviate the situation.

Dr. Barnette said he knew certain conservative and radical factions would not agree with his thought of political and education racial equality, while keeping the races distinct.

[*Nota bene*: The reporter wrote that I said "the races should be kept distinct." He repeated the phrase at the article's end. Read carefully my remarks below from the speech given earlier to the Florida Baptist Convention and later to the WMU for what I really said.]

Race Relations
Report to Florida Baptist Convention
Daytona Beach, 16 November 1949
Dr. Henlee H. Barnette
Professor of Religion, Stetson University
DeLand, Florida

The race problem is universal in scope and exceedingly acute at the present time. With the spread of the democratic philosophy on a worldwide scale, all peoples of the earth are demanding freedom, justice, opportunity and equality. At no place, perhaps, is the race situation more critical than in our own Southland. Minority groups are no longer content with their lot. There is a growing unrest at the status to which they have been assigned in our political, education and social life.

Florida is no exception, for this State has its race problem. It involves a number of racial groups, but the largest by far is that of the Negro. The minority groups are pressing for a larger measure of economic security, civil rights and educational opportunities. But the race problem is not just an economic and scientific problem. Gunnar Myrdal in his great work, *An American Dilemma*, points out that the American Negro problem is "a problem in the heart of the American. It is there that the interracial tension has its focus." Therefore, the race problem is a moral and spiritual one, and the Christian forces should take the lead in its solution. Certainly the solution to this problem should not be left to social agencies, political leaders, the forces of organized labor and outsiders. If the Baptists of Florida fail in offering leadership in this pressing issue, they will shirk their moral duty and will lose the good will of the racial groups of the State.

Baptists of the South have not seriously studied the problems of race. Hitherto their efforts in the interest of minority groups have been restricted largely to strictly religious work. They have not come to grips with the basic issues growing out of social relationships. However, they are becoming more socially minded. There is a growing awareness among us that we need to study the whole racial situation in its moral and religious aspects and to

A Pilgrimage of Faith

face the question of Baptist responsibility in the solution of the problems which it presents. Indicative of the growing interest of Florida Baptists in the improvement of race relations is the action taken by this Convention last year in Miami when it adopted the "Charter of Principles on Race Relations" which the Southern Baptist Convention adopted in 1947 and reaffirmed in 1948. At this same Convention a Special Committee on Race Relations was appointed to study the race situation and to work in co-operation with the Social Service Commission of the Southern Baptist Convention.

At present many of our Baptist people are sincerely asking, "What are the next steps in race relations?" In the first place, we must discover the scientific and Christian basis for action in human relations. What are these basic scientific and scriptural truths governing race relations?

For years our ablest historians, sociologists, anthropologists and psychologists have studied the race problem. What are their conclusions? Only a few can be listed: all peoples of the earth are a single family with a common origin; there are no pure races for the ancestry of all peoples is mixed; no one race can be considered inferior or superior to any other race; all human blood is the same (There are four basic types of blood, A, B, AB and O. Every one of these types is present in all racial groups); neither mentality or personality of peoples is determined by any racial characteristics such as the shape of the head, color of the skin, or the texture of the hair.

What are the Biblical and Baptist views concerning race and race relations? A few may be listed: all men are God's creatures, potential members of God's kingdom, capable of becoming the sons of God; every person is of supreme worth and should be treated as an end and never as a mere means; the love of God is inseparable from the love of man, so that failure to love man is proof that there is no genuine love of God; Christians are to practice the golden rule and treat others as they would have others treat them; God is no respecter of persons; the Bible summons all Christians to practice justice toward all people of all races; and, finally, Baptists believe in democracy and the constitutional rights of all citizens irrespective of racial characteristics. These are the scientific and scriptural truths concerning the race situation.

But how can these principles become more than mere generalities? How may they be applied in personal and social relationships? Let it be made clear that there is no easy and final solution to the race problem. The Christian ideal in race relations is radical and does not permit an easy application. Nevertheless there are certain practical steps which can be taken toward improving human relations in Florida. The following suggestions, some of which grew out of the Race Relations Conference, Ridgecrest, NC, August 1949 may be helpful.

I. At the Individual Level

1. Accept individuals on the basis of their ability as persons, not on the basis of their color.

2. Avoid jokes that belittle members of minority groups and perpetuate prejudice and stereotypes.

3. Use the proper title of "Mr." Or "Mrs." When addressing Negroes, Jews, etc.

4. Cultivate the acquaintance of several representatives of minority groups in the community and get to know them on an informal, friendly basis.

5. Participate in organizations that work for the advancement and better understanding between races.

II. At the Level of Our Local Churches

1. Conduct study courses for each age level in the church on Race Relations.

2. Conduct a Community Audit or Self-Survey. This should be done by a bi-racial committee with a view to determining the good and bad points in health, recreation, education, participation in government and community life, housing, employment opportunities together with moral and spiritual improvements.

3. Exchange pulpits on Race Relations Sunday with ministers from the minority group churches.

4. Exchange choirs from time to time.

5. Invite the minority group leaders to address organizations and church groups on topics other than race relations.

6. Observe Brotherhood Week with special emphasis on immediate community needs.

7. Plan for inter-group work and worship projects for young people such as painting a church, repairing pews, cleaning off a cemetery, etc.

8. Urge members to volunteer for social and religious work in the missions that are located in minority group areas.

9. Provide courses to train their leaders for Vacation Bible Schools, Every Member Canvass, Census, etc.

10. Invite all Baptist Churches to participate in simultaneous revival plans.

11. Encourage joint ministerial conferences.

12. Devise community demonstrations projects where possible to employ these suggestions.

III. At the Christian College Level

1. Offer courses in human relations. Such courses should include a scientific study of the problem and the practical application of Christian principles with the view to eliminating prejudice and coming to a better understanding between the races.

2. Provide religious and recreational activities which will be open to all racial groups represented on the campus.

3. Plan inter-group work, worship projects with students in nearby Negro colleges and universities. For example, the BSU could help establish a similar organization in a Negro school.

4. College students should be urged to work in missions located in minority group areas which seek to improve the moral and spiritual situation in those areas.

IV. At the Convention Level

1. Let the Florida Baptist State Convention recognize its responsibility for the promotion of better racial understanding and urge our Baptist constituency to be Christian in attitude and action toward members of other races.

2. The Convention should continue to appoint committees to study the race problem and to keep the churches informed as to matters touching race relations, human rights, spiritual needs and citizenship of minority groups.

3. And finally, the Convention can continue to express its approval of and work in co-operation with various agencies as the Home Mission Board, WMS, Social Service Commission, et cetera, which are working with minority groups throughout the Southern Baptist Convention.

These are some of the practical steps which can be taken by Florida Baptists to become more Christian in race relations. But let us never forget that the first essential is social change in a changed individual. We cannot have a Christian community without Christians. Therefore, the primary task of the churches is to bring men into a personal, first-hand experience with God in Christ. But the process does not end there. The Christian does not live in a vacuum, but in a vast web of social relationships in which he must seek to be Christian. Therefore the Christian must be led to see that in all areas of his life God expects him "to do justly, and to love kindness, and to walk humbly with thy God."

The Goal and the Pace of the Advance

Given to WMU convention Winter Haven, FL on Tuesday 4 April 1950:

Among the proposed solutions for the race problem in the South are: (1) extinction of minorities; (2) expulsion and colonization; (3) patching and perfecting the caste system; (4) the forty-ninth state; (5) parallel civilizations; (6) amalgamation; and, (7) integration.[1]

None of these is wholly satisfactory. Perhaps at present the most practical goal is that of parallel civilizations with equality and integration along economic, legal and political levels. This means a distinct separation of races with the recognition that each has a definite contribution to make to our civilization.[2] At this specific stage in the South's development it may be the only practical plan, which on the whole, will make for peace and progress. Though this position falls short of the Christian ideal, it is within the realm of the possible and it will lay the foundation for further social progress in the South.

What about the pace of advance toward the Christian ideal in human relations? Southern Baptists will be wise and avoid the rock-ribbed conservative view which seeks to maintain the *status quo* in race relations, and the radical liberal view which insists upon absolute social equality immediately. Rather the road to a peaceful solution to this problem is the progressive-conservative position which urges a progressive application of the Christian ideal to human relations. This means we must keep a tension between what is and what ought to be. Then we will move inevitably in the

---

[1] G. Gallagher Buell, *Color and Conscience* (New York: Harper and Row, 1946). See Chapters 7 and 8 for a good discussion of these solutions.
[2] See *Color and Conscience* (New York: Harper and Row, 1946) Chapter 7; and his *Problems of the Present South*, 273–74; J. H. Oldham, *Christianity and Race Relations* (London: Christian Student Movement, 1924) 170–71; Howard Odum, *Race and Rumors of Race* (Chapel Hill: University of North Carolina Press, 1943).

direction of the Kingdom of God on earth, which, simply stated, is a Godly people in a righteous community.

Index

early schooling, 14–15; family move to Kannapolis (NC), 20–21; FBI investigation of, 99–100; festschrifts for, 226; first sermon, 32; foundational teaching principle, 14–15; friendship with Fletcher, 156–57, 159–60; going away sermon for D. E. King, 216–18; graduate dissertation, 51; Haymarket district ministry (Louisville, KY), 54–62; health problems, 239; Howard College teaching position, 63–64, 66, 68; humorous anecdotes, 243–47; inaugural address (1954) at Southern Seminary, 87–88; inaugural address for Willie Lawnsie Holmes, 218–19; interim pastor at San Mateo (FL) Baptist Church, 72; involvement in civil rights issues (Alabama, 1940s), 65–69; involvement in protests and social action, 136–44; M. L. King's death, actions and writings in aftermath of, 131–32; move to Stetson University, 70–74; ordination, 33; pastoral duties during college, 41–43; political involvement, 166–72; race relations, reports on (1949, 1950), 275–81; reaction to sons' stances on Vietnam War, 185–86, 188, 195–97; reaction to wars during lifetime, 190–95; reference works on, 255–56; resignation from Central Baptist Mission, 60–62; response to Debusman's dismissal from Southern Seminary, 153–54; response to nuclear test ban treaty, 206–8; restarting education, 31–32; retirement from Southern Seminary, 227–34; return to Southern Baptist Theological Seminary, 75–78; seminary education, 44–53; speaking on race relations to Southern Baptist Convention (1957), 117; speeches on race relations (Florida, 1949–50), 72–73; studies at Union Theological Seminary (NY), 77–78; teaching ecology/ethics course at Stetson, 163–64; theological consult, 237–38; travel to Poland (1957), 98–99; travel to Russia (1957), 95–99, 246, 257–68; visiting professor at University of Florida, 162–64; at Wake

Forest College, 34–41, 42–43; working in cotton mills, 23–24, 25–26; working on dissertation, 63, 71

Barnette, James Randolph (author's son), 68, 93, 116

Barnette, Jennifer, 100

Barnette, John Alexander (author's son), 64, 80, 82, 83, 85–86, 92–93, 173–82

Barnette, John Andrew (Drew), 182

Barnette, Loomis, 12

Barnette, Martha, (author's daughter) 170

Barnette, Mazo, 11, 12, 81, 86, 130

Barnette, Romulus, 10

Barnette, Roy, 81

Barnette, Wayne (author's son), 64, 80, 83, 85, 92, 99, 100, 182–89

Barnette, William Alexander (author's father), 5, 10, 11, 17, 26, 81; jobs and businesses, 18–19; officeholder, 12–13; profession of faith, 29

Barnette, Winnie Helen Kerley (author's mother), 4, 10–12, 26, 27–28, 29, 81

Barnett(e) family Civil War soldiers in, 3; history of, 1–2

Barth, Karl, 133, 160

Baylor University, job offer from, 108

Beach, Henry, 167

Beard, Luke, 66

"The Beeches." *See* Southern Baptist Theological Seminary

Bellevue Baptist Church (Memphis, TN), 74

Bennett, John, 77–78

Bennett, Willis, 104, 129, 151

Bently, Fred, 12

Berrigan, Dan, 215

Berrigan, Philip, 215

Berry, John, 168

Biblical Perspectives on Bioethical Problems (Barnette), 225

Binkley, Joseph M., 52

Binkley, Olin T., 36, 49, 50–52, 75

Binkley, Pauline, 52

bioethics, 224

biomedical ethics, 156–57

Birch, John, 138

A Pilgrimage of Faith

Dahunsi, Emmanuel, 118n2
Daley, Chauncey, 148
Davis, Harwell G., 63
Davis, Jerome, 95, 96, 98
Davis, William Hersey, 48–49
death, as celebration, 251–52
Debusman, Paul, 153–54, 226
Deering, Ronald, 105, 106
Diehl, Amanda Magnolia, 4
Diehl, Lettie Webster, 4
Diehl, Miles, 4
Diehl, William, 4
Diehl (Deal) family, 4
Dixon, Thomas, 35
Dobbins, Gaines, 53, 75, 77, 90
Dole, Robert, 172
Dorris, Glen, 172
Duncan, Pope, 70
Dunn, George, 239
Dunster, Henry, 109
Durham, Henry, 105

Ecoclub, 161, 224
ecology, 161–65
eco-theology, 164n1
Edmunds (president of Stetson Univ.), 73
Edwards, (Big) John, 16, 17
Edwards, Doc, 12, 13, 16
Elliff, Tom, 153
Ellis, Earle, 105
end of life, approaching, 249–53
Enlow, Eugene, 80
Enthoven, Alain, 205
Environment, Power and Society (Odum), 162
Ericsson, Hans, 183
Ericsson, Karin, 183
Ericsson, Yurli, 183
ethics, influential books on, 160
Ethics Luncheon, 223–24
Euzelian Literary Society, 35, 36
Exploring Medical Ethics (Barnette), 224–25, 236–37, 240–42, 243

"faith," 1
faith, factors shaping, 1, 5–6
First Baptist Church (DeLand, FL), 70

First Baptist Church of Landis (NC), 33
"The Firstborn" (Barnette), 174
Fisher, Bill, 73–74
Fitzgerald, Thomas, 100
Fleck, James C., 205
Fleming, Ellen Grace, 223–24
Fletcher, Joseph, 156–57
Flewelling, Ralph Tyler, 87–88
Flint, Cort, 80, 81
Florida Baptist Convention (1949), 72–73
Flowers, Nancy, 237, 239
Folk, Edgar Estes, Jr., 36, 40
Folk, Edgar Estes, Sr., 40
Ford, Charlotte. *See* Barnette, Charlotte Ford
Ford, Wendell, 168
Francisco, Clyde, 105, 232
Franklin, James H., 44
Frog Holler (West Point, NC), 30
Fuller, Ellis, Sr., 51
Fuller, Mrs. Ellis A., 81
Fussell, Warner, 55

Gaba, Charles, 239
Gardner, E. Clinton, 237
Garland, Diana, 139, 153
Garrett, James Leo, Jr., 105, 119, 129
Gay, Julian Brown, 128
Georgetown College, 214–15
Get Off Your But (Cosby), 226
Gheens, Charles (Mr. and Mrs.), 55
Glass, Edith, 64
Glass, Victor, 64
globalization, 204–5
Goatley, Wilbert H., 119
Goerner, H. C., 52, 84, 102
Grand Rounds, 236, 240–42
Graves, Allen, 103, 118, 129
Gray, Laman, 239
Gulf War, 193
Gulley, N. Y., 39

Hall, Thomas O., Jr., 103, 104
Hamilton, Prof, 58–59
Harvard University, research fellowship at, 106–14
Haymarket (Louisville, KY), 45, 54–62

Owens, John J., 83, 103

Pappy Circle, 36
Paschal, George, 36, 40–41
patriotism, 202
peacemaking, 201–2
Peach Tree Baptist Church, 43
Peacock, Heber, 104, 106
Pedigo, Merle, 55
Perry, Emmett, 68
Perspectives on Christian Ethics, 226
Pharr, J. W., 11
Philamathesian Literary Society, 35
Pilcher, W. E., 59, 62
"pilgrimage," 1
Poarch, Helen. *See* Barnette, Helen Poarch
Poarch, Mrs. O. G., 91
Poarch, O. G., 49, 91–92
Poteat, Hubert, 36, 39
Poteat, William (Billy) Lewis, 36. 37–38, 39
prayer, 249
prescription drug costs, 140–41
Price, T. D., 47, 83, 101, 103, 104
protests, 136–44
Pusey, Nathan, 107

race relations, 117–27
racism, rural North Carolina (1930s), 42
Ramsey, Paul, 205
Randles, Elwood Eton, 59–60
Randles, Helen Rufena, 60
Randles, Mary, 59–60
Randles, Raymond, 60
Randles, Samuel, 59–60
Ranson, Guy H., 83, 84, 103, 104
Rauschenbusch, Walter, 51, 131–32, 133
Reid, A. C., 36, 39–40
Review and Expositor, 225–26
Ridgecrest (NC), integration of Southern
   Baptist retreat at, 143
Robinette, David, 32
Roebuck, Claude, 36
Rogers, Adrian, 74, 147–51
Rogers, Carl, 14
Rogers, Turner C., 14, 191
Roosevelt, Eleanor, 97

Rouse, J. E., 65
Russell, C. Allyn, 104
Russell, Claude, 32
Rust, David, 176
Rust, Eric, 119, 144, 146

Samford University, 68
Sampey, John Richard, 45–47, 55, 216, 220,
   249
Sampey, Mrs. John R., 55
San Mateo (FL) Baptist Church, 72
Saved by His Life, 108
Schaly, Harald, 36–37
Schmidt, Kermit, 55
Schrum, David, 36
Schurz, Carl, 199, 202
Schwab, John, 235–36, 239, 240
Schwartzschild, Henry, 196
Scorboro, Ray, 35
the shacks (Kannapolis, NC), 27, 28
Shelp, Earl, 224
Simmons, Paul, 137, 146, 153, 223, 224, 226,
   231–32
situation ethics, 157–59
Situation Ethics: The New Morality (Fletcher),
   156, 159
Sloan, Jean, 239
Sloane, Harvey, 168, 232
Smith, John, 2
Smith, Stephen L., 237
Smith, T. C., 56, 104
Snowden, Grady, 70
solitude, 249
Southard, Samuel, 105
Southern Baptist Convention Christian Life
   Commission, 143; dealing with race
   relations (1957), 117–18; fundamentalist
   takeover of, 148; Weatherspoon's
   influence on, 50
Southern Baptists World Peace Committee,
   201
Southern Baptist Theological Seminary
   (Louisville, KY), 44–53; "Abstract of
   Principles," for teaching at, 76;
   administrative conflicts in School of
   Theology, 101–6; attempt to begin

international relations curriculum, 204;
Barnette's retirement from, 227–35; Black
Church Studies program, 119–20; Carver
School of Social Work, 139–40; Clarence
Jordan Center, 223; Ecoclub, 161, 224;
Ethics Club, 223; fundamentalist control
of, 152–55; fundamentalist takeover of,
171; honoring King, 134; integrating the
faculty, 118–19; M. L. King speaking at,
15, 116, 128–31; parking problems at,
141–43; programs introduced by Barnette,
220–24; protests at, 136–37; students
(1950s) favoring racial integration, 120;
target for heresy hunters, 145–46; weekly
chapel services, 77
Spangler, Otto, 129
"spirituality," 1
Spurgeon, Charles Haddon, 97
St. Amant, Penrose, 105, 119
Stagg, Bob, 176
Stagg, Frank, 106, 146, 201, 222
Stanfield, Latrell, 83, 84
Stanley, Frank, Jr., 130, 216
Stansbury, William, 167
"The Star Spangled Banner," 203
Stassen, Glen, 162, 165, 204, 215
Stealey, Syndor, 51, 53
Stetson University, 70–74, 163
Stokely, Edith, 56
Stout, W. W., 244
Stovall, Thelma, 167–68
Sugar Loaf Township (NC), 3–4
Sullivan, Clayton, 105
Summers, Ray, 104
Sunday, Billy, 22

Taking Time Seriously (Adams), 113
Tate, Marvin, 232
Taylor, Claude, 77
Taylor, Eldred, 83
Taylorsville (NC), 5, 13–14
Terkel, Studs, 249
Thompson, George, 119
Tillich, Paul, 107, 108, 111–12, 133
Toy, Crawford Howell, 145–46
Tribble, Harold, 40, 53

Trueblood, Elton, 92
Turlington, Henry E., 55–56, 75, 104, 106

Union Gospel Mission (Louisville, KY), 45,
54–59, 215–16
United Nations, 208–11
University of Florida, 162–64
US-USSR exchanges, 96–97, 204

Valentine, Foy, 232
Vardaman, Jerry, 105
Vaught, W. O., 137–38
Vestal, Daniel, 222
Vietnam War, 136, 175, 184–88, 191–93

Wagemaker, Herbert, 239
Wake Forest College, 34–41, 44
Walker, John, 56
Walker, O. L., 70
Walker, Peahead, 35
Walker, T. Vaughn, 120
Wallace, William, 221
Waller (Rabbi), 240
Walters, David A., 99
Wamble, G. Hugh, 104
war. *See* Gulf War, Iraq War, just war, Korean
War, Vietnam War, War on Terrorism,
World War I, World War II
War on Terrorism, 193–94
Ward, Mrs. Jasper, 121
Ward, Tom, 167–68
Ward, Wayne, 80, 81, 83, 84, 119, 129
Ward-Pugh, Tina, 170–71
Watts, J. Washington, 105
Watts, Lula, 13–14
Wauford, Charles, 84
Waverly Tuberculosis Hospital, 45
Weatherspoon, Jesse Burton, 49–50, 51, 83,
130
Webster, Alexander, 7–8, 18
Webster, Charles, 7
Webster, Francis Marimane, 7, 8–9
Webster, Nancy. *See* Barnett, Nancy (Webster)
West Point (NC) Baptist Church, 33
White Citizens Council, 15
White, Lincoln, 96